DATE			

HWLC

WINDOWS
& DOORS

Other Publications:

MYSTERIES OF THE UNKNOWN

TIME FRAME

FIX IT YOURSELF

FITNESS, HEALTH & NUTRITION

SUCCESSFUL PARENTING

HEALTHY HOME COOKING

UNDERSTANDING COMPUTERS

LIBRARY OF NATIONS

THE ENCHANTED WORLD

THE KODAK LIBRARY OF CREATIVE PHOTOGRAPHY

GREAT MEALS IN MINUTES

THE CIVIL WAR

PLANET EARTH

COLLECTOR'S LIBRARY OF THE CIVIL WAR

THE EPIC OF FLIGHT

THE GOOD COOK

WORLD WAR II

HOME REPAIR AND IMPROVEMENT

THE OLD WEST

WINDOWS & DOORS

TIME-LIFE BOOKS
ALEXANDRIA, VIRGINIA

Fix It Yourself was produced by
ST. REMY PRESS

MANAGING EDITOR	Kenneth Winchester
MANAGING ART DIRECTOR	Pierre Léveillé

Staff for *Windows & Doors*

Series Editor	Kathleen M. Kiely
Editor	Elizabeth W. Lewis
Art Director	Odette Sévigny
Research Editor	Katherine Zmetana
Designer	Solange Pelland
Contributing Writers	Cathleen Farrell, Elyse Greenberg, Carol Halls, Joan Irving, Eric Lowdon, Grant Loewen, Noel Meyer, Michael Mouland, Peter Orr, Wayne Voce, Rachel Wareham, Sharon Wickham-Foxwell
Contributing Illustrators	Gérard Mariscalchi, Jacques Proulx
Technical Illustrator	Robert Paquet
Cover	Robert Monté
Index	Dale Huston, Christine M. Jacobs
Administrator	Denise Rainville
Coordinator	Michelle Turbide
Systems Manager	Shirley Grynspan
Systems Analyst	Simon Lapierre
Studio Director	Daniel Bazinet
Photographer	Maryo Proulx

Time-Life Books Inc. is a wholly owned subsidiary of
TIME INCORPORATED

Founder	Henry R. Luce 1898-1967
Editor-in-Chief	Henry Anatole Grunwald
Chairman and Chief Executive Officer	J. Richard Munro
President and Chief Operating Officer	N. J. Nicholas Jr.
Chairman of the Executive Committee	Ralph P. Davidson
Corporate Editor	Ray Cave
Group Vice President, Books	Kelso F. Sutton
Vice President, Books	George Artandi

TIME-LIFE BOOKS INC

EDITOR	George Constable
Executive Editor	Ellen Phillips
Director of Design	Louis Klein
Director of Editorial Resources	Phyllis K. Wise
Editorial Board	Russell B. Adams Jr., Thomas H. Flaherty, Lee Hassig, Donia Ann Steele, Rosalind Stubenberg, Kit van Tulleken, Henry Woodhead
Director of Photography and Research	John Conrad Weiser
PRESIDENT	Christopher T. Linen
Chief Operating Officer	John M. Fahey Jr.
Senior Vice Presidents	James L. Mercer, Leopoldo Toralballa
Vice Presidents	Stephen L. Bair, Ralph J. Cuomo, Neal Goff, Stephen L. Goldstein, Juanita T. James, Hallett Johnson III, Carol Kaplan, Susan J. Maruyama, Robert H. Smith, Paul R. Stewart, Joseph J. Ward
Director of Production Services	Robert J. Passantino

Editorial Operations

Copy Chief	Diane Ullius
Editorial Operations	Caroline A. Boubin
Production	Celia Beattie
Quality Control	James J. Cox (director)
Library	Louise D. Forstall
Correspondents	Elizabeth Kraemer-Singh (Bonn); Maria Vincenza Aloisi (Paris); Ann Natanson (Rome).

THE CONSULTANTS

Consulting Editor David L. Harrison is Managing Editor of Bibliographics Inc. in Alexandria, Virginia. He served as an editor of several Time-Life Books do-it-yourself series, including *Home Repair and Improvement*, *The Encyclopedia of Gardening* and *The Art of Sewing*.

Brian Pickens is general manager of Pickens Window Service in Cincinnati, Ohio. A second-generation window repair specialist, he has repaired hundreds of models of windows and patio doors, and supplied discontinued and hard-to-find replacement parts internationally.

Ron Straight has lived in and worked on century-old houses and is, of necessity, an avid do-it-yourselfer. Most recently, he completely renovated an 1887 row house in Washington, D.C. He has encountered and overcome nearly every problem described in this volume.

Evan Powell is the Director of Chestnut Mountain Research Inc. in Taylors, South Carolina, a firm that specializes in the development and evaluation of home and building products. He is contributing editor to several do-it-yourself magazines and the author of two books on home repair.

Mark M. Steele, a professional home inspector in the Washington, D.C. area, is an editor of home improvement articles and books.

Library of Congress Cataloguing in Publication Data
Windows & doors
    (Fix it yourself)
    Includes index
    1. Windows–Maintenance and repair. 2. Doors–Maintenance and repair. I. Time-Life Books.
II. Title: Windows and doors. III. Series
TH2270.W63   1987   643'.7   87-17981
ISBN 0-8094-6216-8
ISBN 0-8094-6217-6 (lib. bdg.)

For information about any Time-Life Book, please write:
Reader Information
541 North Fairbanks Court
Chicago, Illinois 60611

CONTENTS

HOW TO USE THIS BOOK

Windows & Doors is divided into three sections. The Emergency Guide on pages 8-11 provides information that can be indispensable, even lifesaving, in the event of a household emergency. Take the time to study this section *before* you need the important advice it contains.

The Repairs section—the heart of the book—is a system for troubleshooting and repairing doors, windows, locks and weatherproofing. Pictured below are four sample pages from the chapter on interior doors, with captions describing the various features of the book and how they work. If your door sticks or binds, for example, the Troubleshooting Guide will

offer a number of possible causes. If the problem is a new door that's too large, you will be directed to page 50 for detailed step-by-step directions for cutting it to size.

Each job has been rated by degree of difficulty and the average time it will take for a do-it-yourselfer to complete. Keep in mind that this rating is only a suggestion. Before deciding whether you should attempt a repair, first read all the instructions carefully. Then be guided by your own confidence, and the tools and time available to you. For more complex or time-consuming repairs, such as replacing a window or rebuilding a door jamb, you may wish to call for pro-

---

Introductory text
Describes the construction of windows and doors, their most common problems and basic repair procedures.

Troubleshooting Guide
To use this chart, locate the symptom that most closely resembles your door or window problem, review the possible causes in column 2, then follow the recommended procedures in column 3. Simple fixes may be explained on the chart; in most cases you will be directed to an illustrated, step-by-step repair sequence.

"Exploded" and cutaway diagrams
Locate and describe the internal and external components of the door or window.

INTERIOR DOORS

The simple opening and closing of an interior door can invite visitors into a room, declare privacy or hide a less-than-orderly area of the house.

Doors may be solid or hollow. Solid panel doors commonly grace the interiors of older homes, while modern homes use hollow doors, often filled with corrugated cardboard. Other styles include top-hung sliding doors for closets and folding doors used for closets and pantries.

In principle, interior doors should remain trouble free for years. In practice, however, hinges sag, houses settle and solid doors warp and shrink due to temperature and humidity.

As a rule, when a hinged door refuses to open and close as it should, first work on the hinges, then the door and finally the door frame. Hinges and strike plates can be shimmed (*page 47*) or their mortises deepened (*page 46*). Doors can be cut (*page 50*), or planed (*page 53*) and jambs can be shifted in or out (*page 49*). Occasionally a bowed door will need to be

straightened with weights or clamps (*page 54*) or its joints will require gluing or bolting (*page 52*). However, wood has a long memory and straightening a warped door should be seen only as a temporary measure. Eventually the door must be replaced.

Match a new door to the other doors in your home. For older styles cull through demolition yards and antique stores. If the door you choose doesn't fit, you may have to cut it to size (*page 50*). Measure the doorway between the side jambs and from head jamb to floor; subtract 1/2 inch for rug or threshold clearance. Don't cut more than an inch off the height of a panel or hollow door—although you can cut up to 2 inches from the width. Reuse old hinge and strike plate mortises, replugging worn screw holes if necessary (*page 123*). Chisel hinge mortises on the door in exact alignment with those on the jamb (*page 122*). Install new doorknobs according to manufacturer's instructions. New doors can also be bought as prehung units and installed yourself (*page 86*).

TROUBLESHOOTING GUIDE

SYMPTOM	POSSIBLE CAUSE	PROCEDURE
Door hinges squeak	Rust or paint buildup around hinges	Remove one hinge pin at a time (p. 45); clean and oil the pin □○
Doorknob or handle loose	Retaining setscrew loose	Tighten setscrew (p. 42) □○
Door won't close properly	Dirt or paint buildup around latch	Clean and lubricate latch (p. 42) □○
	Latch broken	Replace latch (p. 43) □○
	Latch spring broken	Replace latch spring (p. 42) □○
	Latch mechanism stuck	Lubricate interior of lock case (p. 42) □○
	Hinges set too deep	Shim hinges (p. 47) □○
	Strike plate needs adjusting	Adjust strike plate by filing or repositioning (p. 43) ▣○
	Door warped	Shim strike plate (p. 47) ▣○; reposition door stop (p. 48) ▣○; straighten door (p. 54) ▣●
Door rattles	Strike plate misaligned	Adjust strike plate (p. 47) ▣○
	Door shrunk or house settled	Weather-strip door (p. 109) □○; shim hinges or strike plate (p. 47) ▣○; shim jamb (p. 49) ▣▣; reposition stop (p. 48) ▣○
Door sticks or binds	Door hinge screws loose	Repair worn screw holes (p. 123) ▣○; replace screws
	Door warped	Determine and correct binding area (p. 46) ▣○
	House settled	Determine and correct binding area (p. 46) ▣○
	New door too large	Cut door (p. 50) ▣▣▲ or plane door (p. 53) ▣▣▲
Door drags	New carpet too thick	Cut door (p. 50) ▣▣▲ or plane door (p. 53) ▣▣▲; raise floor bracket (folding door, p. 56; sliding door, p. 57)
Hole in hollow door	Heavy blow against veneer surface	Patch door (p. 55) ▣○
Top-hung sliding door drags	Roller wheel or bracket needs adjusting	Adjust roller wheel or bracket (p. 57) ▣○
Top-hung sliding door jammed	Roller wheel jumped from track	Remove and rehang door (p. 57) □○
	Bottom guide askew	Adjust bottom guide (p. 57) □○
Folding door drags	Slider screw or spring-pivot pin loose	Tighten screw or replace pin in slider (p. 56) □○
Folding door corner broken off	Excessive force used to unjam door	Glue corner back and clamp (p. 56) ▣○
Fixed-louver broken	Heavy blow against louvered surface	Replace louver (p. 57) ▣●

DEGREE OF DIFFICULTY: □ Easy ▣ Moderate ■ Complex
ESTIMATED TIME: ○ Less than 1 hour ◐ 1 to 3 hours ● Over 3 hours ▲ Special tool required

40

41

Degree of difficulty and time
Rate the complexity of each repair, and how much time the job should take for a homeowner with average do-it-yourself skills.

Special tool required
Some repairs, particularly those involving glass or screens, require specialized tools (*page 118*).

Variations
Differences in popular windows or doors are described throughout the book, particularly if a repair procedure varies from one type to another, or from older to newer models.

ssional service. You will still have saved time and money by
agnosing the problem yourself.

Most of the repairs in *Windows & Doors* can be made with a
crewdriver, a wood chisel, a hammer and a backsaw. For
pairing cracks and splinters, and joining wood, you will
ed clamps, carpenter's glue and a solid workbench or table.
ou may also need power tools for some of the heavier
pairs. Basic carpentry tools—and the proper way to use
em—are presented in the Tools & Techniques section start-
g on page 118. If you are a novice when it comes to home
pair, read this section in preparation for a major job.

Home repair can lead to serious injury unless you take
certain basic precautions. Wear safety goggles when cutting
wood, and put on a pair of work gloves to prevent cuts, especially when handling glass. If you are using strong chemicals,
such as paint stripper, protect your hands with thick rubber
gloves, and work in a well-ventilated area. When removing
lead paint also wear a respirator. Be kind to your back—work
with a helper when lifting heavy windows and doors. Remember to take special precautions when working in wet condi-
tions or on the roof. Most important, follow all safety tips in
the Emergency Guide and throughout the book.

me of repair
u will be referred by the
publeshooting Guide to the first
ge of a specific repair job.

Tools and techniques
When a tool or method is required for a job,
it is described within the step-by-step repair.
General information on carpentry techniques,
including the use of power tools, is covered in
the Tools & Techniques section *(page 118)*.

Step-by-step procedures
Follow the numbered repair sequence carefully.
Depending on the result of each step, you may
be directed to a later step, or to another part of
the book, to complete the repair.

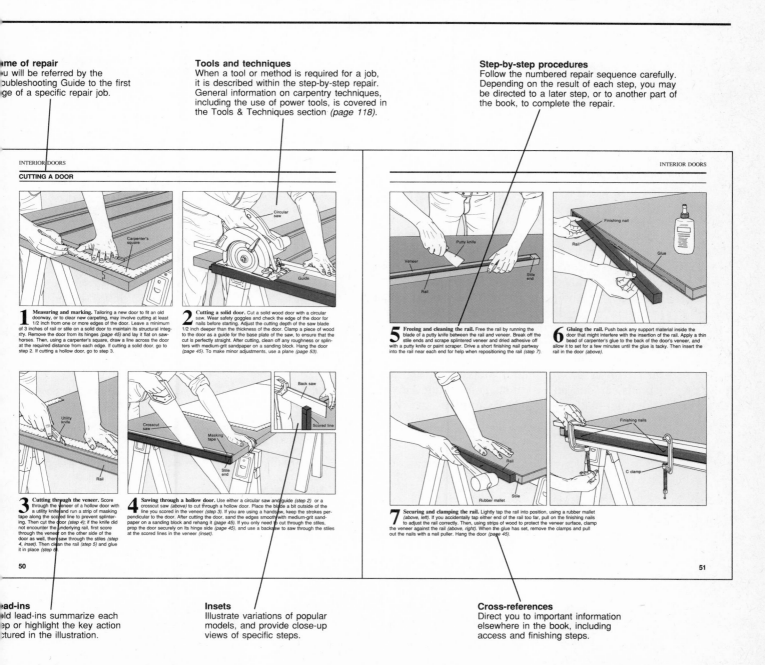

ad-ins
ld lead-ins summarize each
ep or highlight the key action
ctured in the illustration.

Insets
Illustrate variations of popular
models, and provide close-up
views of specific steps.

Cross-references
Direct you to important information
elsewhere in the book, including
access and finishing steps.

EMERGENCY GUIDE

Preventing window and door problems. When a window or door needs fixing, it rarely creates a serious problem. It may not work smoothly or look elegant, but usually the repair can be put off until tomorrow. Occasionally, however, a real emergency will arise. A window pane may break during a heavy rainstorm, demanding immediate action to protect the inside of the home against water damage. Or burglars may splinter a front door, leaving the home and its residents temporarily without protection. More commonly, the planned removal of a door or a window for repair or replacement requires the services of a plywood panel nailed over the opening *(page 10)*.

Door locks, or their failure, are more likely to cause headaches than doors themselves. Most people have experienced the frustration of being locked out of their own home, or the fright of finding that a stranger has broken in. A broken lock can rarely be fixed, but installing a padlock hasp until you can replace the old lock can be done in a matter of an hour or so. Simply removing a broken key or other foreign material from a keyhole, or thawing a frozen lock, are easy fixes that take more patience than skill. These emergency lock repairs are detailed on page 11.

Read the safety tips at right for suggestions on how to prevent problems that might arise when fixing a window or door, as well as how to make them safer. Simple, easily installed accessories that increase the security of a window or door are shown in the inventory on page 9. For advice on how to deal with an emergency when it does arise, review the Troubleshooting Guide on page 9. It lists quick-action steps to take, and directs you to procedures described in this chapter and elsewhere in the book. Study the Tools & Techniques chapter *(page 118)* for the right choice and proper use of the tools needed to fix a window or door.

When in doubt about your ability to handle an emergency, don't hesitate to call for help. Post numbers for the police and fire departments, a 24-hour locksmith and the poison control center near the telephone. Even in non-emergency situations, these professionals can answer questions concerning the safe use of tools and repair materials and the security of your doors and windows.

SAFETY TIPS

1. Before attempting any repair in this book, read the entire repair procedure. Familiarize yourself with the specific safety information presented in each chapter.

2. Carefully read the label on any paint, solvent, patching compound, adhesive or other material used to make a repair. Follow manufacturer's instructions to the letter, and pay special attention to hazard warnings and storage instructions.

3. Before cutting into a wall, switch off power at the main service panel. Leave a note on the panel so that no one turns on the power while you are working.

4. Guard against electrical shock when using power tools. Plug power tools into grounded outlets only, and never cut off or bypass the third, or grounding, prong on a power tool's plug. A tool with a two-prong plug must be labeled "double insulated". Do not use any power tool in a damp area.

5. Wear the proper protective gear for the job: safety goggles when operating power tools such as a router or a circular saw; heavy work gloves to handle broken glass, fiberglass or metal flashing; heavy rubber gloves when applying chemical strippers, solvents, and cleaning solutions.

6. Wear a respirator when working with fiberglass insulation or doing jobs that generate dust or toxic fumes. Select a respirator filter specially made to block the particles or vapors being produced. Replace filters according to the manufacturer's instructions.

7. Do not drink alcoholic beverages while using paints, solvents, strippers or adhesives that produce fumes—the combination can cause illness. If you feel faint or sick, leave the room and get fresh air, then improve ventilation before continuing work.

8. When working with flammable chemicals or with power tools, have on hand a fire extinguisher rated ABC, and know how to use it before you begin work.

9. Keep garage door opener transmitters away from children.

10. Stick tape or colorful decals on clear glass doors and windows that may appear transparent to a running child.

11. Prune branches away from windows to prevent obstruction and glass breakage.

12. Don't rely on weak, easily picked locks, such as spring-latch locks, to secure exterior doors. Choose deadbolt locks and install strike plates with 3-inch screws.

13. Don't leave valuables near windows where they can be seen.

14. Keep a roll of 4- to 6-mil plastic sheeting on hand as a temporary cover for blown-in windows.

15. If a lock requires a key to open it from the inside, keep the key nearby for emergency escape.

16. Install locking interior doors with loose-pin hinges that can be removed from outside the room if someone gets locked inside.

17. Post emergency, utility company and repair service numbers near the telephone.

TROUBLESHOOTING GUIDE

SYMPTOM	PROCEDURE
Person locked in a room	Insert nail or hairpin into slot in center of doorknob to open door; or slip a credit card between latch and strike plate and pull door open
	Remove door from hinges (p. 45)
	Call locksmith or fire department to unlock door
Person cut by glass	Apply pressure with clean cloth and elevate limb until bleeding stops; clean injury with soap and water if minor; if cut is serious or contains glass fragments, go to hospital emergency room
Person fallen from window or roof	Do not move victim; call for emergency medical service
Person locked out of the house	Call locksmith to unlock door
Lock frozen	Chip away any ice from face of lockset, dip key in alcohol and insert into keyhole
	Heat key with lighter and insert into keyhole (p. 11)
Key broken in lock	Use a hooked darning needle to lift cylinder pins and extract key fragment (p. 11)
Exterior door lock broken	Install temporary hasp and lock (p. 11)
Sliding window or door lock inadequate	Secure window or door with a broomstick or other piece of wood (p. 10) until new lock can be installed
Window pane broken	Remove broken glass; cover opening with plastic sheeting or plywood (p. 10) until you replace pane (p. 78)
Exterior door or window severely damaged, or removed for repair or replacement	Cover opening with plastic sheeting or plywood panel (p. 10) until you repair or replace the door or window

SECURITY AND SAFETY ACCESSORIES

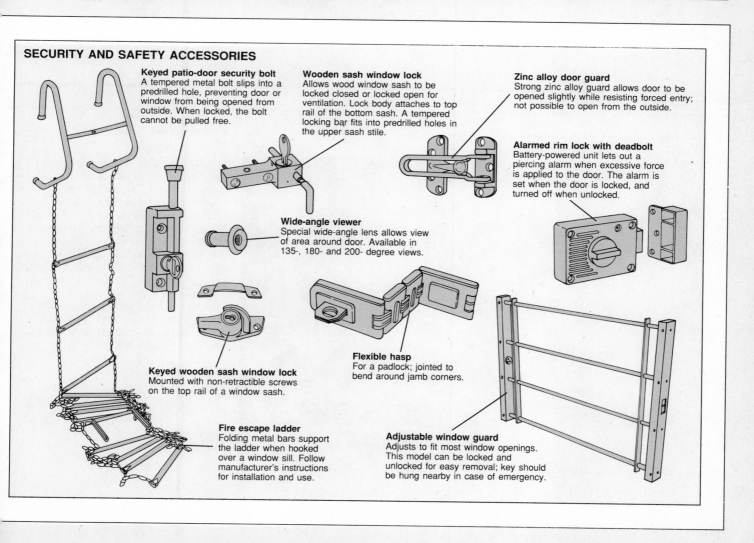

Keyed patio-door security bolt
A tempered metal bolt slips into a predrilled hole, preventing door or window from being opened from outside. When locked, the bolt cannot be pulled free.

Wooden sash window lock
Allows wood window sash to be locked closed or locked open for ventilation. Lock body attaches to top rail of the bottom sash. A tempered locking bar fits into predrilled holes in the upper sash stile.

Zinc alloy door guard
Strong zinc alloy guard allows door to be opened slightly while resisting forced entry; not possible to open from the outside.

Alarmed rim lock with deadbolt
Battery-powered unit lets out a piercing alarm when excessive force is applied to the door. The alarm is set when the door is locked, and turned off when unlocked.

Wide-angle viewer
Special wide-angle lens allows view of area around door. Available in 135-, 180- and 200- degree views.

Keyed wooden sash window lock
Mounted with non-retractible screws on the top rail of a window sash.

Flexible hasp
For a padlock; jointed to bend around jamb corners.

Fire escape ladder
Folding metal bars support the ladder when hooked over a window sill. Follow manufacturer's instructions for installation and use.

Adjustable window guard
Adjusts to fit most window openings. This model can be locked and unlocked for easy removal; key should be hung nearby in case of emergency.

PROTECTING WINDOWS AND DOORS AGAINST STORMY WEATHER

Shielding unprotected openings. To prevent storm damage, cover windows and doors with 1/2-inch plywood sheets cut to fit. Nail the plywood to the exterior wood frame *(far left)*, using 2-inch common nails spaced about 12 inches apart. Remove nails and plywood with a pry bar or claw hammer after the storm has subsided, and fill nail holes with wood filler *(page 123)*. To attach plywood sheets to metal frames, drill pilot holes and use screws; caulk the holes when the plywood is removed. In hurricane regions, install shutters or window shields that can be closed in the event of a storm.

Use 4- to 6-mil plastic sheeting to seal a broken window. Staple the plastic around the window frame, or tuck the plastic under 1-by-2 wood slats, nailing 1 1/2-inch common nails through the slats and plastic into the window frame *(near left)*. Cover the floor and sill under the window with rags or towels if it rains. Remove the slats with a pry bar or claw hammer to reglaze *(page 76)*.

SECURING A SLIDING WINDOW OR PATIO DOOR

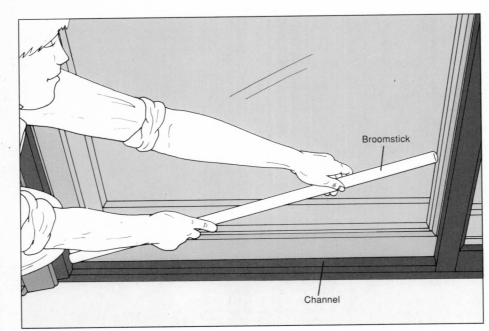

Burglar-proofing a patio door. If a sliding patio door or sliding window can be jimmied open, secure it temporarily with a broomstick or other piece of wood cut to fit the interior floor channel.

Measure the length of the channel with the door closed and locked. Using a handsaw, cut a broomstick or other piece of wood to fit snugly in this space. Wedge the wood into place, as shown, making sure it lies flat in the channel.

For better, more permanent protection, install a commercially available locking security bar in the channel, or install a patio door security bolt *(page 9)*.

INSTALLING A TEMPORARY DOOR LOCK

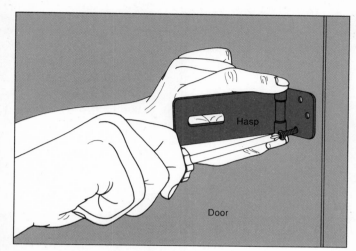

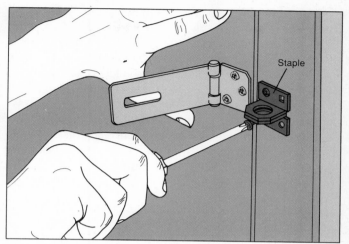

1 **Installing a hasp.** Position the screw-hole leaf of the hasp closest to the door edge. Drill pilot holes, then drive 1-inch screws through the holes into the door; check that the screws are covered when the hasp is closed. If the surfaces of the door and the jamb are not flush when the door is closed, install a flexible hasp *(page 9)* on the jamb.

2 **Installing the staple.** Close the hasp and mark where the staple should be screwed into the door frame. Attach the staple to the door frame with 1-inch screws. Close the hasp over the staple and secure the door with a padlock.

FREEING A LOCK

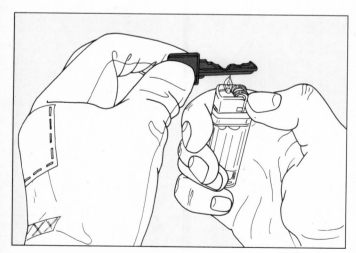

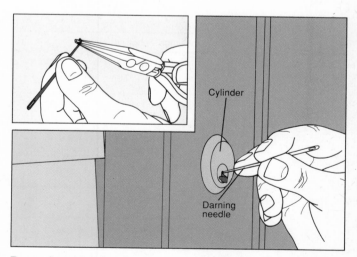

Unfreezing a lock. To unfreeze an exterior door lock, first chip any ice off the lockset. Using a pocket lighter, heat the door key, wearing a glove to protect your hand *(above)*. Slowly work the heated key into the cylinder. Repeat several times, if necessary, until the key turns in the cylinder. Lock de-icer, available in tubes, or denatured alcohol, can also be used to unfreeze locks.

Removing a broken key from a lock. Bend a metal darning needle point by heating it with a lighter and twisting the point into a hook with needle-nose pliers *(inset)*. Lubricate the keyhole with a lubricant spray. Insert the needle in the top of the cylinder hole, the hook pointing down. Push up the cylinder pins and pull out the key fragment with the hook. Alternatively, dismantle the lock and push the key through from the back of the cylinder or replace the cylinder *(page 66)*.

DOUBLE-HUNG WINDOWS

A double-hung window, with movable upper and lower sashes, opens at a touch with help from one of several balance systems, illustrated at right. Single-hung windows, on which only the lower sash is movable and has a balance system, work similarly and are maintained the same way. An old-style weight-and-pulley balance may be repaired, or it may be replaced by one of the more modern balance systems shown. On a small, light window, replacement channels *(page 20)*, which work by friction, can replace a balance system entirely.

A wood double-hung window suffers from the problems typical of any wood window: The wood shrinks, rots or warps, window joints loosen and paint buildup makes sashes stick shut. In addition, the balance system can wear out or break—a broken sash cord is very common. The Troubleshooting Guide below lists fixes in this chapter for these problems a more. Before performing any complicated procedures— example, routing a rabbet in a sash *(page 20)*—make sure window is sound enough to make repair worthwhile. Have professional evaluate the window if necessary—some windows are best replaced entirely *(page 86)*. For proble with window panes, see Panes and Screens *(page 76)*.

Installed over a double-hung window, an aluminum sto window takes the brunt of moisture and temperature extrem Regular cleaning and lubrication of the sash channels keep a storm window operating smoothly. Many storm sash can be disassembled for repair *(page 24)* or for replacement panes or screens *(page 76)*, and new storm windows are difficult to install *(page 25)*.

TROUBLESHOOTING GUIDE

SYMPTOM	POSSIBLE CAUSE	PROCEDURE
Window doesn't open or opens with difficulty	Sash channels need lubricating	Lubricate channels with paraffin wax or silicone spray
	Wood window painted shut	Break paint bond *(p. 14)* □○
	Paint buildup in wood sash channels	Strip channels *(p. 14)* ■◐
	Wood stop and/or sash warped	Reposition interior stop *(p. 48)* ■○; plane sash *(p. 16)* ■◐▲
	Wood sash separating at joint	Glue and clamp joint *(p. 52)* ■○; reinforce joint *(p. 16)* ■○
	Sash cord broken	Replace sash cord *(p. 18)* ■◐; or replace balance with clockspri balance *(p. 19)* ■○, replacement channels *(p. 20)* ■◐▲, or spir balance *(p. 21)* ■◐▲
	Block-and-tackle balance faulty	Replace balance *(p. 23)* ■○
	Spiral balance faulty	Lubricate balance with silicone spray; adjust or replace balance *(older window, p. 21* ■○; *tilt-in window, p. 22* ■○▲ *)*
	Clockspring balance faulty	Replace balance *(p. 19)* ■○; or replace with replacement channe *(p. 20)* ■◐▲, or spiral balance *(p. 21)* ■◐▲
	Weather stripping faulty	Replace weather stripping *(p. 112)* ■◐
Lower sash doesn't stay open, upper sash falls down	Sash cord broken	Replace sash cord *(p. 18)* ■◐; or replace balance with clockspri balance *(p. 19)* ■○, replacement channels *(p. 20)* ■◐▲, or spir balance *(p. 21)* ■◐▲
	Clockspring balance faulty	Replace balance *(p. 19)* ■○; or replace with replacement channe *(p. 20)* ■◐▲, or spiral balance *(p. 21)* ■◐▲
	Replacement channels faulty	Replace channels *(p. 20)* ■○; or replace with spiral balance *(p. 21)* ■◐▲
	Spiral balance faulty	Adjust or replace balance *(older window, p. 21* ■○; *tilt-in window p. 22* ■○▲ *)*
Wood sash rattles	Wood has shrunk	Reposition interior stop *(p. 48)* ■○; or install weather stripping *(p. 112)* ■○
	Wood sash rotted	Remove rotted wood and patch with epoxy *(p. 123)* □○; replace sill *(p. 17)* ■◐
Metal storm sash doesn't open or opens with difficulty	Sash channels dirty or clogged	Clean channels and lubricate with silicone spray
	Slide tab broken	Replace slide tab *(p. 24)* ■○
	Metal frame out of square	Realign frame or replace window *(p. 25)* ■◐
Metal storm sash rattles or sash rails loose	Rubber gasket dried out	Replace gasket *(p. 80)* ■○
	Corner key broken	Replace corner key *(p. 24)* ■○

DEGREE OF DIFFICULTY: □ Easy ■ Moderate ■ Complex
ESTIMATED TIME: ○ Less than 1 hour ◐ 1 to 3 hours ● Over 3 hours ▲ Special tool requ

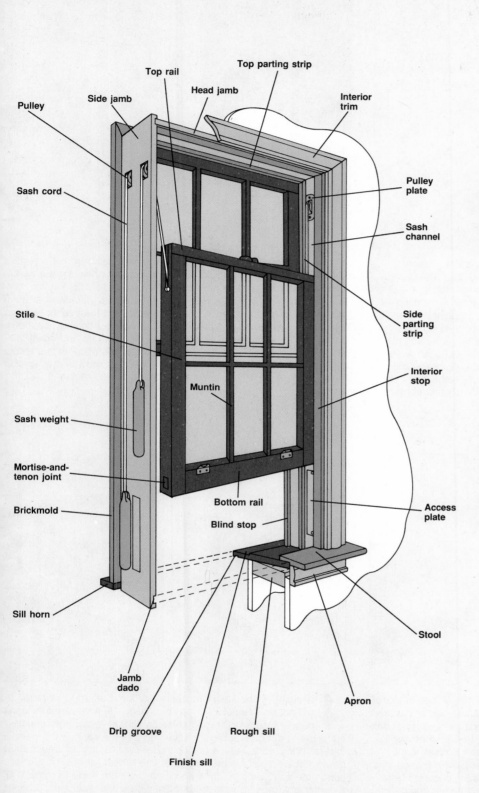

Pulley

Side jamb

Top rail

Head jamb

Top parting strip

Interior trim

Sash cord

Pulley plate

Sash channel

Stile

Side parting strip

Muntin

Interior stop

Sash weight

Mortise-and-tenon joint

Bottom rail

Brickmold

Blind stop

Access plate

Sill horn

Stool

Jamb dado

Drip groove

Rough sill

Apron

Finish sill

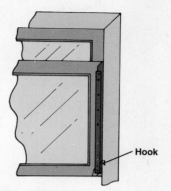

Hook

Block-and-tackle balance
Typical of many aluminum-window balances, this model rides in a groove in the stile and is attached to the jamb by a clip at the top and a hook at the bottom. When the sash is removed, the balance remains connected to the jamb. Its tension cannot be adjusted.

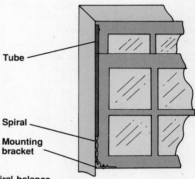

Tube

Spiral

Mounting bracket

Spiral balance
Hangs in a tube secured to the top of the jamb. On a typical older model *(above)*, the spiral connects to a mounting bracket on the sash. On modern tilt-in sashes *(page 22)*, it hooks into a plastic block, or shoe, that rides in a jamb channel. The older type may be used as a replacement balance for weight-and-pulley and clockspring balances. The tension of both spiral balances can be adjusted.

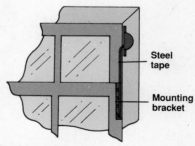

Steel tape

Mounting bracket

Clockspring balance
Mounted on the side jamb, or more rarely on the top jamb. Usually operates using a steel spring tape that is fastened to a bracket on the sash. Generally a more expensive balance, it is frequently a replacement for weight-and-pulley balances. It is weight-specific, but can be adjusted plus or minus 2 pounds. To increase the balance tension, turn the adjusting screws *(page 19)* clockwise. Reverse to decrease tension.

UNBINDING A WOOD SASH

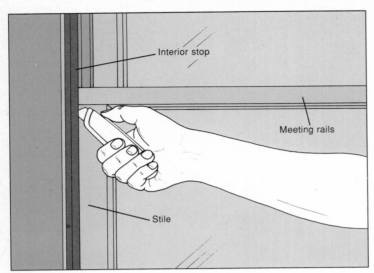

1 Breaking a paint bond. Carelessly applied paint will seal a window shut. Use a utility knife to slice through the paint bond. Place the blade of the knife between the interior stop and the top of the lower sash *(above)*. Draw the knife straight down, taking care not to gouge either the stop or the sash. Cut the paint between stop and sash all the way around both sashes, inside and outside. If the meeting rails are stuck together by paint, use the utility knife to break the paint bond. Push up the window; if it still doesn't open, continue to step 2. If the window opens, but with difficulty, examine the channels. If old paint has built up there, go to step 4. If not, try lubricating the channels with household paraffin wax or with silicone spray.

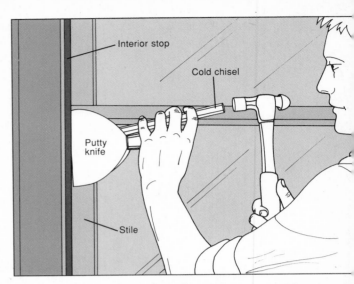

2 Separating stop from sash. Wood sashes and stops swell with humidity, making a window difficult to open. Free a lower sash by separating the interior stops from the sash stiles. Remove any weather stripping that may be in the way. Wedge two wide putty knives together between the sash and the interior stop. Drive them apart with a cold chisel and ball-peen hammer, as shown forcing the stop slightly away from the sash. Work up and down the length of the window and repeat at the other side. Repeat this technique on the exterior as well, between the upper sash and blind stop. Push up the window. If it still doesn't open, continue to step 3.

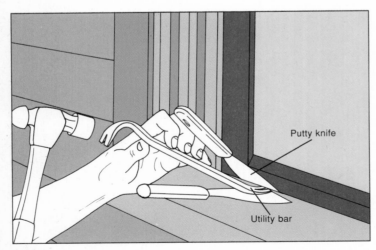

3 Forcing up the sash. From outside the house, wedge a pair of wide putty knives between the sill and the bottom rail of the sash near one corner. Drive the knives apart with a utility bar and ball-peen hammer *(above)*. The utility bar will force up the edge of the sash. Work gently; too much force may separate the window joints. Work on one corner at a time until the sash comes free. If the top sash is balky, use the same technique to separate the sash's top rail from the top jamb. If the sash remains frozen, strip the channels *(step 4)* or remove the sash *(page 15)* to plane it *(page 16)*.

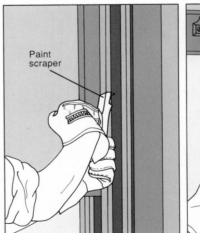

4 Stripping the sash channels. Work the sash up as far as it will go; only remove the sashes *(page 15)* if the window won't budge. Use an old wood chisel to scrape away minor paint buildup and dirt obstructing the movement of the sash. If the paint thick or bumpy, try using a paint scraper *(above, left)* to smooth it down. If the problem is more severe, use a heat gun *(page 125)* to soften the paint *(above, right)* and a narrow putty knife to remove it If necessary, remove vestiges of paint with a chemical paint stripper *(page 60)*, then sand and repaint *(page 124)*. Finish the job by lubricating the channels with paraffin wax or silicone spray.

REMOVING UPPER AND LOWER SASHES

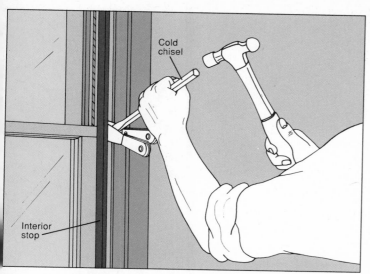

1 Prying off the interior stop. If the window has a spiral balance, go to step 2. To take out a lower sash, first remove one of the interior stops. If you are servicing a balance, remove the stop on the side of the broken balance. Begin by breaking any paint sealing the interior stop to the jamb (page 14, step 1). Remove any screws that secure the stop. Then push a pair of putty knives between stop and jamb and drive them apart with a cold chisel and ball-peen hammer (above). Start at the middle of the stop and work up and down. If the top of the stop has a mitered corner, carefully bow the stop to slip the tip out of the joint.

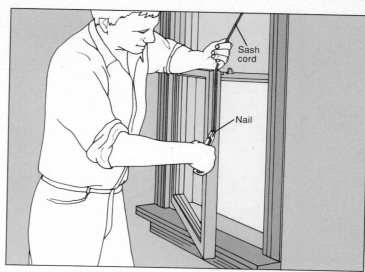

2 Removing the sash. Pull the sash out of the frame on the side where the stop was removed. Remove any screws or nails securing the end of the sash cord or chain to the sash (above). Push a nail through the cord or chain and feed it slowly up to the pulley; the nail will prevent it from being pulled through. Lift out the other side of the window sash and remove the cord or chain the same way. If the window operates with a clockspring balance, unhook the tape from the sash and feed it back into the drum. If the sash has a spiral balance, unscrew its tube from the top of the jamb and unscrew its mounting bracket from under the corner of the bottom rail. Then pry off the interior stop (step 1).

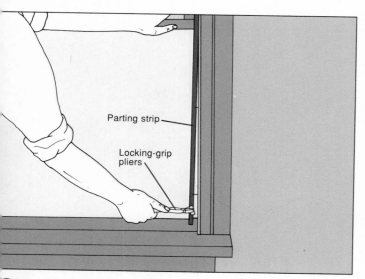

3 Pulling out the parting strip. If the upper sash uses a spiral balance, disengage the balance as in step 2 before removing the parting strip. To remove an upper sash that uses a weight-and-pulley or clockspring balance, first pry the parting stop out of the jamb on the same side as the interior stop. Remove any screws from the strip and break the paint bond (page 14). Pressing against the lower rail of the upper sash, use a pair of locking-grip pliers padded with wood shims to pull the bottom of the strip out of its groove in the jamb (above). Lower the upper sash, angle it out and remove the balance attachments as described in step 2. Then lift it out of the window.

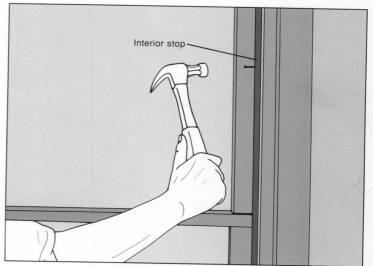

4 Replacing the sash and resecuring the interior stop. After completing repair, reassemble the sashes in their frame by reversing the steps you took to remove them. Take this opportunity to lubricate the sash channels with paraffin wax or silicone spray and to touch up paint or varnish. Use a nail puller to remove old nails from the interior stop (page 48, step 2). Be careful to replace the stop close enough to the sash to keep the sash from rattling, while leaving sufficient space for the sash to move freely. Secure the stop with finishing nails (above) or wood screws, opening and closing the sash after driving each nail or screw to test the fit.

PLANING A SASH TO SHAPE

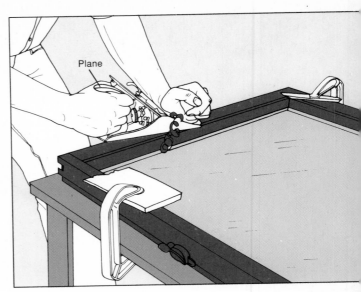

1 **Marking the warp.** Remove the binding sash from its frame *(page 15)* and clamp it to a work table with C clamps padded with scrap wood. Align a straightedge along the side of the warped stile and draw a line indicating the warp *(above)*. To preserve the finish on the front of the sash, you can plane the back; draw the line accordingly. Sometimes sanding the stile with medium-grit sandpaper on a sanding block is all you need to do. If sanding isn't enough, use a plane to shave away the binding area *(step 2)*. If the warp is more than 1/4 inch high, consider replacing your window *(page 86)*.

2 **Planing the sash.** Set the blade of a jack plane for fine planing and practice on a scrap of wood *(page 122)*. Holding the plane firmly in two hands, push it over the warped area in the direction of the grain *(above)*. Lift the nose of the plane off the wood as you finish the stroke to avoid gouging. After each stroke, check the line that marks the warp. When the warp has been flattened, smooth the sash with fine sandpaper on a sanding block. Touch up the paint or varnish and reinstall the sash.

REINFORCING THE JOINTS OF A WOOD SASH

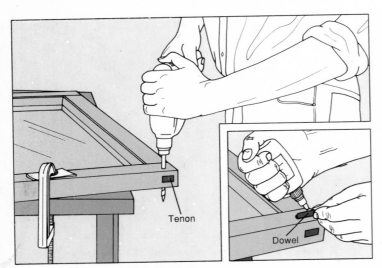

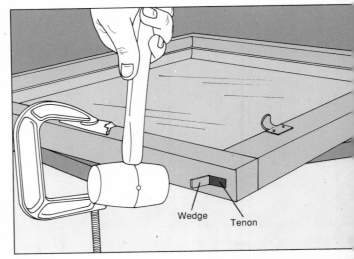

Doweling a sash joint. Remove the sash from the window *(page 15)*. Clamp the sash to a work table with C clamps padded with scrap wood, the joint you are strengthening extending over the edge. Using a power drill fitted with a 1/4-inch bit, drill a hole for the dowel straight through the mortise-and-tenon joint *(above)*. Use a backsaw to cut a piece of 1/4-inch dowel slightly longer than the thickness of the sash. Round one end slightly with sandpaper for easier insertion. Coat the dowel with carpenter's glue *(inset)* and tap it into the hole using a rubber mallet. Clean off excess glue with a damp rag. When the glue is dry, use fine sandpaper on a sanding block to trim it flush with the sash.

Adding a wedge to a sash joint. Remove the sash from the window *(page 15)* and inspect the joints for looseness. Inserting a wedge between tenon and mortise will strengthen the joint. Use long-nose pliers to pull out any loose old wedges. With a utility knife, cut a 1-inch wedge from cedar shim or scrap wood, 1/8 inch thick at the thicker end. Coat both sides of the wedge with carpenter's glue and use a rubber mallet to hammer it into the joint next to the tenon *(above)*. Hammer gently; too much force could crack the sash. When the glue has dried, use fine sandpaper on a sanding block to smooth the wedge flush with the sash.

EPLACING A WINDOW SILL

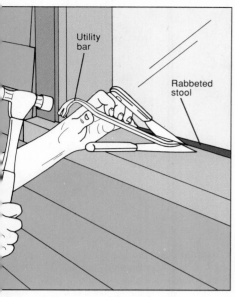

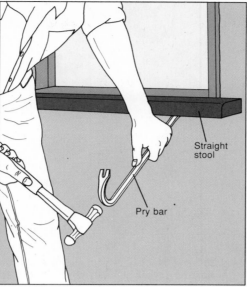

1 **Removing the stool and sill.** Inspect the finish sill closely; if it has minor rot, cut it away to healthy wood and patch with epoxy *(page 123)*. If the damage is severe, replace the sill to prevent t from spreading to the house framing. The sill may fit into sloped does in the jambs, may simply butt against the jambs or may be ld by corner rabbets. To gain access to the sill, first remove the win- w's interior side trim and apron *(page 89)*, the stops *(page 15)* and e stool. To remove a rabbetted stool that overlaps the indoor edge of e sill, go outside and wedge a pair of wide putty knives between the

sill and the stool, and drive them apart with a utility bar and ball-peen hammer *(above, left)*. If the window is inaccessible from the ground, lean out the window from inside to dislodge the stool. Use a hammer and pry bar to free a straight stool that is nailed flush to the sill *(above, center)*. Measure the width and thickness of the sill and its length both inside and outside. The difference between these two measurements (if there is one) is the length of the sill horns. Using a crosscut saw, cut through the finish sill down to the rough sill *(above, right)* in two places.

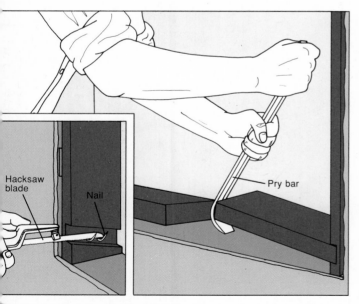

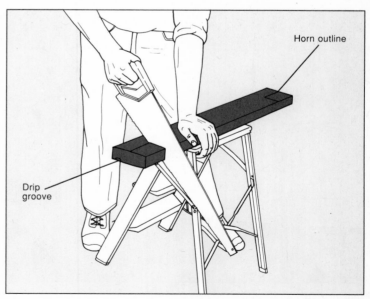

2 **Prying out the finish sill.** With a pry bar, lever the middle portion of the sill up and out, and then lift up each of the two remaining sections *(above)*. Pull these end pieces free by hand avoid damaging the jambs. Keep the pieces of the sill, if in good ndition, to use as a template for the new sill. If the jambs shifted ward, tap them back out with a rubber mallet. After the finish sill is noved, use a hacksaw blade with a handle *(inset)* to cut off any ls sticking out of the jamb.

3 **Cutting the horns for the new finish sill.** Buy sill stock of the same dimensions as the original sill; the wood must be straight-grained and knot-free. Lay the pieces of old sill on the sill stock and trace its outline. If the sill horns have disintegrated too much to use as a template, draw a pattern on cardboard using the measurements you took in step 1. Use a fine-toothed crosscut saw to cut out the horns for the new sill *(above)*. Sand rough edges smooth and apply two coats of a wood preservative compatible with the paint or varnish you will apply.

REPLACING A WINDOW SILL (continued)

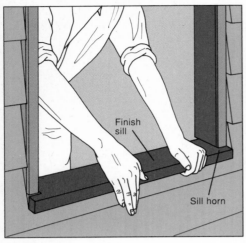

Finish
sill

Sill horn

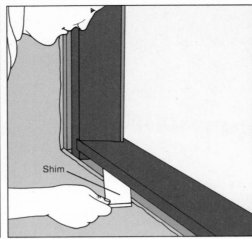

Shim

4 **Installing the sill.** Vacuum the jamb dadoes, if any, and the rough sill. Hold the sill outside the window and slide it into the dadoes *(above, left)*. If necessary, use a rubber mallet and a block of wood to tap it into place. If the ends of the sill are too thick to fit into the dadoes, trim their edges with medium-grit sandpaper on a sanding block. For extra support, insert wood shims snugly beneath the center of the sill *(above, center)*. Take care not to force the sill out of alignment.

If the sill butts against the jamb or fits into rabbets rather than dadoes, shim the full length of the sill. Toenail each end of the sill to its jamb with three or four finishing nails *(above, right)*. Caulk all exterior joints between the sill and the window frame and reinstall the stool, stops, interior trim and apron. If necessary, retrim the window *(page 99)*. Then paint the sill with exterior paint.

REPLACING A BROKEN SASH CORD ON A WEIGHT-AND-PULLEY BALANCE

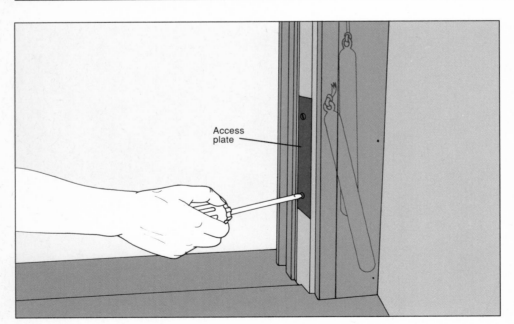

Access
plate

Chain

String

1 **Removing the access plate.** If one sash cord breaks, install all new cords to prevent future problems. Sash cords may be replaced with more durable flat-link sash chain, or you may replace the entire system with clockspring balances *(page 19)*, replacement channels *(page 20)* or spiral balances *(page 21)*. To determine the length of a replacement cord, measure from the top of the pulley to the bottom of the sash channel and add 6 inches. If one of the lower sash cords is broken, remove the lower sash; if an upper sash cord is broken, remove both sashes *(page 15)*. Unscrew the access plate in the sash channel on the side of the broken cord *(above)*. If necessary, strip away old paint first *(page 14)*. If no screws are visible, the plate may be nailed shut; use an old screwdriver to pry the plate out. If there is no access plate, remove the window trim *(page 89)* to expose the pocket. Lift out the weight and untie the broken cord from its eye.

2 **Feeding the sash chain or cord.** Tie a nail or screw to the end of a long piece of string. Tie its other end to the end of the new sash chain or cord. Feed the weighted end of the string over the pulley and down into the pocket. Reach into the pocket and pull the string *(above)* until the sash chain or cord appears.

REPLACING A BROKEN SASH CORD ON A WEIGHT-AND-PULLEY BALANCE (continued)

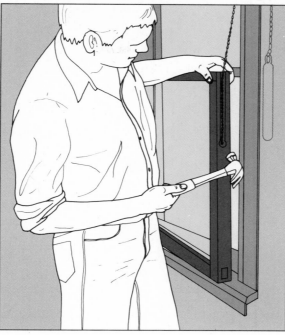

3 **Connecting the chain or cord.** Untie the sash chain or cord from the string and pass it through the eye of the weight. Wrap copper wire through the links of a chain to secure it to the weight *(far left)*; if you are using a sash cord, knot it. Put the weight back into the pocket. To fasten the chain or cord to the sash, pull down its free end until the weight hits the pulley. Run a nail through a link in the chain, or through the cord, and rest it across the pulley hole to keep the weight from tugging the chain or cord. Place the sash on the sill and feed the free end of the chain into the sash groove, securing it with screws or short nails through two links *(near left)*. For a cord, knot its end and hammer a finishing nail through the knot. Remove the nail at the pulley. Have a helper slowly raise the sash and hold it against the top of the window while you look into the pocket; the weight should hang 3 inches above the sill. If not, adjust the chain or cord at the weight end. Reinstall the access plate and the sashes *(page 15)*.

INSTALLING A CLOCKSPRING BALANCE

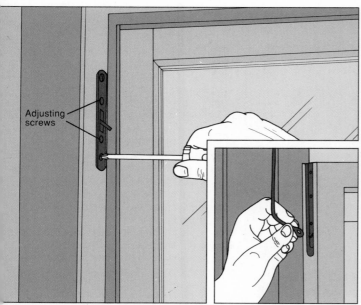

Adjusting screws

Removing and replacing a clockspring balance. Take out the sash *(page 15)* and unhook the balance tape from its bracket on the sash *(inset)*. Remove the screws securing the clockspring plate to the jamb *(above, left)* and pull the clockspring drum free of its pocket. Take the drum to a window specialist and buy an exact replacement. Position the new drum in its pocket *(above, right)* and screw the plate to the jamb. Place the sash on the sill, angled out slightly on the side of the new balance. With one hand holding the sash, use the other to pull down the balance tape clip and attach it to the bracket on the side of the sash. If the sash is heavy you may have to use considerable force to pull down the tape. Reinstall the sash *(page 15)*. To replace worn-out weight-and-pulley balances with clockspring balances, weigh the sash and buy a pair of clockspring balances and mounting brackets made to support that weight. Unscrew the pulley plate from the jamb and let the sash cord drop into the pocket. Screw the clockspring plate to the jamb. If it doesn't fit into the pulley-plate mortise, enlarge the mortise as you would for a strike plate *(page 44)*. Screw the bracket into the sash groove for the tape clip. Then complete the installation as described above. If you are installing clockspring balances on both sashes, work on the upper sash first.

INSTALLING REPLACEMENT CHANNELS

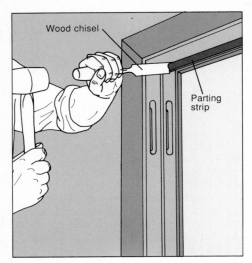

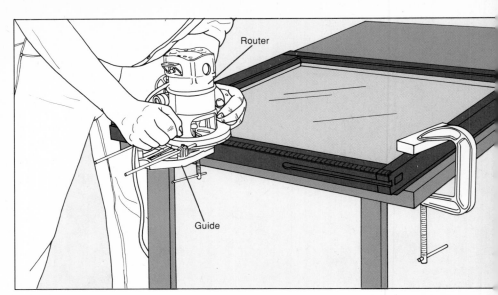

1 **Trimming the top parting strip.**
Replacement channels can take the place of worn-out balances. Measure between top jamb and sill to determine what height replacement channel you need. Remove the sashes *(page 15)* and the old balance system. Using a sharp wood chisel and rubber mallet, cut 1/2 inch off each end of the top parting strip *(above)*. To install the channels on a typical 1 3/8-inch-thick sash, go to step 3. If your sash is thicker than this, use a router to cut rabbets in the sash stiles to fit the replacement channels *(step 2)*.

2 **Routing the sash.** To cut a rabbet, use a router fitted with a guide or a self-guiding rabbet bit *(page 121)*. When positioning the sash, remember that the rabbets must be cut in the interior side of the lower sash, and in the exterior side of the upper sash. Clamp the lower sash to a work table, using C clamps padded with blocks of wood. Pull out any nails in the stile; hitting metal will throw the router off course. Measure the thickness of the sash stiles and subtract 1 3/8 inches to determine the depth to cut each rabbet. Since the inner and outer flanges (or stops) of the replacement channels protrude 1/4 inch, use a 1/4-inch rabbet bit. Move the router slowly and evenly along the sash stile *(above)*, deepening the rabbet in 3/8-inch increments. Cut rabbets in both stiles of both sashes.

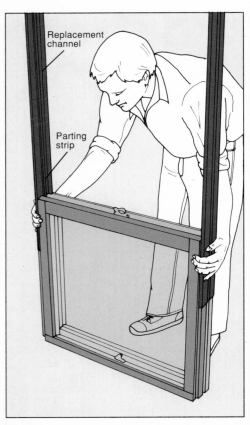

3 **Installing replacement channels.**
Hold the upper and lower sashes together, the exterior side of the lower sash against the interior side of the upper sash. Fit the replacement channels along the sash stiles *(far left)*. The replacement channels are angled at the bottom to fit the slope of the sill; position the channels correctly in relationship to the sashes. The parting strip—spring-loaded in the model shown here—fits between the sashes, and the channels' flanges act as stops. Lift the sashes and replacement channels onto the window sill, tilting them into the window frame *(near left)* until they come to rest against the blind stop. Secure the channels to the jamb using the nails or screws supplied with the replacement channel kit. If you routed the sash stiles to fit the replacement channels, reinstall the interior stops *(page 15)* to hide the grooves.

To replace damaged replacement channels, remove the nails or screws securing the channels to the jamb. Take off any interior stops, slide both sashes to the middle of the window and, with a helper, tilt the sashes and channels out of the window as a unit. Then slide the channels up off the sashes. Install new replacement channels as described above.

INSTALLING A SPIRAL BALANCE

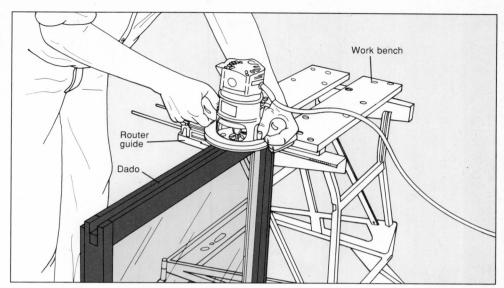

1 Patching the jamb. Measure the height of the sash stiles and subtract 2 inches. Buy four spiral balances of this size, with mounting brackets. Take out the sashes *(page 15)* and the old balance system. To patch a mortise left by an old pulley plate or clockspring plate, measure the mortise and draw its outline on a 1/4-inch piece of wood. Cut out the patch with a backsaw. Glue it in the mortise with carpenter's glue. When the glue is dry, use a sharp wood chisel to level the patch flush with the jamb *(above)*. Sand the area smooth and touch up the paint *(page 124)*.

2 Routing a dado for a spiral balance. To adapt a wood sash for spiral balances, cut a channel, or dado *(page 121)*, in each stile. Clamp the sash with the stile you are working on facing up. Pull out any nails in the stile; hitting metal will throw the router off course. Measure the thickness of the stile and draw a line down its center. Position the balance exactly on the center line and draw two lines outlining it along the stile. These lines mark the width of the channel to be routed. Choose a dado bit of the right size to cut this width. Then measure the thickness of the balance. This will be the depth of the channel; cut to this depth in 3/8-inch increments. Turn on the router and align the bit with the lines. Rout along the stile from left to right, repeating to the channel's final depth *(above)*. Check that the balance fits into the channel; when installed it must be flush with the stile. If necessary, use a wood chisel to square off the corners of the channel. Cut dadoes in the other stile and both stiles of the upper sash the same way.

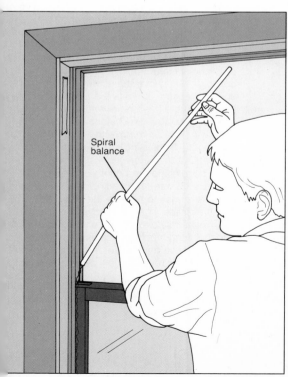

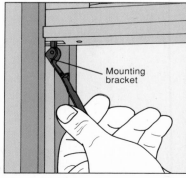

3 Installing a spiral balance. Reinstall the upper sash and the parting strip *(page 15)*. Insert the bottom end of the spiral balance into the stile channel *(far left)*; the spiral will drop down. Center the balance in the sash channel and nail or screw it in place *(near left, top)*. Repeat for the other side of the sash. Raise the sash about a foot and rest it on a block of wood. Rotate the mounting bracket near each corner of the sash's bottom rail clockwise until it rises to the rail *(near left, bottom)*. Secure each bracket to the bottom of the sash with one screw. Remove the block of wood and move the sash down and up. If the sash does not open or close easily, the balance is too tight. Remove the bracket screw, being careful not to let the balance unwind. Rotate the bracket counterclockwise one or two turns and reattach it. Adjust the other balance and try the window again. If the window will not stay open, increase the tension by rotating the brackets clockwise. Repeat until the window opens and closes smoothly, then install the other screws. After the upper sash is adjusted, replace the lower sash and interior stop *(page 15)*, and install and adjust the lower sash balances the same way.

SERVICING A SPIRAL BALANCE ON A TILT-IN WINDOW

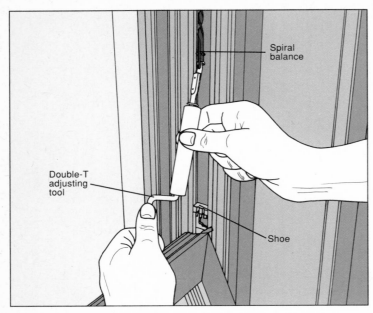

1 **Adjusting the spiral balance.** The sashes of some modern double-hung windows can be tilted indoors for cleaning or for servicing of their spiral balances. To adjust a balance, release the slide catches on the top rail of the lower sash and carefully lower the window. To tilt in an upper sash, slide it halfway down and tilt it in as well. If the sash does not open or close easily, loosen the tension on the balance by using a double-T adjusting tool. Unhook the balance from the shoe on the jamb and rotate it counterclockwise two turns *(above)*. If the window does not stay open, tighten the tension by rotating the balance clockwise two turns. Do the same on both sides. Resecure the sash to the jambs and test its operation. Repeat the adjustment until the window opens and closes smoothly.

2 **Removing the lower sash.** If the spiral balance breaks, replace it with an exact duplicate. To remove the broken balance on the type of lower sash shown here, tilt down the sash until it is parallel to the ground, then lift up one side of the sash until the corner pivot that connects it to the shoe is freed. Lift out the other side and store the sash in a safe place. Lower the top sash and remove it the same way. Use the double-T adjusting tool to unhook the broken balance from the shoe on the jamb *(step 1)*.

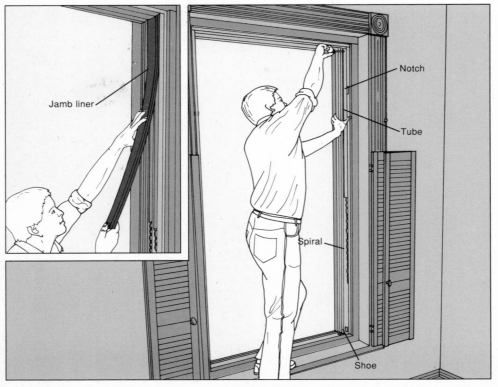

3 **Replacing the spiral balance.** To remove a broken spiral balance on a tilt-in sash, remove the jamb liner, if it has one, by slipping a screwdriver under the edge of the liner and prying up one end. Lift the liner free as shown *(inset)*. If it is screwed to the jamb, unscrew it. Remove the screw at the top of the spiral balance that holds the tube end of the balance to the jamb *(left)*, and lift out the balance. To install a new balance, reverse the steps you took to remove the broken one. Use the double-T adjusting tool to rotate the spiral five or six turns before hooking it to the shoe. If the shoe fell to the bottom of the jamb when the balance was removed, slide it up to the same level as the shoe in the other jamb. To lock it in place, fit a screwdriver into its hole and rotate it clockwise. If a shoe breaks, slide it to the open notch two thirds of the way up the jamb, and pull it free. Install an exact replacement by reversing the steps you took to remove it. Lock it in place, then use the double-T adjusting tool to rehook the spiral end of the balance into the slot in the shoe. Adjust the balance tension as described in step 1.

SERVICING A BLOCK-AND-TACKLE BALANCE

Clip

1 **Removing the lower sash.** A block-and-tackle balance *(page 13)* cannot be adjusted; if the window does not open and close properly or does not stay open, one or more of the balances is probably broken and must be replaced. To remove the lower sash, first flip up the clip at the top of each sash channel *(inset)*. If the clip is hidden by a sash stop, remove its screws and lift it off, then pull up the clip. Flip up the second clip the same way. Raise the sash high; the clips will catch the tops of the balances and disengage them from the sash. Push one side of the sash against the jamb and pull the other side out of the frame *(left)*. If the upper sash doesn't work properly, lower the sash to flip up the clips, then take out the sash as described above.

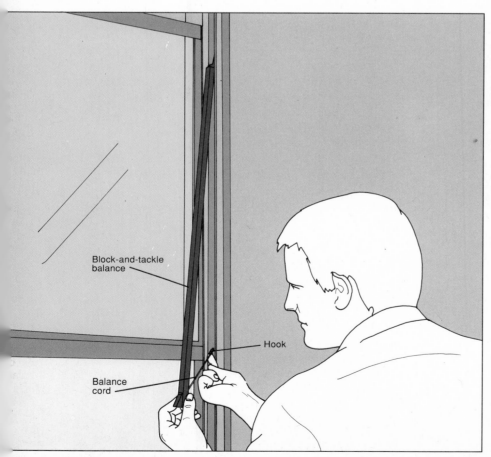

Block-and-tackle balance

Hook

Balance cord

2 **Removing the balance.** Pull the bottom of the balance away from the jamb to expose the balance cord, which is hooked into a notch in the jamb *(left)*. Push the hook up and out of the notch and lift the balance free. Disengage the second balance the same way. Inspect the balances for damage; take a broken balance to a window specialist and buy an exact replacement, or buy just the broken part, if possible. To reinstall a balance, push the top of the balance under the clip. Hold the balance with one hand while you pull the balance cord hook and engage it in the notch in the jamb. Install the second balance the same way. Reinstall the sash by pushing one side of it into the jamb channel above the balance and swinging the other side of the sash into the frame. Then lower the sash and reinstall the sash stops, if any. Replace the upper sash the same way.

SERVICING A METAL STORM WINDOW

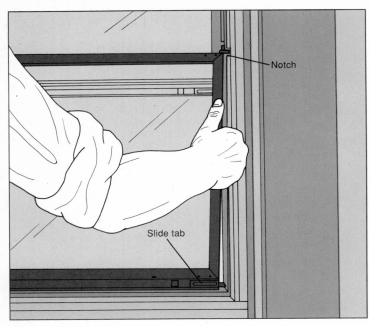

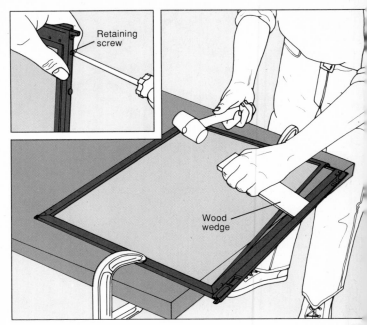

1 **Removing the sash.** To remove an upper or lower sash from a double-track window, shown above, release the slide tabs and slide the sash up or down to align the swivel keys with the notches in the frame. Then pull out the bottom of the sash and tilt it to pull the swivel keys out through the notches *(above)*. Many triple-track windows have an opening along one side of the frame for each track; slide the sash up or down to the opening and lift it out.

2 **Disassembling the sash.** Unscrew any retaining screws at the top and bottom of the stile edges *(inset)* and gently pull the top and bottom sash rails off the pane of glass. If a screw is stuck, apply penetrating oil and wait 15 minutes before unscrewing it. To remove a stubborn bottom rail, clamp the sash to a work bench or table. Place a wedge of wood against the lip of the bottom rail *(above)* or in the slide tab channel, and tap it gently to free the rail. If the corner keys are crimped to the rails, follow step 3 to replace the corner keys and slide tabs. To replace the pane and rubber gasket, go to page 80.

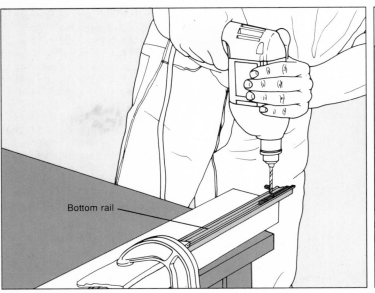

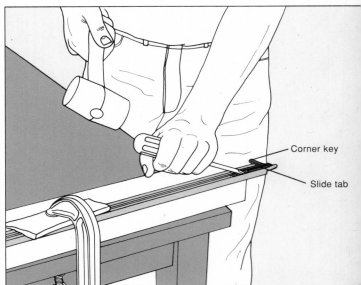

3 **Removing corner keys and slide tabs.** In most cases, the L-shaped corner keys inside the sash corners are crimped to the rails and—unless there are retaining screws *(step 2)*—to the stiles. You will see two small indentations at each end of the rail. To remove the corner keys and slide tabs, fasten the rail securely to a block of wood with a C clamp. Wearing safety goggles, drill through each indentation *(above, left)*, using a power drill at slow speed, with a bit exactly the same diameter as the indentations. Then place an old screwdriver against the slide tab *(above, right)* and, using a mallet, knock out the slide tab and corner key. The spring may fall out—if so, replace it as well. Repeat at the other end. If necessary, remove the top rail's T-shaped swivel keys the same way.

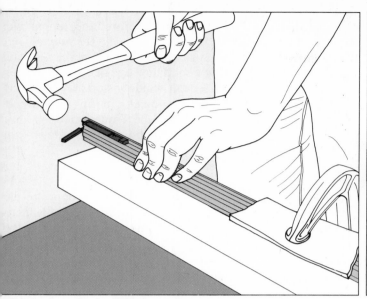

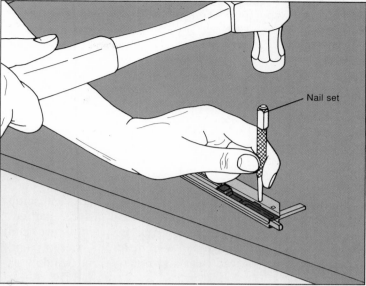

Nail set

4 **Reassembling the sash.** Take the old slide tabs and corner keys to a window specialist for exact replacements. Slide in the new corner key and slide tab, tapping them into place with a hammer *(above, left)*. To recrimp the corner key, lay the rail on a flat surface and secure it with a C clamp. Place a nail set over each hole left by the drill, and tap it firmly with a hammer *(above, right)*, crimping the rail against the corner key. Place the rails and stiles back in the pane, tucking the rubber gasket into place, and replace the stile screws or crimp the stiles against the corner keys.

INSTALLING A METAL STORM WINDOW

Flange

Installing a storm window. If you are replacing an old storm window, measure its height and width from the outside edges of the flanges and replace it with a window of the same model and size. Otherwise, go outside and measure the window opening height at both jambs, and the opening width across top and bottom, recording the smallest measurement from each. Buy a storm window to fit this opening size.

Drill 3/16-inch screwholes at the corners and midpoint of each flange and midway between these holes, 3/4 inch from the outside edge of the flange *(inset)*. Apply a 3/8-inch bead of caulk along the inside flange edge. With a helper inside to hold the storm window, place it against the window frame. Fasten the storm window with a screw in the middle hole of one side *(left)*, then align the storm window evenly against the window frame and install the middle screw on the other side. Be careful not to push the sides of the window toward each other as you drive the second screw; this will cause the sashes to bind in their channels. Have your helper test all sashes to ensure that they slide smoothly. Then secure the window through the remaining screw holes and caulk around the outside flange edges.

SWINGERS AND SLIDERS

To maintain the seemingly effortless motion made by windows that swing and windows and doors that slide, a homeowner must regularly clean and lubricate a variety of mechanical parts. Swingers (casement, awning, jalousie and hopper windows) swing open on hinges, sometimes guided by a metal rod and propelled by a crank operator or, less commonly, controlled by a lever mechanism. Sliders (sliding windows and patio doors) run on glides or rollers.

Dust and grease accumulate in operators and clog the splines of the gears. Periodically lubricating the operator in place with silicone spray is a good practice. A thorough cleaning once a year, as described in this chapter, requires a careful disassembly of the operator from the window. Dirt also builds up in tracks and around the window. Vacuum tracks and scrub sashes and frames with mild detergent. Steel surfaces, particularly common on basement hoppers, frequently rust, and should be scraped and repainted with rustproof exterior paint.

In many ways you can treat a swinging wood window as you would a double-hung window or even a convention[al] interior door. Inspect hinges for sagging, and replug wor[n] hinge-screw holes if necessary *(Tools and Techniques, pag[e] 123)*. If the sash binds against the jamb or sill, perhaps becaus[e] it is swollen with moisture, sand the edge of the sash where [it] rubs. Repositioning a casement window stop as you would [a] door stop *(page 48)* may help to quiet a rattling window. If [a] problem arises that is not listed in the Troubleshooting Guid[e] below, consult the chapters on Double-hung Windows *(pag[e] 13)* and Interior Doors *(page 40)*.

Even the best maintenance practices can't prevent par[ts] from breaking down, but they can usually be repaired. Fo[r] each type of window and door shown on the opposite pag[e] there are numerous other models, with their own distinctiv[e] parts. Save broken parts to help you find matching replace[-] ments; if your local hardware store doesn't stock the sam[e] model, take the part to a window repair specialist. As a fina[l] resort, consult the manufacturer.

TROUBLESHOOTING GUIDE

SYMPTOM	POSSIBLE CAUSE	PROCEDURE
CASEMENT, AWNING AND JALOUSIE WINDOWS		
Window doesn't open or close smoothly	Operator loose	Tighten operator mounting screws
	Operator dirty	Clean and lubricate operator *(casement, p. 28; awning, p. 29; jalousie, p. 30)* ◨○
	Operator worn	Replace gear or operator *(casement, p. 28; awning, p. 29; jalousie, p. 30)* ◨○
	Extension-arm shoe jammed	Release shoe *(p. 28)* □○; clean and lubricate track with silicone spray
Operator handle slips	Handle setscrew loose	Tighten setscrew
	Gear stem dirty	Remove handle, clean and lubricate stem *(p. 28)* □○
	Gear stem worn	Replace gear or operator *(casement, p. 28; awning, p. 29; jalousie, p. 30)* ◨○
Multi-vent awning window grinds when opened or closed; one or more vents are crooked; window rattles	Linkage system faulty	Lubricate linkage; adjust if necessary *(p. 29)* ◨○
Glass slat of jalousie window loose or falls out	Jalousie clip or rivet broken	Replace broken part *(p. 31)* ◨○
Hopper window doesn't open or close smoothly	Accumulation of rust or paint on sash or sill	Use coarse steel wool to remove rust deposits; scrape off paint and repaint with rustproof exterior paint □◓
SLIDING WINDOWS AND DOORS		
Slider doesn't open or close smoothly	Glides worn	Replace glides *(p. 31)* ◨○
	Roller assembly faulty	Adjust roller assembly *(p. 33)* □○
	Roller assembly broken	Replace roller assembly *(p. 33)* ◨○
	Track damaged	Install steel cap *(p. 32)* ◨○; repair track *(p. 32)* ◼◓
Slider rattles	Weather stripping worn	Replace weather stripping *(p. 115)* □○
	Insulation foam worn	Replace foam *(p. 31)* ◨○
	Track damaged	Install steel cap *(p. 32)* ◨○; repair track *(p. 32)* ◼◓
	Roller assembly faulty	Adjust roller assembly *(p. 33)* □○
	Track bowed	Hammer down if minor; call for service

DEGREE OF DIFFICULTY: □ Easy ◨ Moderate ◼ Complex
ESTIMATED TIME: ○ Less than 1 hour ◓ 1 to 3 hours ● Over 3 hours

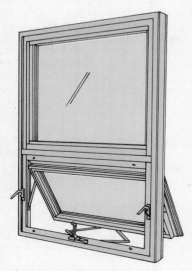

Awning windows (single-vent)
Pivot at the top and swing upward and out, shielding the inside from rain even when open; their crank operator commonly uses scissor arms clipped or screwed to the sash, or a sliding arm that runs along a track on the sash.

Awning windows (multi-vent)
Open and close by a complicated series of linkages that run vertically along both sides of the window unit; the torque bar lining the bottom of the frame connects them and transfers the crank operator movement evenly to the sashes.

Casement windows
Swing open on side hinges; usually use a crank operator which consists of gears and an extension arm that slides through a track fastened to the lower part of the sash. Older casements may operate with a lever that controls the motion of the sash.

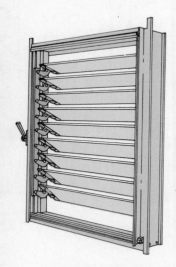

Jalousie windows
Resemble a multi-vent awning; the narrow panes are held in place by clips or metal channels; a linkage system runs up only one side of the frame; the glass-to-glass joints tend to leak air and so are usually found in porches, breezeways and other unheated areas.

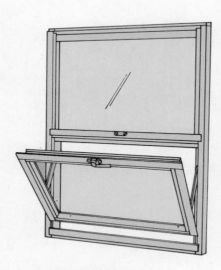

Hopper windows
Are used in basements or in combination with non-moving windows; they pivot at the bottom and swing inward, and rarely use an operator; often made of steel, they require regular maintenance to prevent damage by rust.

Sliding windows and patio doors
Ventilate through 50 percent of the window opening; the window or door moves along a track, usually on rollers or plastic glides; some come with one fixed and one sliding sash or door, others have two moving sections.

SERVICING A CASEMENT WINDOW

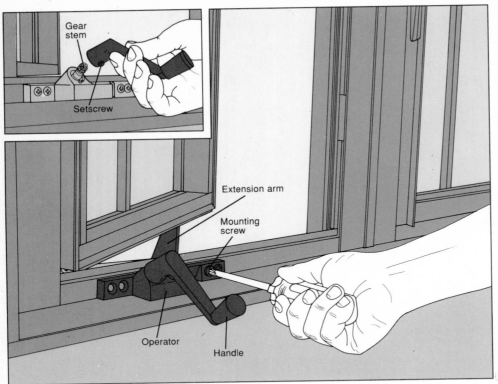

1 **Freeing the operator.** Clean and lubricate a casement window's working parts at least once a year. Open the window and clean the extension-arm track of old paint and hardened grease with a wire brush. Spray silicone lubricant on all moving parts, along the track and where the extension arm exits from the back of the operator on the window frame. Loosen the handle setscrew and pull off the handle *(inset)*. Spray lubricant along the gear-stem splines. If the operator is broken or a thorough cleaning of its gears is required, you will have to remove it. With the window opened, remove the two, three or four screws that secure the operator to the inside bottom edge of the frame *(left)*. If your casement works with a lever instead of a crank operator, remove the screws that attach the pivot mount to the sill.

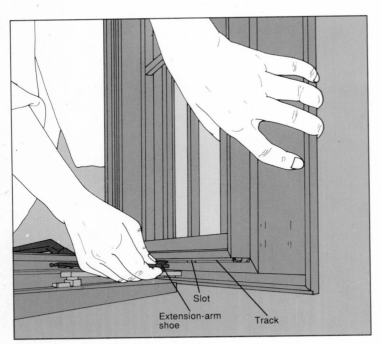

2 **Removing the extension-arm shoe.** To disengage the extension arm from the sash, slide it along the sash until it reaches the access slot. Push the extension arm down and pull its shoe through the slot *(above)*. Some models don't have a slot in the track. Instead, free the extension arm by sliding it off the end of the track. If the window is lever-operated, you will have to unscrew the pivot plate that secures the lever arm to the sash. Set aside all screws for reassembly later.

3 **Replacing the operator.** Pull the operator free of its slot in the window frame *(above)*. Remove the handle *(step 1, inset)*. Examine the splines of the operator gears and gear stem *(inse* if clogged with old grease and dirt, soak the operator in commercial mineral spirits or kerosene. Dry it completely before applying white grease or petroleum jelly to the main gear only. If gear or stem spline are rounded or broken, consult a window specialist or the manufactur for repair or replacement. To reinstall the operator, reverse the steps taken for removal.

ERVICING AN AWNING WINDOW (Single-vent)

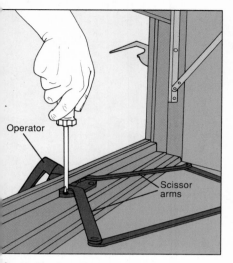

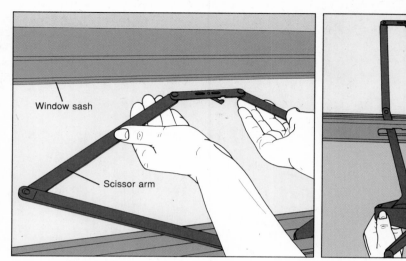

Window sash

Scissor arm

Scissor arms

Operator

Releasing the operator. Open the window as wide as possible. If the sash hinges are old and worn, brace the ndow with blocks of wood so that the win- w will not slam shut when the scissor arms d operator are removed. Remove the ounting screws that secure the operator to e window frame *(above)*.

2 Replacing the operator. Reach under the sash and unhook the scissor arms from their clips on the sash *(above, left)*. For scissor arms that are screwed to the sash, remove the screws. If the window has extension arms that slide along a track on the sash, spread the arms and slide their shoes off each end of the track. In the type shown, straighten the scissor arms, and pull them clear of the window frame *(above, right)*. Clean and lubricate awning window operators as you would casement window operators *(page 28)*. If gear or stem splines are rounded or broken, consult a window specialist or the manufacturer for repair or replacement. To reinstall the operator, reverse the steps you took to remove it.

ERVICING AN AWNING WINDOW (Multi-vent)

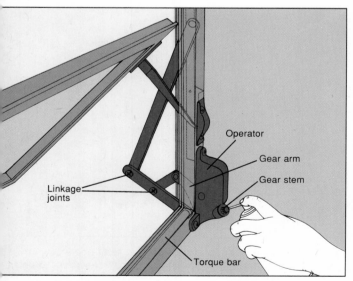

Operator

Gear arm

Gear stem

Linkage joints

Torque bar

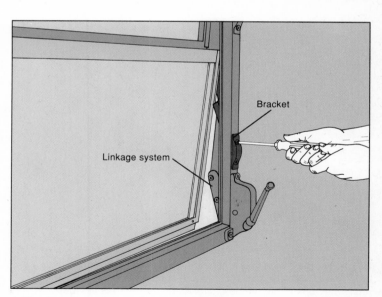

Bracket

Linkage system

bricating the operator and linkage system. Lubricate the win- w's moving parts at least once a year. Open the window and spray cone lubricant through the opening where the gear arm exits from back of the operator. Remove the operator handle *(page 28)* and ay lubricant on the stem splines *(above)*. Also lubricate the linkage ts on both sides of the ventilators and the torque bar that runs ng the bottom of the window frame. If the torque bar is covered by a tal casing, first pry it off with an old screwdriver. Snap it back on er lubricating the bar.

Adjusting the vents. To determine which vents need to be adjusted, crank the window closed and test the vents' linkage system by pushing firmly on each vent in turn. If a vent flops rather than snaps back into place, use a screwdriver to adjust the screws on the brackets around the frame *(above)*. To stop a vent from rattling, lower its brackets about 1/16 inch. To loosen a vent that is too tight, raise its bracket the same distance. If any vents are crooked, loosen the bracket screws, align the brackets and retighten the screws. Whenever you make any adjustment, test each of the vents in turn; moving one vent's brackets will affect the tension of the other vents.

SERVICING AN AWNING WINDOW (Multi-vent, continued)

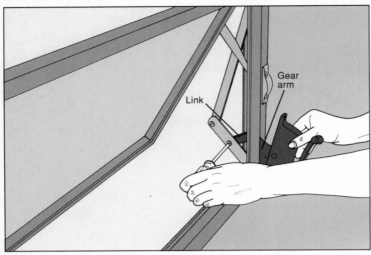

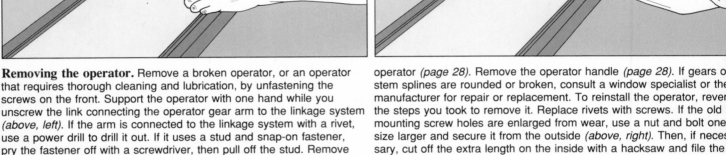

Removing the operator. Remove a broken operator, or an operator that requires thorough cleaning and lubrication, by unfastening the screws on the front. Support the operator with one hand while you unscrew the link connecting the operator gear arm to the linkage system *(above, left)*. If the arm is connected to the linkage system with a rivet, use a power drill to drill it out. If it uses a stud and snap-on fastener, pry the fastener off with a screwdriver, then pull off the stud. Remove the operator from its slot in the window frame. Clean and lubricate a multi-vent awning window operator as you would a casement window

operator *(page 28)*. Remove the operator handle *(page 28)*. If gears or stem splines are rounded or broken, consult a window specialist or the manufacturer for repair or replacement. To reinstall the operator, reverse the steps you took to remove it. Replace rivets with screws. If the old mounting screw holes are enlarged from wear, use a nut and bolt one size larger and secure it from the outside *(above, right)*. Then, if necessary, cut off the extra length on the inside with a hacksaw and file the bolt flush with the nut.

SERVICING A JALOUSIE WINDOW

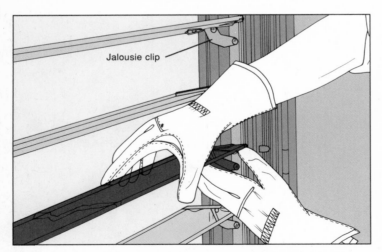

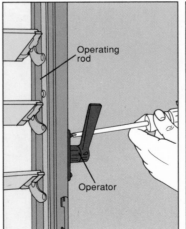

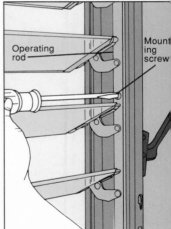

Replacing a broken pane. Wearing heavy work gloves, pull down the lip of the jalousie clip and slide out the cracked or broken glass *(above)*. Measure one of the unbroken panes of glass and buy one cut to size. The exposed edges of jalousie panes are rounded for safety. If you cut your own pane *(page 77)*, smooth the edges with an oilstone dipped in water before installing it.

Servicing an operator. To remove either a lever operator *(above)* or a crank operator from a jalousie window, use a screwdriver to unfasten its mounting screws *(above, left)*. Then remove the mounting screw from the operating rod *(above, right)*. If it is connected with a rivet, use a power drill to drill it out. If it is connected with a stud and snap-on fastener, pry off the fastener with a screwdriver first, then pull off the stud. Pull the operator from its slot in the window frame. Clean and lubricate a jalousie operator as you would a casement window operator *(page 28)*. If any internal parts are worn or broken, consult a window specialist or the manufacturer for repair or replacement. To reinstall the operator, reverse the steps you took to remove it, substituting screws for any rivets you had to drill out.

ERVICING A JALOUSIE WINDOW (continued)

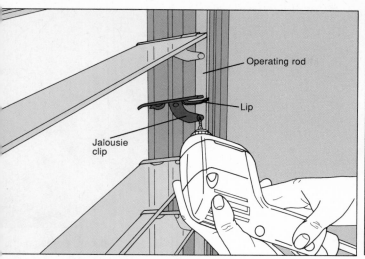

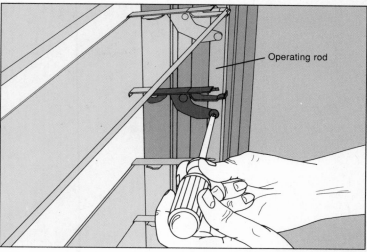

placing a jalousie clip. The lip of a jalousie clip may break off if you nd it too far or too often when replacing a pane. To remove the clip, st remove the glass pane *(page 30)*. Then use a power drill to drill out e rivet that holds the clip to the operating rod *(above, left)*. If it has a d instead, pry off the snap-on fastener with a screwdriver, then pull the stud. If it has a screw, unscrew it. Pull out the jalousie clip.

Consult a window specialist or the jalousie window manufacturer for a replacement. Insert the new jalousie clip into its slot in the frame and replace the stud or rivet with a sheet-metal screw. Screw the clip back into the operating rod *(above, right)*. Pull down on the lip of the jalousie clip and slide the pane into place. Do not bend the lip of the clip more than necessary.

ERVICING A SLIDING WINDOW

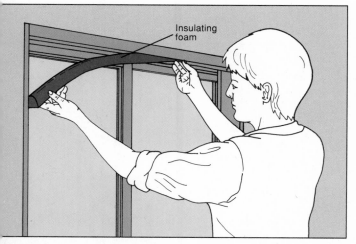

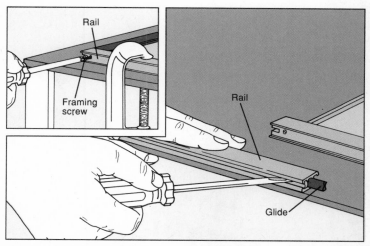

placing the insulating foam. If the insulating foam in your sliding dow wears out, the sash may rattle in its frame. To replace the m, remove the sash by pushing it up while swinging the bottom out. h the sash out, the liner that holds the foam in place can sometimes ply be twisted out of the top jamb. On some models, you may have nscrew the liner to expose the foam. Pull it free, as shown. If the m is glued, pry it out with a screwdriver. If the foam is held in place screws, remove the screws. Choose a replacement foam of the e type, about 1/2 inch thicker than the original. Use scissors to cut the length of the top jamb and install it by reversing the steps you k for removal.

Replacing window glides. Bottom rail glides wear out and can be replaced. Remove the sash as described at left. Clamp the sash down on a flat surface with C clamps and remove the framing screws that secure the rails to the stiles *(inset)*. Using a rubber mallet and a block of wood to protect the window, knock the bottom rail free *(page 33, step 2)*. Insert a screwdriver into the channel in the bottom rail and force out the glide *(above)*. Some sliding windows run on as many as four glides in each rail. Take the worn guide to a window specialist or contact the manufacturer for an exact replacement. To install a new guide, reverse the steps you took to remove the old one.

SERVICING A PATIO DOOR TRACK

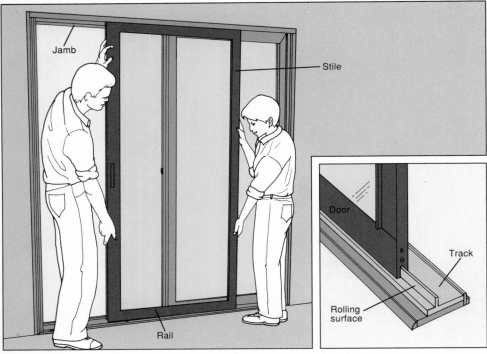

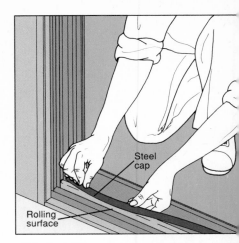

1 **Removing a patio door.** Slide the door about halfway along the track. With a helper, lift the door up off the rolling surface *(inset),* pushing it into the top jamb, as shown. Carefully swing the bottom of the door out. Some very old patio doors can only be removed from the outside. If there is a fixed panel, unscrew any brackets that hold it in place, slide it to the center of the track and lift it out. Then lift out the patio door itself. After completing the necessary repairs *(step 2 or step 3),* replace the door, reversing the steps you took to remove it.

2 **Installing a steel cap.** Sometimes th protruding rolling surface of a sliding door's track gets dented by constant wear and tear. If the damage isn't too sever fit the track with a U-shaped steel cap for th door to run along. Consult a window special ist to choose a cap that will fit your door's rollers. Have a cap cut to the length of your track. Snap the cap onto the rolling surface as shown above and press it down firmly. In most cases the weight of the door will keep the cap in place. If it doesn't, drill a hole into the side jamb just above the steel cap. Inser a screw so that its head holds down the cap Replace the door and slide it along the track If the door fits too tightly, adjust the roller assembly *(page 33, step 1).*

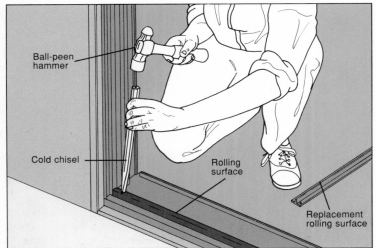

3 **Repairing the track.** When damage to the rolling surface of the track hampers the opening and closing of your patio door, cut off and replace the rolling surface. Using a sharp cold chisel and a ball-peen hammer, cut the rolling surface away from the track. Begin at one end *(above, left)* and cut along its base until it separates from the track. Smooth any jagged edges left on the track surface with a metal file or a power drill with a grinder attachment. Leave one inch of roughness at each end to serve as a guide when laying down the replacement piece. Take the old rolling surface to a window and door

specialist or contact the patio door manufacturer; you need an exact match. Have it cut 1 inch shorter than the original piece. Place it on the track surface, using the rough edges at each end to line it up. If your new piece doesn't come predrilled, wear safety goggles and use a powe drill to countersink holes 8 to 10 inches apart through the edges of the rolling surface and into the track *(above, right).* Insert one screw at eac end. Replace the door and slide it along to see that it operates smooth With the door in place, install the rest of the screws the same way.

ERVICING A PATIO DOOR ROLLER ASSEMBLY

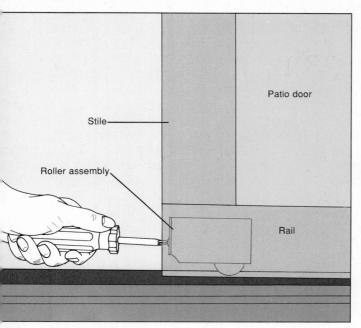

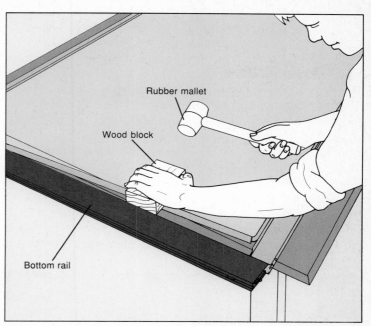

1 Adjusting the rollers. If your patio door has trouble running smoothly, adjust the roller assembly screws. If it sticks at the top, insert a screwdriver into the adjusting screw in the roller at the bottom and turn it counterclockwise. If it rubs too tightly in the track at the bottom, turn the screws clockwise. You may need help to raise the door slightly to take the pressure off the roller assembly so the screws can be adjusted. Get a helper to wedge a strong screwdriver or utility bar between the door and the track. Be careful, the door is heavy. Slide the door along the track to see that it is even. If the roller assembly needs servicing, go on to step 2.

2 Removing the bottom rail. Remove a roller assembly for cleaning or replacement. Take down the door *(page 32)*, and lay it flat on a work table with its bottom over the edge as shown. Unscrew the framing screws that secure the bottom rail to the stiles. Hammer off the bottom rail with a rubber mallet, using a block of wood to protect the door and glass. On some doors, like this one, you may first have to knock the stiles out slightly to keep the roller adjusting screws from interfering with the removal of the bottom rail.

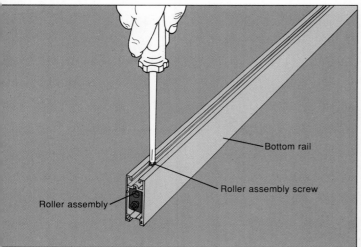

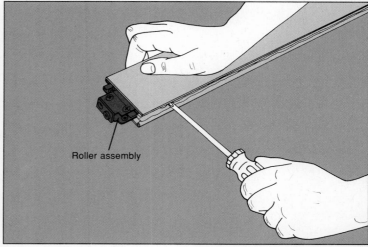

3 Removing a patio door roller. Use a screwdriver to remove the screw that holds the roller assembly in the rail *(above, left)*. If the roller is held in place with a steel pin, turn the rail on its side and raise it on a small block of wood. Then drive the pin out with a hammer and nail set. Slide the roller assembly out with a screwdriver *(above, right)*. Repeat for the other roller. Inspect them carefully; they may only need a good cleaning. Soak the assemblies in kerosene or mineral spirits and dry them well. If a roller is damaged, replace it with an exact duplicate. Reinstall the rollers and the rail by reversing the steps you took to remove them.

SKYLIGHTS

A skylight lends a sense of spaciousness to a room or hallway by breaking the confinement of a closed ceiling. The traditional multi-paned glass structure has been superseded by modern styles with a clear acrylic, double-glazed dome and a prefabricated aluminum frame. Two variations are shown below. One is mounted on a raised wood frame called a curb; the other has a built-in aluminum curb *(inset)*. The curb helps divert water away from the skylight. To keep it watertight, the wood curb is flashed—wrapped with thin sheets of aluminum overlapped in such a way that they shed water downroof. The aluminum curb has flanges that serve as built-in flashing. Flashing joints are sealed with roofing cement.

Modern non-opening skylights rarely leak; if water gets into the house, fault usually lies with the flashing. Inspect the flashing periodically; if it is damaged, also inspect the wood curb beneath it for rot. Some skylights are installed without a curb. If this type of skylight leaks, it should be replaced with model that requires a curb.

Most houses have asphalt shingles, secured with shingl nails (or staples) and roofing cement. The flashing strips ar layered among the shingles or inserted beneath them. Whe inspecting or removing flashing, take care not to tear th shingles. Loosened shingles may be renailed and cemented but damaged ones must be replaced. If your roof is cedar, slat or tile, consult a roofing expert before servicing a skylight

You can buy new aluminum flashing in rolls and cut an bend it to shape, or it can be custom-made at a metalwor shop. Wear work gloves when handling flashing.

Before working on the roof, read the precautions on pag 35. When you are finished, clean any spilled roofing cemen off an acrylic pane with kerosene. Wash the pane with a mil detergent-and-water solution and wipe it with a chamois.

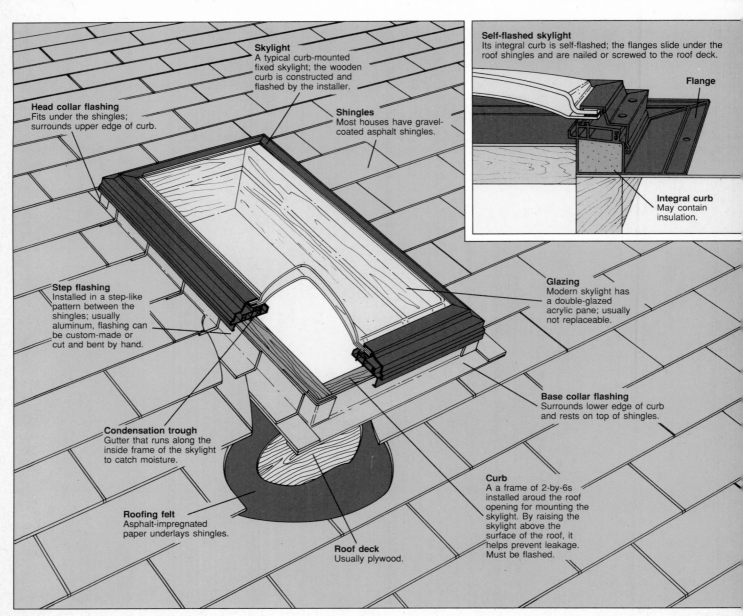

Skylight
A typical curb-mounted fixed skylight; the wooden curb is constructed and flashed by the installer.

Head collar flashing
Fits under the shingles; surrounds upper edge of curb.

Shingles
Most houses have gravel-coated asphalt shingles.

Self-flashed skylight
Its integral curb is self-flashed; the flanges slide under the roof shingles and are nailed or screwed to the roof deck.

Flange

Integral curb
May contain insulation.

Step flashing
Installed in a step-like pattern between the shingles; usually aluminum, flashing can be custom-made or cut and bent by hand.

Glazing
Modern skylight has a double-glazed acrylic pane; usually not replaceable.

Base collar flashing
Surrounds lower edge of curb and rests on top of shingles.

Condensation trough
Gutter that runs along the inside frame of the skylight to catch moisture.

Roofing felt
Asphalt-impregnated paper underlays shingles.

Roof deck
Usually plywood.

Curb
A a frame of 2-by-6s installed aroud the roof opening for mounting the skylight. By raising the skylight above the surface of the roof, it helps prevent leakage. Must be flashed.

TROUBLESHOOTING GUIDE

SYMPTOM	POSSIBLE CAUSE	PROCEDURE
Skylight on low-pitched roof leaks	Self-flashed skylight without a curb	Remove skylight and replace with self-flashed model with an integral curb *(p. 36)* ▬◗ or with one that uses a wood curb. Build wood curb *(p. 37)* ▬◗ and flash *(p. 38)* ■●
	Wood curb rotted due to inadequate flashing	Remove skylight *(p. 36)* ▬○ and curb *(p. 37)* ▬◗; build new curb *(p. 37)* ▬◗ and install new flashing *(p. 38)* ■●
	Roofing cement dried out and cracked; flashing torn or corroded	Seal flashing with roofing cement or patch *(p. 36)* ▬○; install new flashing *(p. 38)* ■●
	Glazing compound around glass pane deteriorated	Remove glazing compound *(p. 124)* ▬○ and recaulk with silicone sealant
Skylight on steeply pitched roof leaks	Roofing cement dried out and cracked; flashing torn or corroded	Call for service to replace flashing
	Self-flashed skylight without a curb	Call for service to replace skylight with self-flashed model with integral curb or with one that uses a wood curb
Condensation drips from skylight	Skylight installed in bathroom, kitchen, laundry room or other humid location	Install a ventilating fan; or replace existing unit with ventilating skylight, or skylight with condensation trough *(p. 36)* ▬◗
Skylight admits too much heat	Skylight faces southwest and transparent glazing does not block sun's rays	Install custom shade following manufacturer's instructions; replace existing unit with ventilating or tinted skylight *(p. 36)* ▬◗
Glass or plastic skylight cracked, discolored, crazed, stained or scratched	Wear and tear caused by ice, hail or fallen branches; mishandling during installation	Replace skylight *(p. 36)* ▬◗ or reglaze if possible, following manufacturer's instructions

DEGREE OF DIFFICULTY: □ **Easy** ▬ **Moderate** ■ **Complex**
ESTIMATED TIME: ○ **Less than 1 hour** ◗ **1 to 3 hours** ● **Over 3 hours**

SECURITY ON THE ROOF

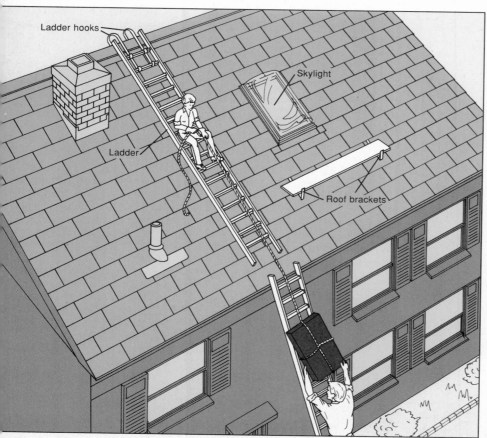

Ladder hooks

Skylight

Ladder

Roof brackets

Working on the roof. Essential for reaching the roof is a heavy-duty extension ladder. A second ladder, fitted with ladder hooks, can be hung from the ridge of the roof for a secure toehold. A 2-by-10 plank supported by a pair of roof brackets provides extra comfort and a platform for work materials. All of these tools can be rented. On a steep roof where the pitch is more than 4 in 12—that is, the roof rises 4 feet for every 12 horizontal feet—enlist the services of a professional. To work on a roof with a lower pitch, take the following precautions:

Plan repairs for when there is no forecast of rain, wind or extreme temperatures. Work with a helper when moving materials between the ground and roof. While on the roof, make sure someone is within earshot and can lend assistance if necessary. Wear soft-soled shoes, and heavy work gloves when handling flashing.

Assemble the tools and materials you need and hoist everything up at the same time. Make sure the ladder is firmly planted on level ground, with the distance from the foot of the ladder to the base of the wall one quarter the length of the ladder. Haul up the skylight and curb with ropes, using the sides of the ladder as guide tracks. Protect the skylight from scratches with blankets or its original container.

REMOVING AND REPLACING A SKYLIGHT

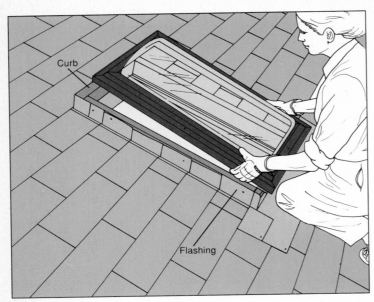

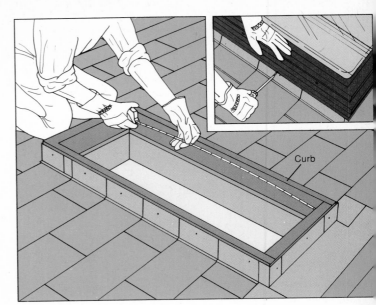

1 **Removing the skylight.** To service a skylight, prepare to work safely on the roof *(page 35)*. A leak may be caused by failure of the skylight, the flashing or the curb. A skylight like the one shown here is most likely to leak because the flashing has deteriorated or was poorly installed. To remove this type of skylight for replacement or service, use a screwdriver to unscrew it from its curb. Lift the skylight off the curb and lay it carefully on the roof.

Some self-flashed skylights rest directly on the roof deck. If this type leaks, replace it with one that requires a curb and flashing *(page 38)*. To remove a self-flashed model, pull back the roofing shingles to expose the flanges. Work carefully, using a utility bar to pry up the shingle nails or staples. Do not tear or crease the shingles. Remove the screws securing the flanges to the roof deck and set the skylight aside. To measure for a new curb or skylight, go to step 2.

2 **Measuring for a new skylight or curb.** Whether replacing a curb *(page 37)* or installing a new skylight of the type shown above, measure the length and width of the curb from the inside edges *(above)*. Then measure the thickness of the lumber used to build the curb. Before installing a skylight in the old curb, use a stiff putty knife to scrape old roofing cement from the curb, and add a fresh layer *(page 37)*. Fasten the skylight to the curb with galvanized wood screws *(inset)*. Build and install a new curb if necessary *(page 37)*. Install a new skylight as above.

To replace a self-flashed skylight, measure the length and width of the opening itself. To install it, slip the flanges beneath the shingles at the top and sides; you may need a helper to pull them back. Rest the lower flange on top of the shingles, leaving it exposed. Screw the flanges to the roof deck with galvanized screws. Nail the shingles in place with roofing nails, through new holes, and cover their heads and the old holes with roofing cement.

SERVICING CURB FLASHING

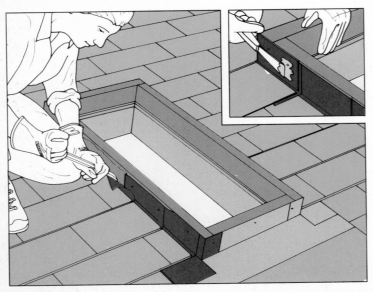

Repairing curb flashing. Remove the skylight *(step 1, above)*. If you have a curbed skylight similar to the one shown, inspect the flashing for corrosion, cracks or missing sections. Use a putty knife to apply a generous amount of roofing cement to seal any small holes or tears where the flashing was nailed to the curb *(inset)*. To repair a larger hole, use tin snips to cut a patch from a piece of flashing. Spread roofing cement around the perimeter of the hole and place the patch on top of the wet cement. Check whether the roofing cement along the curb has deteriorated or was inadequately applied when the skylight was installed. If so, use a pry bar to extract the nails securing the flashing to the curb. Gently bend back the flashing *(left)* and add a dollop of roofing cement to the curb. Then press the flashing back in place and renail it to the curb. Seal all seams between flashing and shingles, and flashing and curb, with roofing cement. If the side flashing is one continuous strip instead of overlapping steps, or if it is badly corroded, reflash around the skylight *(page 38)*. Test the curb for signs of rot by sticking the point of a key or a tool into the wood; if the curb is soft and spongy, replace it *(page 37)*.

REPLACING THE CURB

1 Making a curb. Remove the skylight and measure the old curb *(page 36)*. Working on the ground, mark the measurements on pressure-treated lumber, usually 2-by-6s. Use a backsaw and miter box to cut their ends at right angles at the marks *(inset)*. Butt the ends together so that the inside dimensions of the curb match the skylight opening. Use galvanized nails to secure each butt joint *(above)*. Check that the joints are square by using a carpenter's square, or extend a tape measure diagonally from corner to corner; the diagonal measurements should match. If not, shift the curb until they do. Then brace two opposite corners with wood strips temporarily nailed to the curb to keep the curb square until it is set in place.

2 Removing the old curb. Tie the new curb with rope and, working with a helper, raise it up onto the roof. If installing a new skylight, hoist it, as well as any tools, flashing and roofing cement that you plan to use, at the same time. Remove the skylight *(page 36, step 1)*. Pry out the nails securing the flashing around the old curb and bend back the flashing *(page 36)*, taking great care not to damage it. Then use a pry bar to extract nails holding the curb to the roof, or a screwdriver to unfasten any screws. Reach inside the opening and insert the pry bar between curb and roof, and lever the curb free of the roofing cement. Then take hold of the edges of the curb and pull it away from the roof deck *(above)*. Use a stiff putty knife to scrape any remaining roofing cement off the deck where the curb was resting.

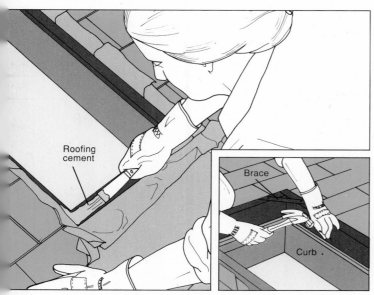

3 Installing the new curb. Use a putty knife to apply a 2-inch-wide bed of roofing cement around the skylight opening *(above, left)*. Set the curb in position, pressing it into the roofing cement. Toenail the curb through the deck into the wood framing of the roof, driving 3-inch galvanized nails at 6-inch intervals *(inset)*. Apply a liberal amount of roofing cement to the outer curb sides; bend the flashing back into place and use roofing nails to secure it to the curb. Cover the nail heads and all holes and joints with roofing cement. If the flashing

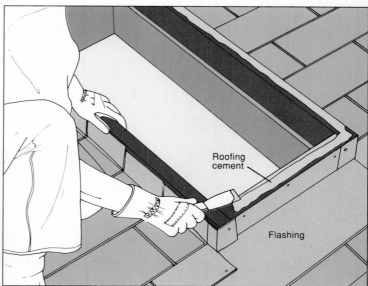

was damaged or inadequate when you removed the old curb, remove and replace it *(page 38)*.

To prepare the curb for the skylight, pry off the corner braces and spread a 1-inch-wide layer of roofing cement *(above, right)* around the top edge of the curb, or apply a thick bead of silicone sealant with a caulking gun. Mount the skylight, with the aid of a helper if it is heavy, and press it onto the curb. Secure the frame of the skylight to the curb with galvanized screws.

INSTALLING FLASHING

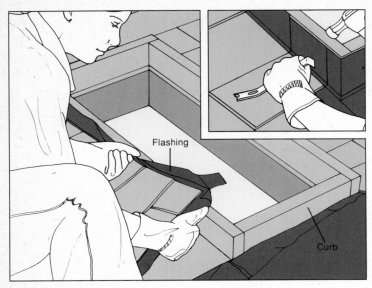

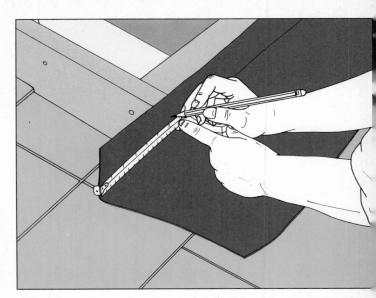

1 **Removing old flashing.** If the flashing has corroded, or if strip flashing was used along the sides instead of step flashing, you will need to remove part or all of the old flashing. First, remove the skylight *(page 36)*. Then loosen the shingles around the sides and top of the curb by prying up the nails with a utility bar *(inset)*. Nail heads may be hidden beneath a quarter-sized dab of roofing cement; scrape away the cement with a stiff putty knife. Pry out the nails attaching the flashing to the curb and, wearing gloves, pull the old flashing free *(above)*. Take care not to damage the shingles.

2 **Measuring and cutting collar flashing.** You will first install base collar flashing across the bottom of the curb, then step flashing along the sides and, finally, head collar flashing across the top. Measure the outside length and width of the curb. Buy custom made collar flashing from a sheet metal shop, or buy flashing in a 12-inch-wide roll and make your own collar flashing: Use tin snips to cut a strip of flashing from the roll, at least 6 inches longer than the base of the curb. Bend the strip lengthwise over a side edge of the curb; one flap should be about 4 inches wide, and the other about 8 inches wide. Center the flashing along the base of the curb, narrow flap up, and mark the flap where it meets the curb corner at each side *(above)*. Cut along the fold to each mark, and wrap the flaps around the corner of the curb. Set this base collar flashing aside and form the head collar flashing the same way.

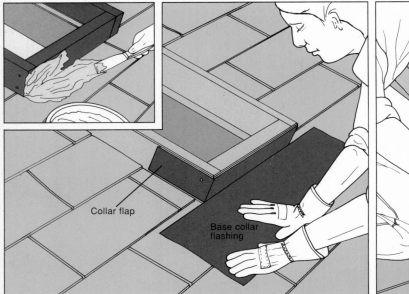

3 **Installing the base collar flashing.** Use a putty knife to apply a liberal coat of roofing cement to the base of the curb and around its corners, and to the shingles below the curb *(inset)*. Reposition the base collar flashing, pressing it into the roofing cement *(above, left)*, and wrapping the collar flaps around the curb edges. Nail the flashing to the curb 1 inch below the top edge, driving galvanized roofing nails at 4-inch intervals *(above, right)*. Cover the heads of all nails with a generous dab of roofing cement.

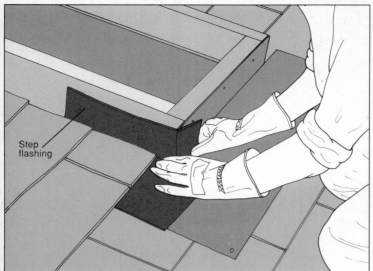

4 **Installing step flashing.** Count the number of courses of shingles along one side of the curb; you will need at least twice as many pieces of step flashing to seal both sides of the curb. Buy flashing in prebent, 10-inch-square pieces from a sheet metal shop. Using tin snips, make a 3-inch cut along the fold on one side of the step flashing. Slip the flashing under the shingles near the bottom of the curb and fold the cut edge around the corner to overlap the base collar flashing *(above)*. Once folded, set the flashing aside and apply roofing cement to the roof deck under the shingles, and to the side of the curb. Slide in the flashing and nail it with galvanized nails at 4-inch intervals, an inch below its top edge. Then apply roofing cement

between the next layer of shingles and the deck, and along the curb, and position the second piece of step flashing *(above, right)*. Work your way up to the top of the curb, always applying the roofing cement before weaving the next piece of step flashing between the shingles. Nail each piece of flashing to the curb as you go. When you get to the top piece of step flashing, cut it as you did the first piece of step flashing, and fold the cut edge around the curb. The top collar flashing, when installed *(step 5)*, will overlap it. Install step flashing on the other side of the curb the same way. When both sides are completed, renail the shingles with galvanized roofing nails; make new holes and cover old ones, and all nail heads, with roofing cement.

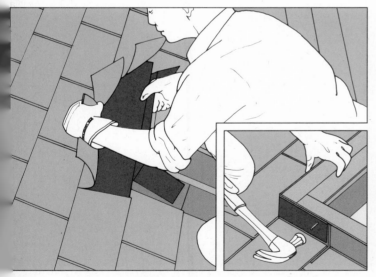

5 **Installing head collar flashing.** Apply a bed of roofing cement to the top edge of the curb and to the roof deck beneath the shingles. Add some to the surface of the upper pieces of step flashing. Using the head flashing you formed in step 2, slide the flap under the shingles *(above)*, and press it into place so it fits snugly against the curb. Then fold the extension flaps around the corners of the curb, overlapping the upper pieces of step flashing. Nail the flashing in place with galvanized roofing nails, 1 inch below its top edge and at 4-inch intervals *(inset)*.

6 **Reinstalling the skylight.** Resecure the shingles with galvanized roofing nails; make new holes and cover old holes and nail heads with roofing cement. Apply roofing cement or silicone sealant to the curb *(page 37, step 3)* and lower the skylight onto the curb *(above)*. Screw the skylight to the curb with galvanized screws.

INTERIOR DOORS

The simple opening and closing of an interior door can invite visitors into a room, declare privacy or hide a less-than-orderly area of the house.

Doors may be solid or hollow. Solid panel doors commonly grace the interiors of older homes, while modern homes use hollow doors, often filled with corrugated cardboard. Other styles include top-hung sliding doors for closets and folding doors used for closets and pantries.

In principle, interior doors should remain trouble free for years. In practice, however, hinges sag, houses settle and solid doors warp and shrink due to temperature and humidity.

As a rule, when a hinged door refuses to open and close as it should, first work on the hinges, then the door and finally the door frame. Hinges and strike plates can be shimmed *(page 47)* or their mortises deepened *(page 46)*. Doors can be cut *(page 50)*, or planed *(page 53)* and jambs can be shifted in or out *(page 49)*. Occasionally a bowed door will need to be straightened with weights or clamps *(page 54)* or its joints will require gluing or bolting *(page 52)*. However, wood has a long memory and straightening a warped door should be seen only as a temporary measure. Eventually the door must be replaced.

Match a new door to the other doors in your home. For older styles, cull through demolition yards and antique stores. If the door you choose doesn't fit, you may have to cut it to size *(page 50)*. Measure the doorway between the side jambs and from head jamb to floor; subtract 1/2 inch for rug or threshold clearance. Don't cut more than an inch off the height of a panel or hollow door—although you can cut up to 2 inches from the width. Reuse old hinge and strike plate mortises, replugging worn screw holes if necessary *(page 123)*. Chisel hinge mortises on the door in exact alignment with those on the jamb *(page 122)*. Install new doorknobs according to manufacturer's instructions. New doors can also be bought as prehung units and installed yourself *(page 86)*.

TROUBLESHOOTING GUIDE

SYMPTOM	POSSIBLE CAUSE	PROCEDURE
Door hinges squeak	Rust or paint buildup around hinges	Remove one hinge pin at a time *(p. 45)*; clean and oil the pin □○
Doorknob or handle loose	Retaining setscrew loose	Tighten setscrew *(p. 42)* □○
Door won't close properly	Dirt or paint buildup around latch	Clean and lubricate latch *(p. 42)* □○
	Latch broken	Replace latch *(p. 43)* ◨○
	Latch spring broken	Replace latch spring *(p. 42)* ◨○
	Latch mechanism stuck	Lubricate interior of lock case *(p. 42)* ◨○
	Hinges set too deep	Shim hinges *(p. 47)* □○
	Strike plate needs adjusting	Adjust strike plate by filing or repositioning *(p. 43)* ◨○
	Door warped	Shim strike plate *(p. 47)* ◨○; reposition door stop *(p. 48)* ◨○; straighten door *(p. 54)* ◨●
Door rattles	Strike plate misaligned	Adjust strike plate *(p. 47)* ◨○
	Door shrunk or house settled	Weather-strip door *(p. 109)* □○; shim hinges or strike plate *(p. 47)* ◨○; shim jamb *(p. 49)* ◨◕; reposition stop *(p. 48)* ◨○
Door sticks or binds	Door hinge screws loose	Repair worn screw holes *(p. 123)* ◨○; replace screws
	Door warped	Determine and correct binding area *(p. 46)* ◨○
	House settled	Determine and correct binding area *(p. 46)* ◨○
	New door too large	Cut door *(p. 50)* ◨◕▲ or plane door *(p. 53)* ◨◕▲
Door drags	New carpet too thick	Cut door *(p. 50)* ◨◕▲ or plane door *(p. 53)* ◨◕▲; raise floor bracket *(folding door, p. 56; sliding door, p. 57)*
Hole in hollow door	Heavy blow against veneer surface	Patch door *(p. 55)* ◨○
Top-hung sliding door drags	Roller wheel or bracket needs adjusting	Adjust roller wheel or bracket *(p. 57)* ◨○
Top-hung sliding door jammed	Roller wheel jumped from track	Remove and rehang door *(p. 57)* □○
	Bottom guide askew	Adjust bottom guide *(p. 57)* □○
Folding door drags	Slider screw or spring-pivot pin loose	Tighten screw or replace pin in slider *(p. 56)* □○
Folding door corner broken off	Excessive force used to unjam door	Glue corner back and clamp *(p. 56)* ◨○
Fixed louver broken	Heavy blow against louvered surface	Replace louver *(p. 57)* ◨◕

DEGREE OF DIFFICULTY: □ Easy ◨ Moderate ■ Complex
ESTIMATED TIME: ○ Less than 1 hour ◕ 1 to 3 hours ● Over 3 hours   ▲ Special tool require

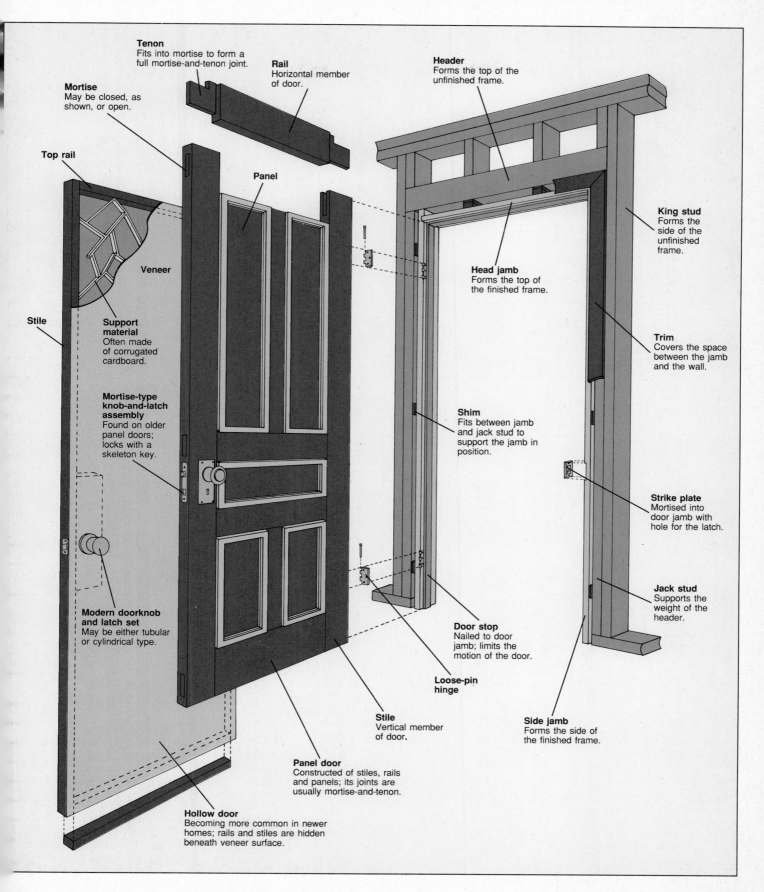

Tenon
Fits into mortise to form a full mortise-and-tenon joint.

Mortise
May be closed, as shown, or open.

Top rail

Rail
Horizontal member of door.

Panel

Veneer

Stile

Support material
Often made of corrugated cardboard.

Mortise-type knob-and-latch assembly
Found on older panel doors; locks with a skeleton key.

Modern doorknob and latch set
May be either tubular or cylindrical type.

Header
Forms the top of the unfinished frame.

King stud
Forms the side of the unfinished frame.

Head jamb
Forms the top of the finished frame.

Trim
Covers the space between the jamb and the wall.

Shim
Fits between jamb and jack stud to support the jamb in position.

Strike plate
Mortised into door jamb with hole for the latch.

Jack stud
Supports the weight of the header.

Door stop
Nailed to door jamb; limits the motion of the door.

Loose-pin hinge

Stile
Vertical member of door.

Side jamb
Forms the side of the finished frame.

Panel door
Constructed of stiles, rails and panels; its joints are usually mortise-and-tenon.

Hollow door
Becoming more common in newer homes; rails and stiles are hidden beneath veneer surface.

SERVICING A KNOB-AND-LATCH ASSEMBLY (Older models)

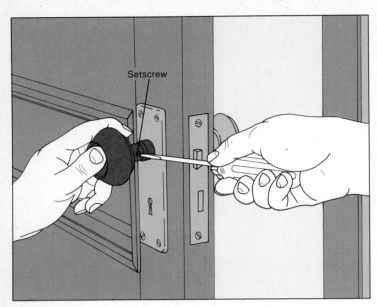

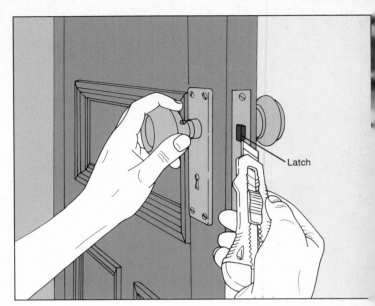

1 **Tightening a loose doorknob.** If its skeleton key has been lost, the mortise-type lock case of an older door may operate as a simple knob-and-latch assembly. To cure the rattling knob of a mortise-type assembly, first loosen the setscrew that secures it to the knob shaft, push the knob snug against its collar on the door, then retighten the screw *(above)*.

2 **Unsticking a latch.** Lubricate sticky door latches periodically with silicone spray. Turn the doorknob so that the latch is withdrawn, and apply the lubricant to the latch opening. Turn the knob back and forth several times to work it in.
Paint buildup is a common cause of a sticking latch. Use a utility knife to break the paint seal around the latch and to scrape paint off its surface *(above)*. If the latch in an old mortise-type lock case continues to stick, remove the lock case for repair or replacement *(step 3)*.

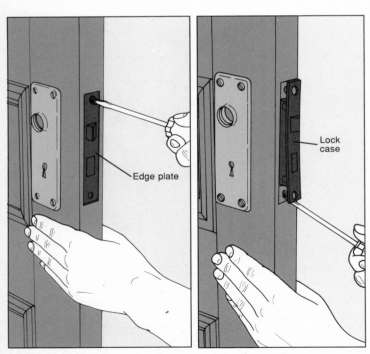

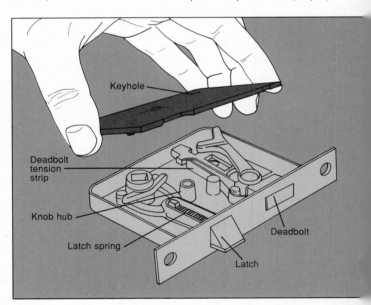

3 **Removing the lock case.** Unscrew one of the doorknobs and pull it off its shaft. Then withdraw the shaft from the door by pulling on the other knob. Using a utility knife or old screwdriver, scrape away any paint blocking the screw slots at the top and bottom of the lock case edge plate. Remove the screws *(above, left)* and carefully pry the lock case free from the door *(above, right)*.

4 **Servicing the lock case.** Lay the lock case on a flat surface, unscrew the cover plate and remove it. Sketch the interior layout in case any part is dislodged, then spray the works with a light coat of silicone lubricant. If either the latch spring or deadbolt tension strip is damaged, replace it. To check the latch insert the knob shaft in the knob hub by hand and turn the shaft. To check the bolt, turn the skeleton key in the keyhole. If either the latch or bolt won't budge, file its openings in the lock case as you would a strike plate *(page 44)*. If the latch or bolt is still stuck, take the lock case to a locksmith who will also be able to replace a lost skeleton key. Once the latch and bolt work smoothly, reassemble the lock case and reinstall it.

SERVICING A KNOB-AND-LATCH ASSEMBLY (Newer models)

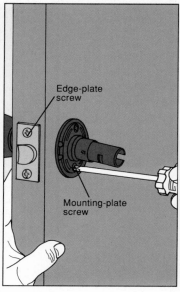

Escutcheon

Release catch

Edge-plate screw

Mounting-plate screw

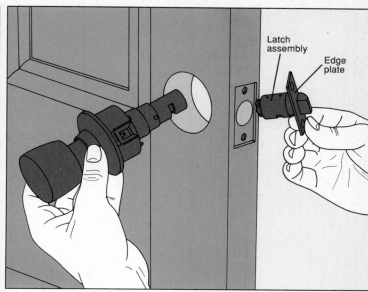

Latch assembly

Edge plate

Repairing a loose knob or broken latch. Sometimes a loose knob can be secured simply by tightening two screws located on the escutcheon. Other types require you to remove the doorknob and escutcheon in order to tighten the mounting plate that connects the knob assembly to the door. For the popular model shown above, you must turn the knob until the slot on the knob shank is aligned with the release catch. Use an awl to depress the catch *(above, left)* and release the knob. Then twist and pull the escutcheon off the shank. Tighten the mounting plate screws to stop the knob assembly from rattling *(above, center)*. If the latch sticks, remove paint buildup *(page 43)*. If this doesn't free it,

the latch may be broken. To remove a broken latch assembly, unscrew the mounting plate screws and the screws securing the latch edge plate. Then pull gently on the remaining knob with one hand, while you wiggle the latch and edge plate free with the other *(above, right)*. Replace the broken latch with an exact duplicate. To reassemble the knob and latch, reverse the steps for disassembly. When reinstalling the escutcheon, make sure you turn it until it catches. Then position the doorknob on the shank, aligning the release catch with the slot, and slide it into place.

ADJUSTING THE STRIKE PLATE

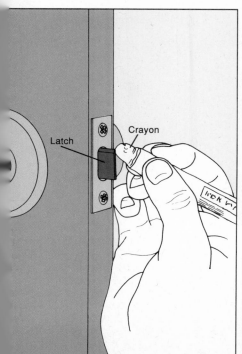

Latch

Crayon

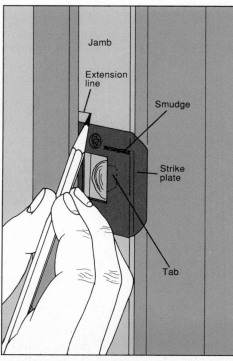

Jamb

Extension line

Smudge

Strike plate

Tab

1 **Determining strike plate problems.** Before adjusting the strike plate, check that the hinge screws are tight *(page 46)*. To pinpoint problems with the strike plate, mortise or latch hole, rub crayon or lipstick on the edge of the latch *(far left)* and close the door. Open the door and examine the smudge on the strike plate. Measure between the smudge and the strike-plate opening to determine the distance the strike must be shifted to fully engage the latch. If that distance is less than 1/8 inch, file the strike plate *(step 2)*. If it is more than that, mark the distance on the jamb *(near left)* and extend the mortise *(step 3)* to reposition the strike plate. To stop a rattling door if your strike plate has a metal tab as shown here, pry the tab outward with an old screwdriver. Push it in slightly if the latch sticks. If only part of the latch reaches into the strike hole when the door is closed, shim the strike plate as you would a door hinge *(page 47)*. Finally, if the latch can't extend its full length because the strike-plate hole is too shallow, deepen the hole *(step 4)*.

ADJUSTING THE STRIKE PLATE (continued)

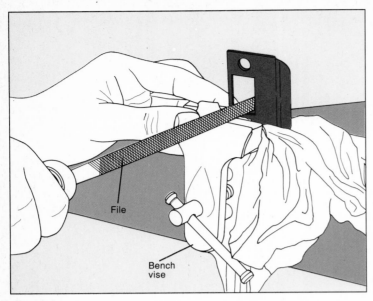

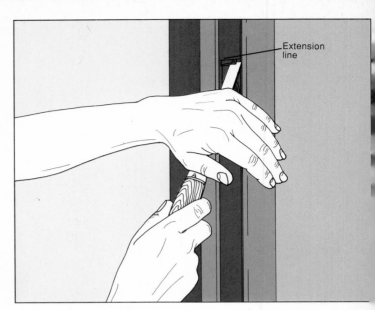

2 Filing the strike plate. Unscrew the strike plate and clamp it in a bench vise, protecting the plate with cloth. Using a metal file, file the edge of the opening to the crayon mark *(above)*. Then resecure the strike plate with the top screw only. Close the door to see whether the latch catches correctly. If it does, replace the bottom screw. If the latch still doesn't catch properly you may have to reposition the strike plate by extending the mortise *(step 3)*.

3 Extending the mortise. Remove the strike plate and pack the screw holes with toothpicks or wooden pegs *(page 123)*. Using a rubber mallet and a wood chisel, cut straight into the extension line you marked on the jamb *(step 1)*. Then with the chisel and hand force only *(above)*, clean out the new mortise shape. Check that the plate sits evenly in its new mortise, then trace the outline of the new strike hole position.

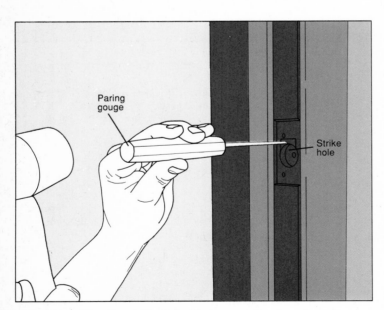

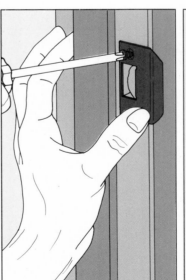

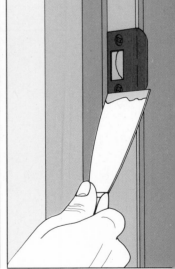

4 Enlarging the strike hole. To increase the diameter or the depth of the strike hole, use a rubber mallet and a narrow wood chisel, or a paring gouge if you have one, to chip away wood to the new strike hole outline *(above)*. Several smaller cuts will produce a cleaner strike hole than a few big ones.

5 Repositioning the strike plate. Place the strike plate in its new location on the door jamb and mark the screw hole locations. Drill a pilot hole for the top screw, then position the plate and drive the screw in *(above, left)*. Then close the door to see whether the latch slides easily into the hole. If it does, add the bottom strike plate screw. If not, adjust the mortise and strike hole as necessary and test again. To fill the gap at the end of the strike plate *(above, right)*, use a putty knife to apply wood putty or spackling compound, depending on whether you plan to stain or paint the wood.

REMOVING AND REHANGING A DOOR

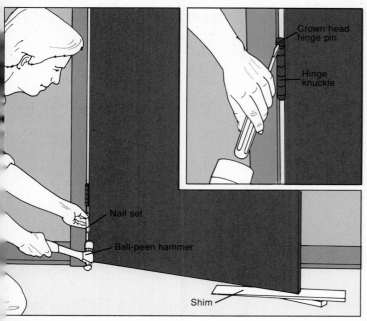

Crown head hinge pin

Hinge knuckle

Nail set

Ball-peen hammer

Shim

Removing the door. Wedge the door open with shims. (Do not force the door upward or it will be difficult to extract the hinge pins.) Most interior doors have loose-pin hinges. Scrape off any paint that may be restricting the pins. Beginning with the lowest hinge, position a nail set on the bottom of the hinge pin (sometimes the knuckle end is open, other styles have only an access hole), and tap it up with a hammer *(above)*, until about 1/2 inch of the pin is exposed. Then pull the pin out by hand. If it won't budge, knock it free with an old screwdriver and a rubber mallet; use this same method to free older crown-head hinge pins whose knuckle bottom is fully sealed *(inset)*. After freeing the bottom hinge pin, free the middle pin (if there is one) and finally the top pin. Then, with a helper if necessary, lift off the door.

Door jack

Propping the door with door jacks. If you plan to turn the door on its side to work, build two door jacks to support the door securely at each end. For each jack, use an 18-inch strip of 1/4-inch plywood or flexible fiberboard with two wood scraps nailed to the bottom as legs. Then nail two scraps of 2-by-4 to the top surface, 2 inches apart. Remove the door *(top)* and position it in the jacks *(above)*. With the door propped in this fashion, you will be able to work safely while protecting the finish of the door and floor.

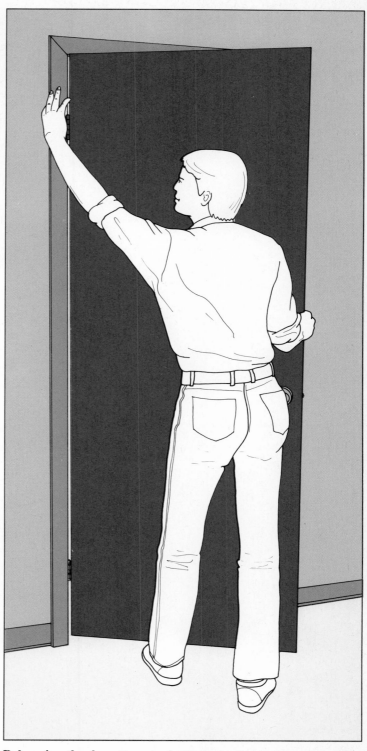

Rehanging the door. If you had difficulty freeing the hinge pins when you removed the door, use a half-round file to make a notch at the top of the hinge knuckle in order to make it easier the next time. Rehang the door: Rest the door on the end of your shoe or on a wedge. Lift the door up so that the top door hinge slips into that on the jamb and drop the hinge pin into the knuckle far enough to grip *(above)*. Then do the same for the bottom and middle hinge, if there is one. Tap the pins in, using a hammer if they will not press in by hand.

DETERMINING THE CAUSE OF BINDING

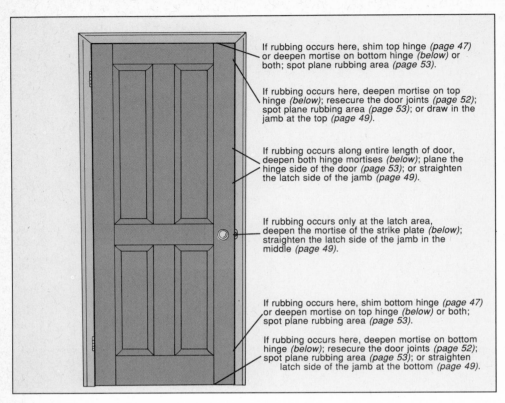

If rubbing occurs here, shim top hinge *(page 47)* or deepen mortise on bottom hinge *(below)* or both; spot plane rubbing area *(page 53)*.

If rubbing occurs here, deepen mortise on top hinge *(below)*; resecure the door joints *(page 52)*; spot plane rubbing area *(page 53)*; or draw in the jamb at the top *(page 49)*.

If rubbing occurs along entire length of door, deepen both hinge mortises *(below)*; plane the hinge side of the door *(page 53)*; or straighten the latch side of the jamb *(page 49)*.

If rubbing occurs only at the latch area, deepen the mortise of the strike plate *(below)*; straighten the latch side of the jamb in the middle *(page 49)*.

If rubbing occurs here, shim bottom hinge *(page 47)* or deepen mortise on top hinge *(below)* or both; spot plane rubbing area *(page 53)*.

If rubbing occurs here, deepen mortise on bottom hinge *(below)*; resecure the door joints *(page 52)*; spot plane rubbing area *(page 53)*; or straighten latch side of the jamb at the bottom *(page 49)*.

Correcting a binding door. Binding may sometimes be corrected by simply tightening the hinge screws on the door or jamb. If a screw hole is too large, remove the loose screw, pack the hole with toothpicks or a wooden peg *(page 123)*, and replace worn screws with new, longer ones. If loose hinges aren't the problem, adjust the door, using the diagram at left as a guide. Work on the door before straightening the jamb. Use a long straightedge to check whether the door is warped. For a slight warp, reposition the door stop as on page 48. If rub marks are not visible on the jamb, slip a nickel around the door between the door and jamb. A properly installed interior door will have a gap of at least 1/16 inch between it and the jamb; the coin will catch where the door is sticking.

DEEPENING A MORTISE FOR A HINGE

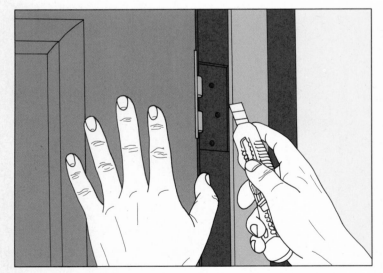

1 **Etching the mortise depth.** Only deepen a hinge mortise when a hinge leaf protrudes slightly from the jamb or door edge; when reinstalled, the hinge must be flush with the surface of the wood. To deepen the mortise on the jamb only, simply wedge the door open. If deepening the mortise on the door, remove the door and prop it securely *(page 45)*. If you need 1/8 inch or more of extra depth, deepen the mortises on both the door and the jamb. To deepen a mortise, first unscrew the hinge leaf and score the perimeter of the mortise with a utility knife *(above)*.

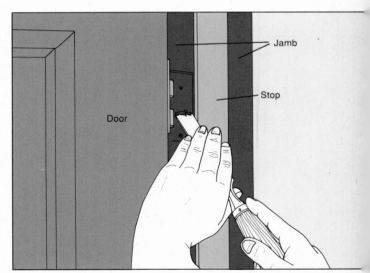

Jamb

Stop

Door

2 **Chiseling the mortise.** Using a wood chisel with the beveled edge facing in and working from the center of the mortise area outward toward the perimeter, clean out the mortise to the required depth. Use hand force only, and do not force the chisel too much. Place the hinge leaf into the mortise, making sure that it sits firmly and evenly in position. If you have made the mortise too deep, shim the hinge flush with the surface of the wood *(page 47)*. Secure the hinge leaf in place with screws; do not reuse screws with worn heads.

HIMMING HINGES

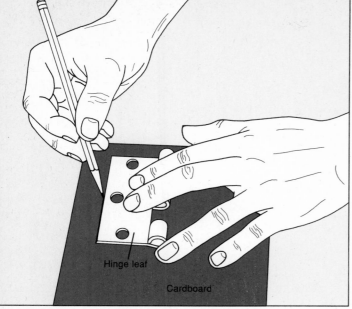

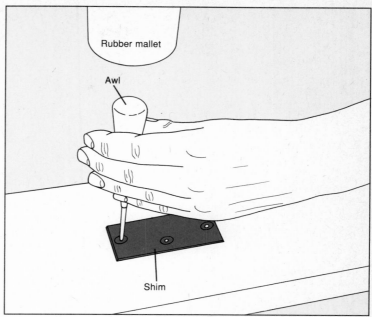

Making the shim. Wedge the door open *(page 45)* and remove the pin of the hinge that requires shimming *(page 45)*. Then unscrew the jamb hinge leaf; you may have to scrape paint m the screw slots. If a screw turns in the hole without coming out, ck the tip of an old screwdriver either under the hinge leaf or under e screw head and pry it up. Use a pair of locking-grip pliers to turn e screw, pulling it out at the same time. If you are shimming the

entire hinge leaf, trace the leaf and its screw holes on a piece of thin cardboard. Then cut out the shim; make two or three for extra thickness. Use an awl to puncture the cardboard at each screw hole position *(above, right)*. If shimming only one edge of the hinge leaf *(below)*, cut out about 1/3 of the traced pattern. To make a shim for a strike plate, unscrew the plate from the jamb and trace its outline as you would for a hinge shim.

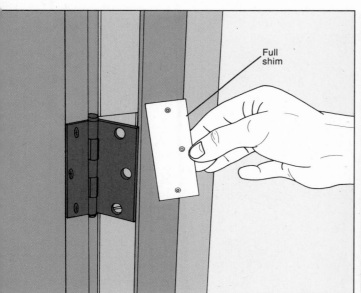

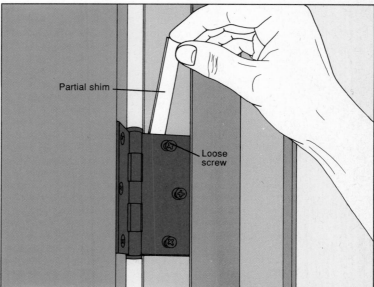

Shimming a hinge. Repin the hinge leaf and place one or more shims in the hinge mortise *(above, left)*. Position the hinge leaf over the shims, and secure it with the hinge screws. If the ew holes are too large, pack them with toothpicks or wooden pegs ge 123), and replace worn screws with new, longer ones. Remove wedges from under the door, and test whether the door closes oothly. Repeat the shimming process until the door works perfectly. shim a strike plate, insert the cardboard shim under the plate.

Resecure the plate to the jamb and test whether the latch catches properly. Add shims until it does, but do not shim out beyond the surface of the jamb. If using partial shims, use them on both the top and bottom hinges. Placed behind the pin edge of the hinge leaf *(above, right)*, partial shims will make the door swing slightly farther into the jamb; placed behind the outer edge of the hinge leaf, they will pull the door slightly away from the door stop. To install a partial shim, loosen the hinge leaf screws and slide the shim behind the leaf.

REPOSITIONING THE DOOR STOP

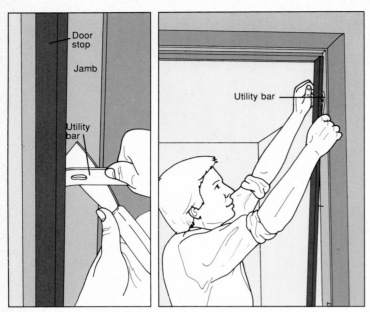

1 **Removing the door stop.** Score paint sealing the edges of the door stop to the jamb with a utility knife. A stop that butts against another stop should be removed first. To pry a stop free, insert a flexible putty knife between it and the jamb, starting at one end. Tap the knife gently with a rubber mallet to open a crack between the stop and the jamb. Then slip a small utility bar into the crack, pivoting the bar on the putty knife blade to protect the wood surface *(above, left)*. Exert gentle pressure, lifting the stop out about 1/4 inch at each nail. Then return to your starting point and pull the stop completely free of the jamb *(above, right)*.

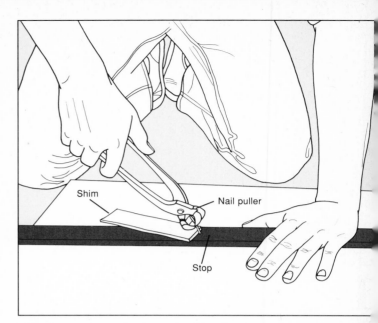

2 **Removing nails from the stop and jamb.** Pull old nails from a door stop that you plan to reuse. Use a nail puller to grip their shanks where they protrude from the back of the stop, rolling the puller's head against a shim to protect the surface of the wood *(above)*. Pull nails from the jamb the same way. If the door stop broke when you removed it, take the pieces to a lumberyard and get an exact replacement.

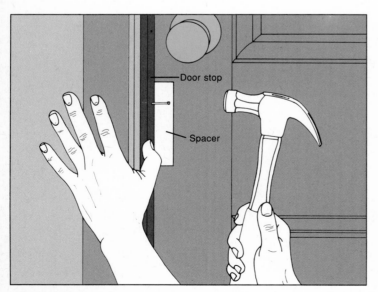

3 **Repositioning and securing the door stop.** Close the door and position the stop against it, using a thin piece of cardboard as a spacer between door and stop. Starting at the middle, near the strike plate, lightly press the stop against the cardboard spacer and drive a slightly larger finishing nail than the ones you removed *(step 2)* into the closest old nail hole. Nail at a slight angle, until only 1/8 inch of the nail protrudes. Continue driving nails through old holes where possible, positioning nails about 16 inches apart. Alternate nailing up and down the stop, forcing it to conform to the shape of the door.

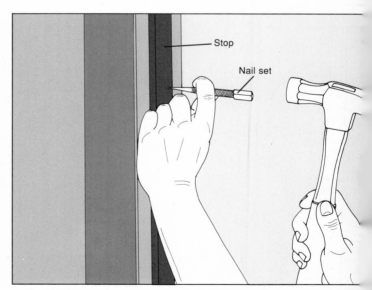

4 **Countersinking and filling nail heads.** When the stop is secured, check to see that the door rests evenly against it. Then use a hammer and nail set to set the nail heads 1/16 inch beneath the surface of the wood. If the wood is to be painted, use a putty knife and spackling compound to fill the countersunk nail holes, as well as any holes left by the old nails. For wood that is to be stained, use wood putty.

HIMMING A DOOR JAMB

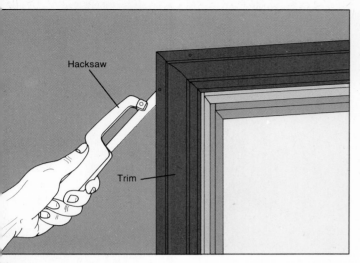

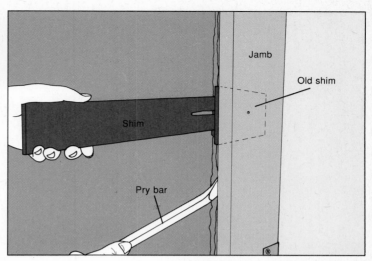

1 **Removing the trim.** If your door no longer makes contact with the door stop, remove the stop *(page 48)* and trim on both sides of the door and shim out the jamb. If the side trim is blind-nailed the top trim at the corners, first cut through built-up paint with a utility ife, then slip a hacksaw behind each corner and cut the face nails as own. Pry up the trim, using the same technique described for reposining the stop *(page 48)*. Use a nail puller to remove the finishing ils from the jamb and the trim *(page 48)*.

2 **Shimming out the jamb and replacing the trim.** Locate the shims between the jamb and the jack stud. With a utility knife, cut a 1/2-inch notch at the thin end of a cedar shim. Insert a pry bar between the jamb and the jack stud at a shim location and lift the jamb out far enough so you can see the shank of the shim nail. Fit the notched end of the shim around the nail *(above)* and test the door for fit. If necessary, add another shim. Drive a finishing nail through the jamb to secure the new shim. Break off the protruding end of the shim. Reinstall the trim, reversing the steps you followed to remove it.

TRAIGHTENING A BOWED DOOR JAMB

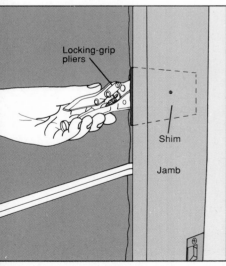

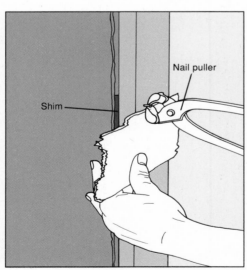

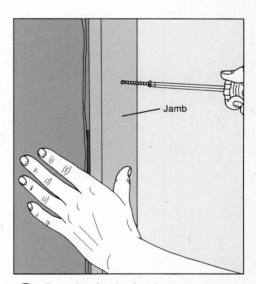

1 **Removing the shims.** Hold a long, straight 2-by-4 against the jamb and mark with a pencil the high point of the bow. If the jamb is only slightly bowed, try reseating it; hold the 2-by-4 against the high point of the bow and hit it once or twice with a rubber mallet. hat doesn't work, you will have to remove some shims. Pry off the stop *(page 48)* and trim ep 1, above). Use a pry bar to lift the jamb out enough to fix a pair of locking-grip pliers onto e shank of the nail securing the shims to the jack stud *(above)*. Push against the jamb until e nail head protrudes. Using a nail puller padded with an old shim, pull the nail head out just ough so a shim falls loose *(above, right)*, and check the straightness of the jamb. If too many ims drop, you may have to replace one *(step 2, above)*.

2 **Drawing in the jamb.** Drill a pilot hole for a 3-inch screw through the high point of the bowed jamb. Drive in the screw until the jamb is pulled straight. Then cover the screw head *(page 48, step 4)*, and replace the trim *(step 2, above)* and the door stop *(page 48)*.

CUTTING A DOOR

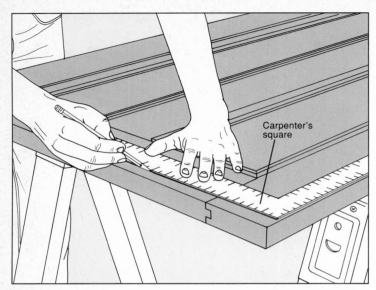

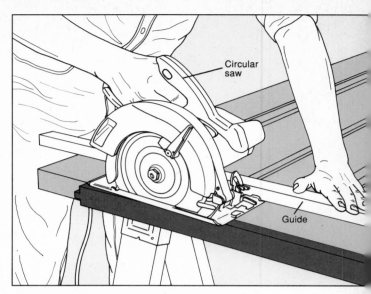

1 **Measuring and marking.** Tailoring a new door to fit an old doorway, or to clear new carpeting, may involve cutting at least 1/2 inch from one or more edges of the door. Leave a minimum of 3 inches of rail or stile on a solid door to maintain its structural integrity. Remove the door from its hinges *(page 45)* and lay it flat on sawhorses. Then, using a carpenter's square, draw a line across the door at the required distance from each edge. If cutting a solid door, go to step 2. If cutting a hollow door, go to step 3.

2 **Cutting a solid door.** Cut a solid wood door with a circular saw. Wear safety goggles and check the edge of the door for nails before starting. Adjust the cutting depth of the saw blade 1/2 inch deeper than the thickness of the door. Clamp a piece of wood to the door as a guide for the base plate of the saw, to ensure that the cut is perfectly straight. After cutting, clean off any roughness or splinters with medium-grit sandpaper on a sanding block. Hang the door *(page 45)*. To make minor adjustments, use a plane *(page 53)*.

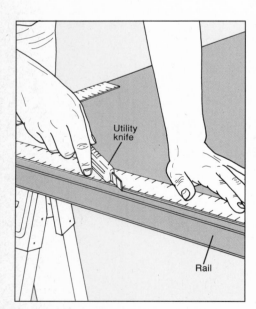

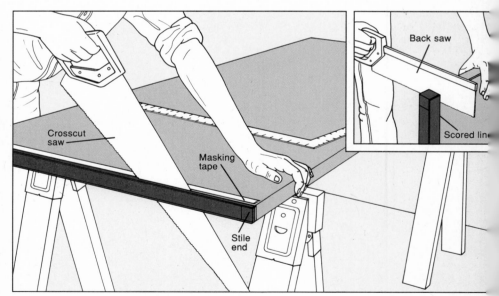

3 **Cutting through the veneer.** Score through the veneer of a hollow door with a utility knife and run a strip of masking tape along the scored line to prevent splintering. Then cut the door *(step 4)*; if the knife did not encounter the underlying rail, first score through the veneer on the other side of the door as well, then saw through the stiles *(step 4, inset)*. Then clean the rail *(step 5)* and glue it in place *(step 6)*.

4 **Sawing through a hollow door.** Use either a circular saw and guide *(step 2)* or a crosscut saw *(above)* to cut through a hollow door. Place the blade a bit outside of the line you scored in the veneer *(step 3)*. If you are using a handsaw, keep the strokes perpendicular to the door. After cutting the door, sand the edges smooth with medium-grit sandpaper on a sanding block and rehang it *(page 45)*. If you only need to cut through the stiles, prop the door securely on its hinge side *(page 45)*, and use a backsaw to saw through the stile at the scored lines in the veneer *(inset)*.

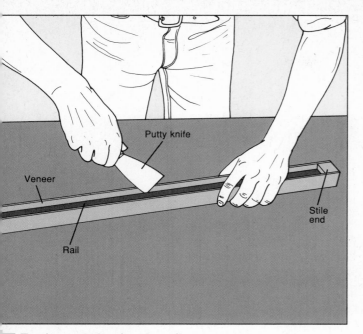

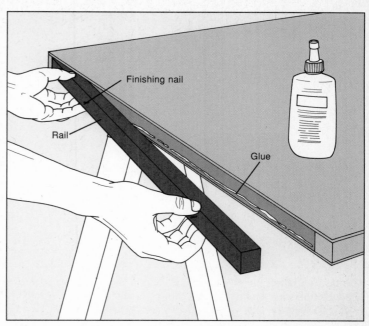

5 **Freeing and cleaning the rail.** Free the rail by running the blade of a putty knife between the rail and veneer. Break off the stile ends and scrape splintered veneer and dried adhesive off ⁓ a putty knife or paint scraper. Drive a short finishing nail partway ⁓ the rail near each end for help when repositioning the rail *(step 7)*.

6 **Gluing the rail.** Push back any support material inside the door that might interfere with the insertion of the rail. Apply a thin bead of carpenter's glue to the back of the door's veneer, and allow it to set for a few minutes until the glue is tacky. Then insert the rail in the door *(above)*.

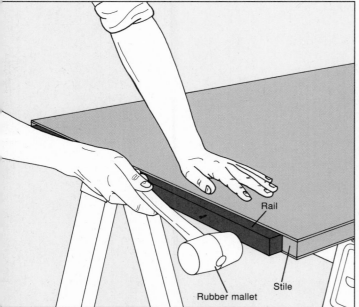

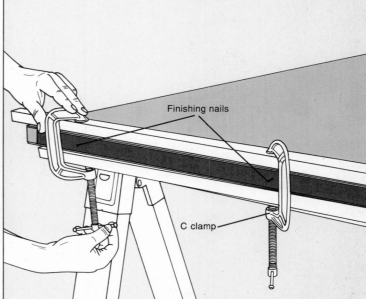

7 **Securing and clamping the rail.** Lightly tap the rail into position, using a rubber mallet *(above, left)*. If you accidentally tap either end of the rail too far, pull on the finishing nails to adjust the rail correctly. Then, using strips of wood to protect the veneer surface, clamp ⁓ veneer against the rail *(above, right)*. When the glue has set, remove the clamps and pull ⁓ the nails with a nail puller. Hang the door *(page 45)*.

REJOINING A DOOR JOINT USING A PIPE CLAMP

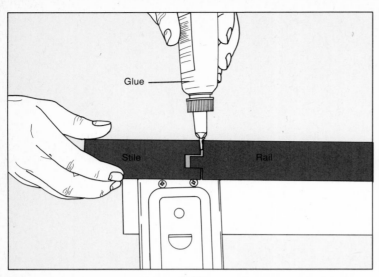

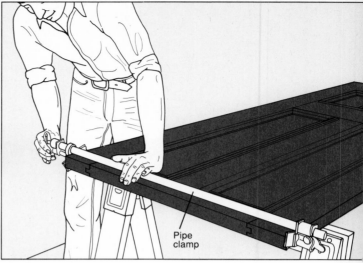

Gluing and clamping the door joint. Panel doors that are subject to excessive humidity or temperature variations can spring open at the joint between the rail and the stile, causing the door to bind on the door jamb. Remove the door *(page 45)* and place it on sawhorses. Using a putty knife, scrape dirt and old glue out of the gap between the stile and rail and brush it out. Apply a thin bead of carpenter's glue in the gap on both sides of the door *(above, left)*. Attach a pipe clamp, its ends padded with scrap wood, across the door from stile to stile *(above, right)*. Tighten the pipe clamp as shown to draw the stile and rail together. Leave the clamp on overnight.

REJOINING A DOOR JOINT USING A RECESSED LAG BOLT

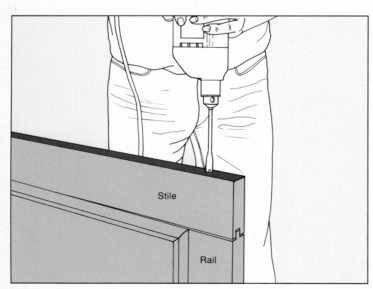

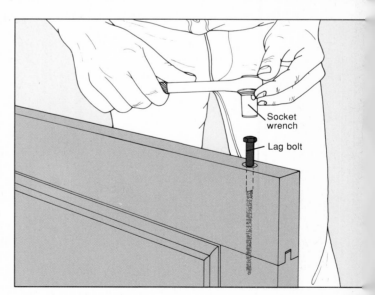

1 **Drilling a hole for the lag bolt.** Installing a recessed lag bolt is a severe measure not suitable for very old, dry doors, but it may be necessary if the stile has warped out badly. The bolt must be at least 1 inch longer than the width of the stile. If the tenon is visible in the edge of the stile *(page 41)* do not use a lag bolt. Remove the door and prop it securely *(page 45)*. Using a power drill with a bit the size of the lag bolt shank, drill through the stile and into the rail. Then use a 1/2-inch bit to countersink for the lag bolt head *(above)*, and to accommodate the socket wrench head used to tighten the lag bolt *(step 2)*.

2 **Installing the bolt.** Clean the gap between rail and stile using a putty knife and brush it out. Use a socket wrench to drive the bolt, tightening it until the stile is drawn snug against the rail *(above)*. It may be necessary to draw in the stile gradually by tightening the bolt several turns a day. Inject glue in the joint just before you draw it closed. When the stile is snug against the rail, and the lag bolt head is beneath the surface of the door, fill the hole with wood putty or spackling compound *(page 48, step 4)*.

PLANING A DOOR TO SHAPE

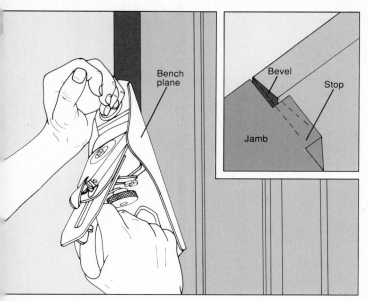

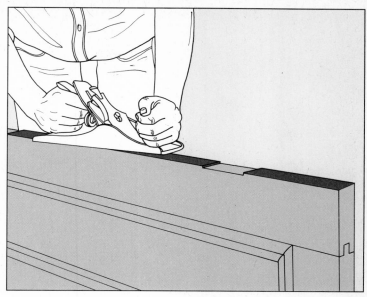

Spot planing a door. Try sanding the rubbing spots on the door with sandpaper on a sanding block. If there is too much to sand, use a bench plane to remove excess wood, but do not plane the latch area. If the door rubs near the latch, remove the door *(page 45)* and its hinges and plane along the hinge side *(right)*. To spot plane, wedge the door open securely *(page 45)*. Set the plane blade cutting depth for very fine planing, and test first on a scrap of wood. The latch edge of a door is beveled so it can swing closed *(inset)*; if you smooth off the bevel, reshape it with coarse sandpaper on a sanding block. Take off just enough wood so that the edge will not catch on the jamb as the door is closed.

Planing the side of the door. Remove the door and its hinges and prop it securely on its latch side *(page 45)*. Set a bench plane blade to the required depth *(page 122)*, and always test its action on a scrap piece of wood before working on the door itself. Plane the entire length of the door; the plane's long base will help you to produce a straight, flat surface. If you plane so much wood from the hinge side that the hinge mortises are about to disappear, pause and deepen the mortises now *(page 46)* before continuing.

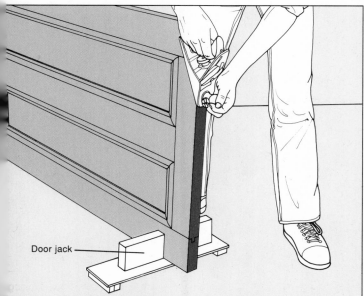

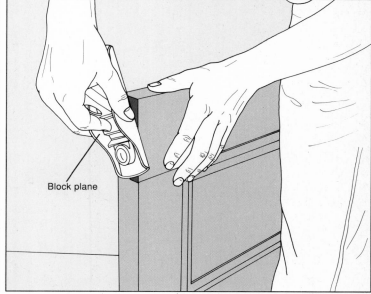

Planing door ends. If more than 1/4 inch of the door must be removed, cut it *(page 50)* rather than planing it. Spot plane *(top, left)* the top of the door with the door still hung; to plane the bottom of the door, remove it and prop it securely with door jacks *(page 45)*. Set the blade of a bench plane to the required depth *(page 122)*, and test its action on a scrap piece of wood before working on the door itself. Plane in toward the middle of the door *(above, left)*. To plane the end grain of a stile, use a block plane *(above, right)* with a freshly sharpened blade only slightly extended *(page 122)*. Shave in small shallow strokes, from the corner inward.

STRAIGHTENING A WARPED DOOR

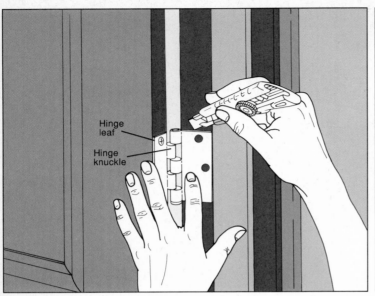

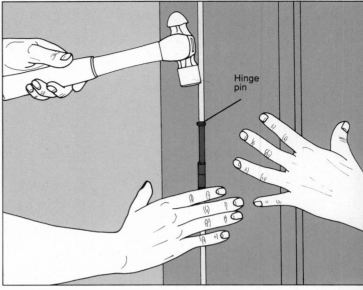

Hinge
leaf

Hinge
knuckle

Hinge
pin

Adding a third hinge. If the door is warped slightly near the middle, adding a middle hinge may solve the problem. Position a hinge leaf against the edge of the door and use a utility knife to score its outline. Chisel a mortise to the same depth as that of the top and bottom hinges *(page 122)*. Screw the leaf to the door. Now press the other leaf against the jamb, engaging the hinge knuckles as shown. Score the leaf outline on the jamb *(above, left)*. Chisel the mortise and screw in the hinge leaf. Have a helper push against the middle of the door, bringing the hinge knuckles in line, so that you can tap in the pin with a hammer *(above, right)*.

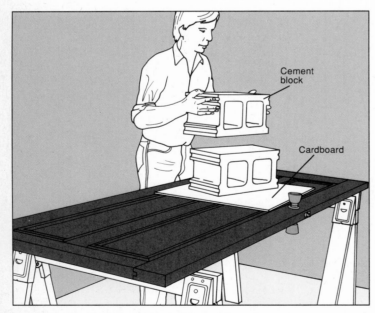

Cement
block

Cardboard

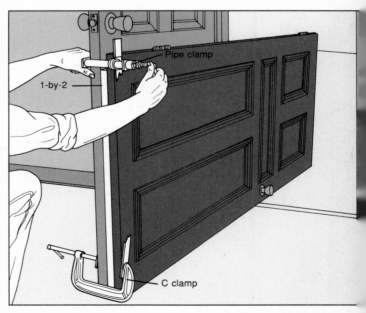

Pipe clamp

1-by-2

C clamp

Straightening a center warp with weights. Remove the door *(page 45)* and lay it flat on sawhorses. Use a carpenter's level to locate the center of the warp. Protecting the door surface with cardboard, place heavy weights—such as concrete blocks, shown here—at the center point of the warp. Check the door every twelve hours, leaving the weights on until the door is slightly warped in the opposite direction.

Correcting a corner warp with clamps. Remove the door *(page 45)* and find the center of the warp as described at left. Then bolster the warped door against a strong, straight door, with the warped corner at the top, warp facing out. Put a 1-by-2 between the doors. Attach a clamp, its jaws padded with scrap wood, to each corner of the door. Tighten the top clamp until the corner is drawn in slightly *(above)*. Over a period of several days, continue tightening the top clamp until the corner is straight.

ATCHING A HOLE IN A HOLLOW DOOR

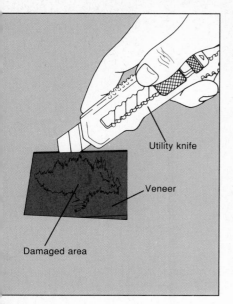

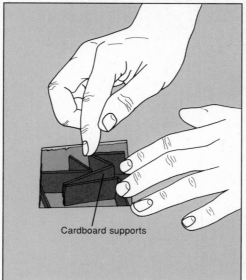

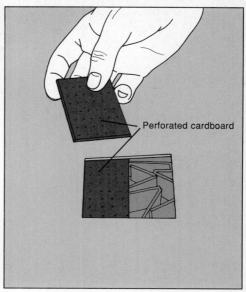

Utility knife

Veneer

Damaged area

Cardboard supports

Perforated cardboard

Cutting out the damaged area.
Using a sharp utility knife, cut out a
rectangle around the damaged area in
veneer. Trim away splinters and push the
pport material inside the door away from
hole.

2 Making and inserting cardboard supports. Measure the depth of the hole and subtract 1/16 inch. Cut strips of 1/8-inch-thick cardboard to this exact width. Fold the strips
loosely and insert them into the hole *(above, left)* to support a new surface. Cut a rectangle of the same cardboard a little larger than the hole. Use an awl to perforate this piece, and
cut it in half. Insert one half into the hole on top of the bent cardboard strips; the fit should be
very tight *(above, right)*. Then slip the second half into place, butting it against the first. Push
on the cardboard; it should resist downward pressure, and allow little sideways movement.

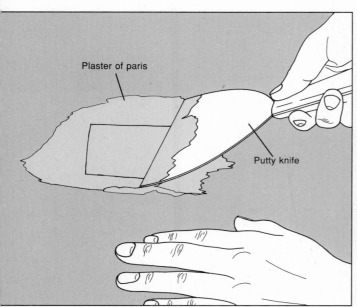

Plaster of paris

Putty knife

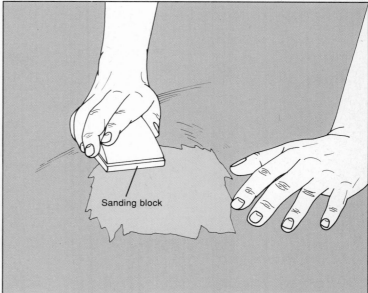

Sanding block

Filling and sanding. Mix enough plaster of paris to cover the perforated cardboard flush
to the veneer surface. Apply plaster to the cardboard with a flexible putty knife, squeezing
it through the perforations *(above, left)*. Work fast; plaster of paris sets quickly. When the
ster is dry, sand it smooth, using fine sandpaper on a sanding block *(above, right)*. Apply a
cond coat of plaster if the surface is not perfectly smooth, and sand again. Then paint the
or *(page 125)*.

SERVICING A FOLDING DOOR

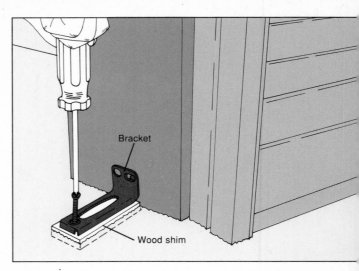

Raising the floor bracket. To prevent the door from dragging or ja
ming on newly-installed carpeting, remove the door *(left)* and cut *(pa
50)* or plane *(page 53)* its bottom edge. To raise the floor bracket, ur
screw it and trace its outline on a scrap of wood the same thickness
the new carpeting. Cut out the wood shim and insert it between the
bracket and the floor. Reinstall the bracket, using screws that are lor
enough to pass through the shim into the floor *(above)*. Replace the
door *(left)*.

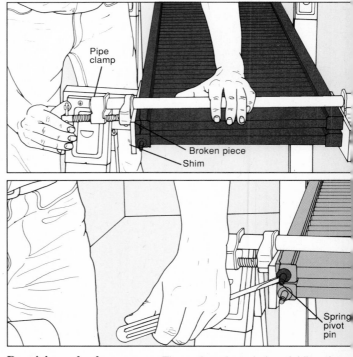

Correcting a jammed or dragging door. A folding door that jams
usually needs only to be removed and rehung properly. Fold the door
open and lift it up out of the floor bracket, then pull it down out of the
track *(above)*. Tighten the screw on the top corner bracket if it is loose.
To rehang the door, fit the top corner pin back in its bracket on the track.
Then lift the door, and insert the pin at the bottom into its bracket on
the floor. Finally, depress the spring-pivot pin at the top with a screwdriver, and slip it back into its slider *(inset)*. If the folding door has more
than two panels, replace the other spring-pivot pins the same way.

Repairing a broken corner. The spring-pivot pin in a folding door
weakens the top corner. If the door is yanked or forced, the corner
may break and the pin fall free. Remove the door as described at lef
and place it on sawhorses or a work bench. Apply a small amount of
carpenter's glue to the broken piece, fit it in place, and then pull it off
When the glue is tacky, press the broken piece back into position, ar
secure the corner with a pipe clamp padded with wood shims *(above
top)*. Before the glue sets, tap the pin in place with an old screwdrive
and a mallet *(above, bottom)*. Leave the clamp on until the glue is dr

REPLACING A FIXED LOUVER

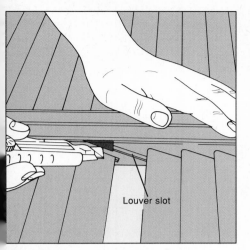

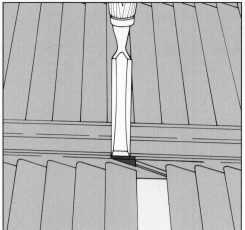

Louver slot

Replacement louver

Stile

1 **Extending the slot.** Remove the door *(page 56)* and place it on sawhorses. Pull out any pieces of broken louver that may still be attached. Working from the less visible side of the door, use a utility knife to score a notch at the louver slot on each side of the door *(above)*.

2 **Cutting and inserting a new louver.** Using a wood chisel and rubber mallet, carefully cut out each notch, extending the louver slot to the edge of the door stile *(above, left)*. Keep the pieces for replacement later. Buy a new louver of the same width as the others. Measure the distance between the stiles of the door, and add 1/8 inch. Using a backsaw and miter box, cut the new louver to size. Stain or paint it to match the finish of the other louvers and push it into the slots *(above, right)*. Glue the chiseled pieces in place and rehang the door *(page 56)*.

SERVICING A TOP-HUNG SLIDING DOOR

Bottom guide

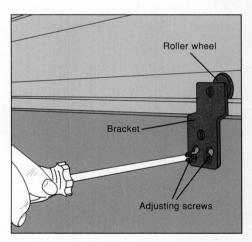

Roller wheel

Bracket

Adjusting screws

Unjamming a top-hung sliding door. Sliding closet doors generally hang from the top, with a simple roller mechanism that moves in a track. Some models also have a bottom guide to maintain alignment. Sliding doors may jam either because one of the rollers jumps out of the track or because the bottom guide comes askew. To reengage the roller wheel, first use a screwdriver to remove the bottom guide *(inset)*. Check from the inside of the closet whether the model you have has access slots in the back of the track to permit reinsertion of the roller wheels. Then swing the door out, lift it upward and fit the wheel through the access slot, before settling the roller back into the track. Then replace the bottom guide.

Correcting a dragging top-hung sliding door. A sliding door may drag because the roller wheel or bracket on the top inside edge of the door requires adjustment to accommodate newly-installed carpeting. Loosening the bottom screws on the bracket *(above)* may allow you to raise (or lower) the door's roller. Check what type of hardware your door has to determine where the adjustment can be made. If the door bottom needs to be raised more than is allowed for by an adjustment to the roller assembly, remove the door *(left)* to cut *(page 50)* or plane it *(page 53)*. Then unscrew any bottom guide from the door *(left, inset)* and raise it with a wood shim the same thickness as the new carpeting. Replace the bottom guide and rehang the door *(left)*.

EXTERIOR DOORS

A door leading into the home welcomes visitors and discourages intruders, keeps storms outside and retains inside warmth. A high-quality exterior door that is properly installed and maintained should remain trouble-free for many years. However, virtually all exterior doors are sources of air infiltration and must be weather-stripped *(page 108)*.

Several styles of exterior door are illustrated below. Solid wood doors are used in the majority of homes. Most wood doors have typical panel-door construction; some newer models have a solid wood core covered with a wood veneer.

Increasing in popularity are insulated steel doors; usually designed to look like wood panel doors, they cost less, insulate better and are often more secure and fire-resistant. Steel doors rarely need repair, but an old wood door can be replaced by a steel door *(page 86)*. Hollow-core doors *(page 40)* do not provide adequate security, and are made only for interior use.

Proper maintenance can extend a wood door's life. Once a year, clean the door and inspect the condition of the door and frame. Also check its paint or varnish finish. A door may need a fresh coat of varnish or paint annually. Use a high-quality

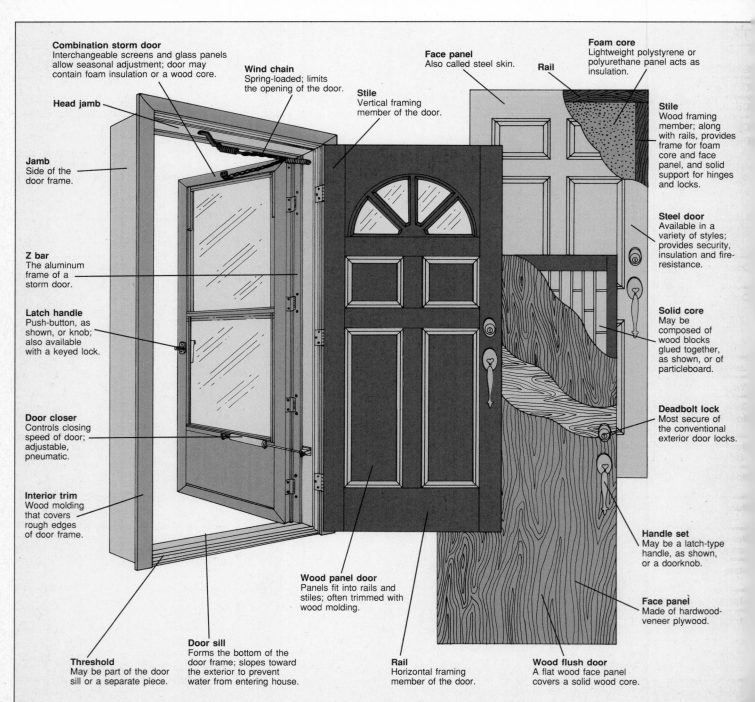

Combination storm door
Interchangeable screens and glass panels allow seasonal adjustment; door may contain foam insulation or a wood core.

Wind chain
Spring-loaded; limits the opening of the door.

Head jamb

Jamb
Side of the door frame.

Z bar
The aluminum frame of a storm door.

Latch handle
Push-button, as shown, or knob; also available with a keyed lock.

Door closer
Controls closing speed of door; adjustable, pneumatic.

Interior trim
Wood molding that covers rough edges of door frame.

Threshold
May be part of the door sill or a separate piece.

Door sill
Forms the bottom of the door frame; slopes toward the exterior to prevent water from entering house.

Wood panel door
Panels fit into rails and stiles; often trimmed with wood molding.

Stile
Vertical framing member of the door.

Face panel
Also called steel skin.

Rail

Foam core
Lightweight polystyrene or polyurethane panel acts as insulation.

Stile
Wood framing member; along with rails, provides frame for foam core and face panel, and solid support for hinges and locks.

Steel door
Available in a variety of styles; provides security, insulation and fire-resistance.

Solid core
May be composed of wood blocks glued together, as shown, or of particleboard.

Deadbolt lock
Most secure of the conventional exterior door locks.

Handle set
May be a latch-type handle, as shown, or a doorknob.

Face panel
Made of hardwood-veneer plywood.

Rail
Horizontal framing member of the door.

Wood flush door
A flat wood face panel covers a solid wood core.

xterior varnish containing an ultra-violet filter, or a high-loss alkyd exterior paint. If your climate is hot and humid, oose a fungicide paint. Wash away surface mildew with a each-and-water solution *(page 124)*. If mildew has spread eneath the finish, or the wood is cracked and grayed, or a avy paint buildup obscures its details, strip and refinish the or *(page 60)*. Refinishing is easier if you take the door off hinges. It can be a weekend job; plan to remove and re-ng the door several times during that period, unless you can ave it off for one or two nights.

The Troubleshooting Guide below lists repairs to exterior doors. An exterior door is usually repaired the same way as an interior door *(page 40)*. But unique to an exterior door is the damage caused by a break-in. In most cases, the door and jamb can be saved; however, repair requires careful carpentry *(page 62)*. When installing a new wood exterior door, paint it before hanging it to avoid exposing the wood to the elements. Treat the end grain with a water-repellent preservative, then paint the edges. Adding a storm door *(page 64)* can increase an exterior door's insulation value and protect its finish.

ROUBLESHOOTING GUIDE

YMPTOM	POSSIBLE CAUSE	PROCEDURE
oor hinges squeak	Rust or paint buildup around hinges	Remove one hinge pin at a time *(p. 45)*; clean and oil the pin □○
oorknob or handle loose	Retaining setscrew loose	Tighten setscrew *(p. 42)* □○
oor doesn't close or lock roperly	Dirt or paint buildup around latch or lock	Clean and lubricate latch *(p. 42)* or lock *(p. 68)* □○
	Latch or bolt assembly broken	Replace latch or bolt assembly *(p. 72)* □○
	Hinges set too deep	Shim hinges *(p. 47)* □○
	Strike plate misaligned	Adjust strike plate *(p. 43)* ◨○
	Strike hole too shallow	Deepen strike hole *(p. 44)* □○
	Door has shrunk or house settled	Weather-strip door *(p. 109)* ◨○; weather-strip threshold *(p. 116)* ◨○; shim door hinges or strike plate *(p. 47)* ◨○; shim door jamb *(p. 49)* ■◐
oor rattles	Door has shrunk or house settled	Weather-strip door *(p. 109)* ◨○, or threshold *(p. 116)* ◨○; shim hinges or strike plate *(p. 47)* ◨○ shim jamb *(p. 49)* ■◐
oor sticks or binds	Hinge screws loose	Repair worn screw holes *(p. 123)* ◨○; replace with longer screws
	Excessive paint or varnish buildup	Strip and refinish door *(p. 60)* ◨●
	Door or frame warped	Determine and correct binding area *(p. 46)* ◨○; replace door with prehung unit *(p. 98)* ■●
eakage around door	Weather stripping worn or absent	Weather-strip door *(p. 109)* ◨○; install storm door *(p. 64)* ◨◐
ater leakage below door	Door sill worn or rotted	Weather-strip threshold *(p. 116)* ◨◐; replace sill *(p. 61)* ◨●
ark, spotty discolorations in oor finish	Mildew on finish surface	Wash door with bleach-and-water solution *(p. 124)* □○
	Mildew below finish surface	Strip and refinish door *(p. 60)* ◨●
oor finish flaking, peeling or scolored	Varnish or paint deteriorated	Touch up finish; strip and refinish door *(p. 60)* ◨●
oor cracked or splintered	Break-in damage	Glue and clamp cracks and splinters *(p. 62)* □●; install reinforcement plate *(p. 62)* ◨◐
oor jamb splintered	Break-in damage	Replace damaged section *(p. 63)* ■●; reinstall strike plate *(p. 70)* ◨○; install reinforcement plate *(p. 63)* ◨○
eadbolt or surrounding area amaged	Break-in damage	Glue and clamp splintered area *(p. 62)* ◨○; plug old hole *(p. 62)* ◨○; install new deadbolt lock *(p. 74)* ◨◐▲
orm door slams	Door closer faulty	Adjust or replace door closer *(p. 65)* □○; adjust or replace wind chain *(p. 65)* □○
orm door binds	Metal door frame twisted or misaligned	Shim metal frame *(p. 64)* ◨○
orm door sags	Hinge screws loose	Replace with larger screws
	Hinges damaged by wind	Replace hinge Z bar *(p. 64)* ◨◐; adjust or replace wind chain *(p. 65)* □○; replace storm door *(p. 64)* ◨◐
	Metal door frame twisted or misaligned	Shim frame *(p. 64)* ◨○; replace frame; replace door *(p. 64)* ◨◐

DEGREE OF DIFFICULTY: □ **Easy** ◨ **Moderate** ■ **Complex**
ESTIMATED TIME: ○ **Less than 1 hour** ◐ **1 to 3 hours** ● **Over 3 hours**   ▲ **Special tool required**

REFINISHING AN EXTERIOR DOOR

1 **Preparing the door.** For slight damage limited to small areas, sand lightly and touch up with the same finish as originally used. To remove the old finish, first take the door off its hinges *(page 45)* and remove all door hardware *(inset)*.

Place the door across two sawhorses or on a flat surface. Work in a well-ventilated area—outdoors if possible, avoiding direct sunlight. If you are working indoors, protect the floor with newspaper, open all windows and aim a fan out the window. Use a paint scraper to remove loose and peeling paint from the door. On surfaces with a heavy paint buildup, use a heat gun *(page 125)* before applying the chemical stripper. Wear heavy gloves, safety goggles and a well-fitting respirator with an organic-vapor filter to apply a non-flammable stripper containing methylene chloride to the painted surface. **Caution:** children, pregnant women and people with heart or lung problems should not use a chemical stripper.

Using an old paintbrush, apply stripper generously in short strokes. Work in one direction, covering one section of the door—rail, stile or panel—at a time. After the application stops bubbling—about 15 minutes—lift off the sludge in smooth strokes with a wide putty knife *(left)*. Place the sludge in a container that can be sealed for disposal.

Clean off any remaining finish with a light application of stripper, scrubbing gently with fine steel wool. Finally, wipe the entire surface with a clean rag soaked in denatured alcohol. Turn the door over and strip the other side if desired, then let the door dry overnight.

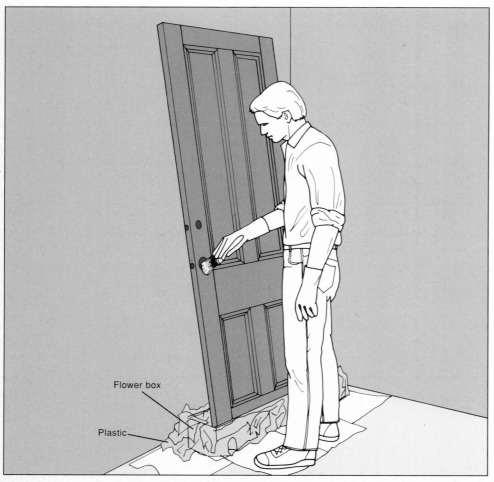

Flower box

Plastic

2 **Applying water-repellent preservative.** Protect your door from moisture and control fungus, mildew and rot by choosing a water-repellent preservative—available at marine or construction supply dealers—that is compatible with the paint or varnish you will apply. If you prefer to use a water repellent without toxic preservative, make your own by mixing 1 cup exterior varnish, 1 ounce shaved paraffin wax and enough paint thinner or turpentine to make one gallon of solution.

Line a flower box with plastic and fill it halfway with the water-repellent solution. Remove the door and stand its bottom edge in the trough for three minutes to treat the end grain of the door. While the door is absorbing the solution, use an old paintbrush to coat thoroughly all door surfaces, including the inside edges of lock and doorknob holes *(left)*. Turn the door upside down to immerse its top edge, and brush all remaining surfaces. Allow the door to dry at least 24 hours (or follow the preservative manufacturer's instructions); rehang the door at the end of the day if necessary. When the wood is dry, paint or varnish the door *(page 125)*.

REPLACING THE DOOR SILL

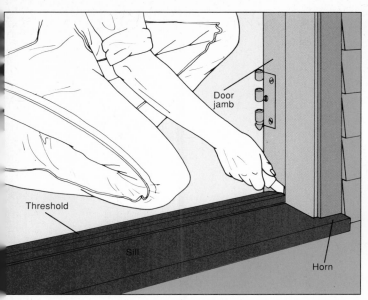

1 Getting at the sill. Use a utility knife to cut away any caulk around the door jamb and threshold or sill edges *(above)*. Remove a wood or metal threshold that has been added to the sill *(page 116)*, and any weather stripping or other protective material attached to the sill. If the exterior edge of the sill is mortared into brick, chip away the mortar with a cold chisel and ball-peen hammer. If you can see where the sill ends, measure the width and thickness of the sill both inside and outside; the difference between these measurements is the combined length of the sill horns. Otherwise, measure the sill after it is removed *(step 4)*.

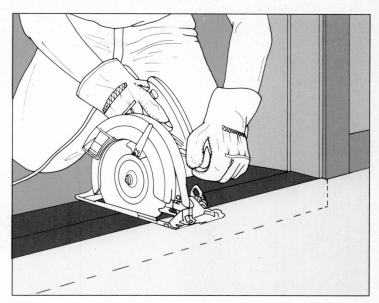

2 Cutting the sill. If the sill is badly rotted, use a cold chisel and ball-peen hammer to break it away in small pieces. Otherwise, use a double-insulated circular saw fitted with an old combination blade, set at a depth of 1/8 inch less than the thickness of the sill. Wearing goggles, cut through the middle of the sill, perpendicular to the wood grain *(above)*.

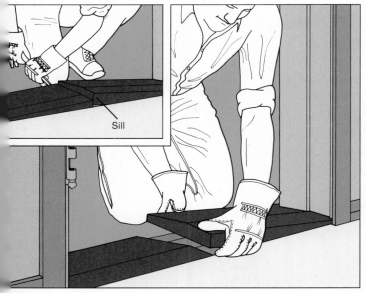

3 Removing the sill. Free the sill by forcing a pry bar under the cut *(inset)*. Pry up the sill just enough to loosen it from the nails fastening it to the jamb; too much force could damage the jamb. Lift each half of the cut sill at the middle and pull it out sideways from under the jamb *(above)*. Cut off protruding nails in the jambs with a hacksaw. Close the door; if it does not close, the jambs have bowed and should be straightened *(page 49)*.

4 Installing the new sill. Mark and cut a new hardwood door sill as for a window sill *(page 17, step 3)*. Clean the sill opening and insert the ends of the new sill under the edges of the jambs. Protecting the sill's finish with scrap wood, tap the sill into place with a hammer *(above)*, working from the center of the sill out to the jambs. If the fit is too tight, take out the sill, cut 1/8 inch from its length, and reinstall it. Drill four pilot holes for nails at each end of the sill, angled into the jamb, and toenail the sill to the jamb with finishing nails *(inset)*.

REPAIRING A CRACKED OR SPLINTERED DOOR

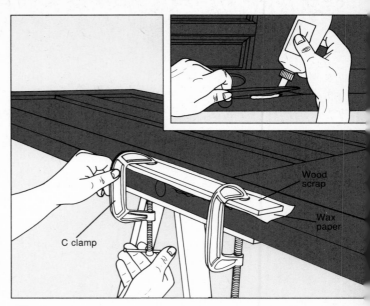

1 **Assessing break-in damage.** If the deadbolt or lockset is broken, repair it *(page 66)* or buy a new one. Remove the locks *(above)* and check the door for cracks and splinters. Examine the wood carefully for hidden cracks that can cause structural weakness. To replace a lock, plug its old hole *(step 3)* and install a new lock in a solid part of the door.

2 **Repairing cracks and splintered edges.** Squeeze a generous amount of carpenter's glue around splinters and into cracks *(inset)*; fit broken pieces back into place. Cover the glued area with wax paper and use C clamps and wood scraps to clamp the repair, as shown. Use masking tape to secure small splinters. To repair a deep vertical crack, insert a utility bar, spread the crack slightly and fill it with carpenter's glue. Wipe off excess glue with a moist cloth and use a pipe clamp to close the crack *(page 52)*. Allow a clamped repair to set for 12 hours, then use a putty knife to lift off any beads of dried glue. Smooth the repair with fine sandpaper.

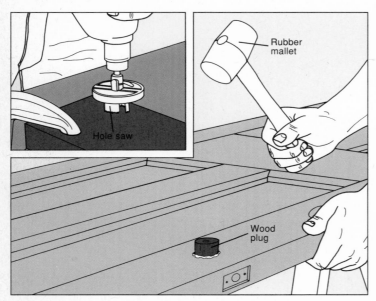

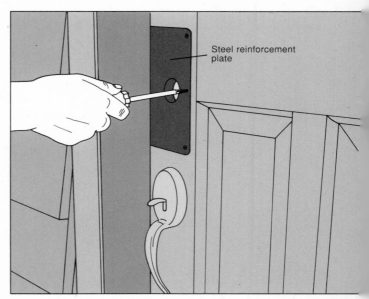

3 **Plugging a hole.** Choose a piece of wood about 1/8 inch thicker than the door. If the door has a clear finish, use the same kind of wood the door is made of. Clamp the piece to a workbench protected by scrap wood. Using a hole saw *(page 120)*, cut a plug the same diameter as the hole in the door *(inset)*. Coat a 1/4-inch dowel with carpenter's glue and tap it into the plug's center hole using a rubber mallet. Then cover the plug's cut edge with carpenter's glue or epoxy glue and tap it firmly into the hole with a rubber mallet, as shown. Let the glue set for 12 hours. Level the plug with a block plane and sand the surface with fine sandpaper.

4 **Installing a reinforcement plate.** Strengthen a door against break-ins by adding a steel reinforcement plate, precut to fit around the deadbolt and door edge, and available from a locksmith. With the door hardware removed, drill holes for the deadbolt cylinder and bolt *(page 73)*, then trace the outline of the reinforcement plate in position on the door. Using a wood chisel *(page 122)*, cut a mortise in the door edge to accommodate the thickness of the reinforcement plate. Within this mortise, cut the mortise for the deadbolt edge plate. Install the edge plate *(page 69)*, then screw the reinforcement plate over it *(above)* and install the deadbolt *(page 74)*.

REPAIRING A SPLINTERED JAMB

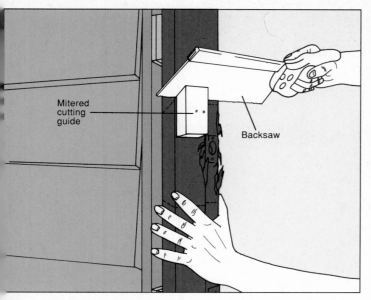

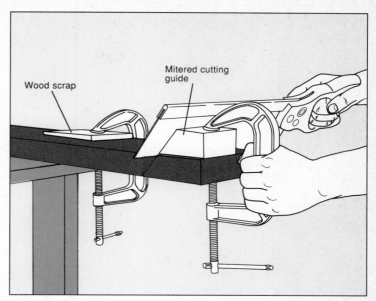

1 Removing the damaged section. After removing the interior trim *(page 49)* and deadbolt strike plate, use a combination square to mark horizontal lines above and below the damaged section of the jamb. Using a miter box and backsaw, cut a block of wood at a 45-degree angle, and nail it to the jamb as a cutting guide. Saw through the jamb at the top line *(above)*, then move the cutting guide to saw at an opposite angle through the bottom line. Pull out the damaged section after removing any screws or nails.

2 Cutting a patch. Buy a piece of wood of the same type, width and thickness as the jamb, and longer than the section you removed. The shape of the built-in stop must be cut into the patch later. Using a combination square, mark guidelines for the length of the patch on the wood. Clamp the cutting guide *(step 1)* just outside each of the guidelines and cut them at opposite angles with a backsaw *(above)*. Then use the backsaw to cut away excess wood to match the shape of the jamb stop—this requires careful measuring and some artistry. Test the fit of the patch and, if necessary, trim the ends until it sits flush with the jamb.

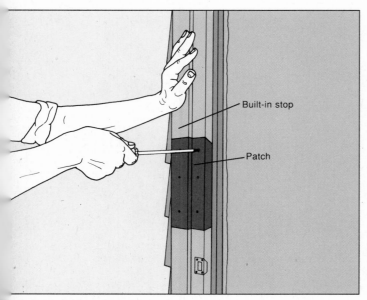

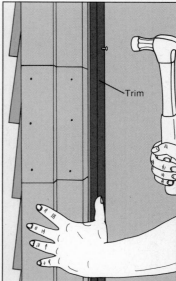

3 Splicing the patch. Holding the patch in place on the jamb, drill pairs of pilot holes through it for screws, using a counterbore bit. Space the holes at 4-inch intervals, 1 inch from the patch edges. Do not drill a hole where the deadbolt strike plate will be installed. Remove the patch and coat its back and ends with carpenter's glue. Reposition the patch and drive screws through the holes into the rough frame. Wipe away excess glue and let it dry for an hour. Use medium-grit sandpaper on a sanding block to refine the shape of the patch. Cover the screw heads with wood putty and reinstall the deadbolt strike plate *(page 75)*.

4 Reinforcing the jamb. Installing a 1-by-1/8-inch steel bar to the indoor edge of the jamb will keep the deadbolt from breaking through the jamb if the door is forced. Buy a bar that extends at least 2 feet above and below the door locks. Mark screw-hole positions along the center of the bar at 6-inch intervals. Drill the holes through the bar, then hold the bar against the jamb, 1/8 inch from its edge, and mark the screw-hole positions on the jamb. Drill pilot holes at the marks and screw the bar to the jamb with 3-inch wood screws *(above, left)*. Cover the bar with the original door trim *(above, right)*; caulk the small gap behind the trim created by the bar.

INSTALLING A STORM DOOR

Z bar

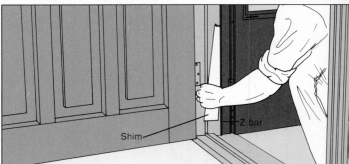

Shim   Z bar

1 **Measuring and cutting the frame.** Measure the inside height of each door jamb *(above, top)*, and the width between the jambs at top, center and bottom. Record the smallest height and width—this is the opening size to order from the door dealer. (If ordering a storm door with hinges attached, order one that opens on the same side as your main door.) Prehung storm doors—such as the one shown here—usually come with a three-sided frame made of aluminum strips called Z bars. The door will come with the side Z bars too long. Turn the door on its side and use a hacksaw to cut the hinge-side and latch-side Z bars 1/4 inch shorter than the opening's height measurement *(above, bottom)*.

2 **Installing the door.** The Z bar frame must be installed perfectly plumb and square, even if the door jamb is crooked. The door itself must clear the frame by 1/8 inch at the latch side, top and ground to open and close properly. To install a typical storm door, unscrew the hinge-side Z bar from the door. Align the Z bar on the jamb with 1/4 inch of space at its top end for the header Z bar. Use a level to plumb the Z bar at both its side and its front, mark its screw-hole positions on the jamb and drill pilot holes. Screw the Z bar back on the door and lift them both into the jambs. Supporting the door on a shim, screw the Z bar to the jamb *(above, top)*; if the door does not hang straight, loosen the screws and shim the Z bar *(above, bottom)*. Install the latch-side Z bar on the other jamb the same way, its top end even with the top end of the hinge-side Z bar. Close the door to check its fit, and shim the Z bar if necessary. Finally, insert the header Z bar across the top of the door and screw it to the head jamb.

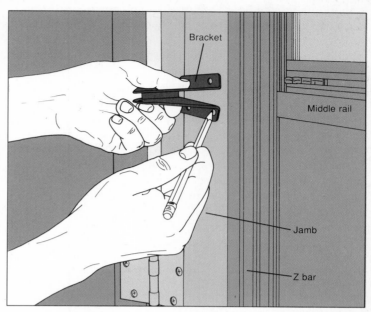

3 Installing the latch and handle. If screw holes are not pre-drilled in the door, position the latch, or template if provided, on the door where it will not hit the main door's knob or lock. Mark the positions of the screw holes. Use a power drill to drill the holes straight through the door from the latch side. Fit the handle and latch through the door together *(inset)*, and install them with the screws provided *(above)*. Then close the door, and position the strike plate on the jamb where it can receive the latch. Drill pilot holes, and screw the strike plate to the jamb. Close the door to check the strike plate position; adjust *(page 43)* or shim *(page 47)* it if necessary.

4 Installing the door closer bracket. Close the storm door and work from inside the house. The door closer may be located on the door's top or middle rail. Position the door closer bracket on the hinge-side door jamb, 1/4 inch from the Z bar, and mark its screw positions with a pencil, as shown. Then drill pilot holes for the screws, and screw the bracket in place.

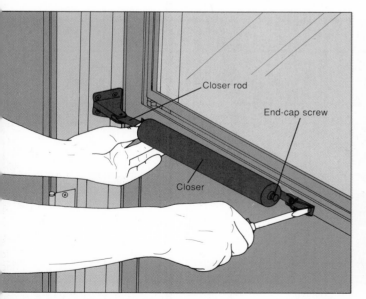

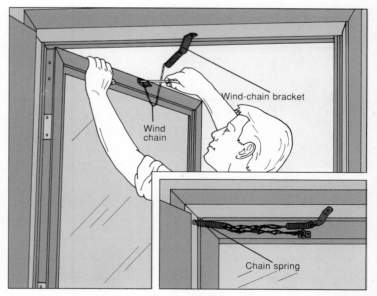

5 Installing the door closer. Slip the hold-open washer onto the door closer rod, then use the pin to attach the rod to the door closer bracket. Hold the free end of the closer against the closed storm door and mark the screw positions on the door. Then remove the closer and drill pilot holes in the door, 1/4 inch farther from the hinge side than you marked. Replace the closer and screw it to the door, as shown. Adjust the closer to the desired closing speed by turning the screw in the end cap. For more tension, remove the closer bracket, turn it and the rod 180 degrees and reinstall it.

6 Installing the wind chain. Screw one wind-chain bracket into the midpoint of the head jamb. Then, with the door closed, mark the screw positions for the other bracket, midpoint at the top of the door; be sure the two brackets will not touch when they are both installed. Screw on the second bracket, as shown. Adjust the length of the chain at this bracket so that the door opens no wider than allowed by the door closer. Then use the attachment provided—in this case, a nail—to attach the chain spring to the side jamb near the upper corner of the door *(inset)*.

DOOR LOCKS

Repairing a broken door lock may seem a daunting prospect. After all, it is designed to keep even the most experienced intruder at bay. However, in most cases, the lock can be disassembled for cleaning and lubrication, and the cylinder and lock case removed by the homeowner for repair or replacement by a locksmith. When security of the existing lock is in question, consider installing a deadbolt as an auxiliary lock.

Most lock problems stem from either inadequate upkeep *(page 68)* or abuse of the lock cylinder. If the lock doesn't work, first inspect your key; it may be burred, bent, or the wrong one entirely. Remove burrs with fine emery cloth and replace bent keys; have copies made by a reputable locksmith. Diagnose your lock's problem with the help of the Troubleshooting Guide *(below)*. It will lead you through the maze of possible solutions, which mostly involve the disassembly of a lock for cleaning or repair. Leave the servicing of lock cases to

a professional. Although the covers of rim and mortise locks can be removed, they enclose an intricate assemblage of levers, slides and springs that are difficult to put back once they've fallen out.

To familiarize yourself with the type of lock securing your door, study the lock anatomies at right—chances are that your lock will resemble one of them. These models are single-cylinder: opened by a key from the outside, and by hand from the inside. A double-cylinder lock needs a key both inside and out to open it. This design is intended to thwart access to the inside by someone breaking through a glass pane. However, it can also keep the household residents locked in. As a safeguard, keep the indoor key hanging near the door. Many double-cylinder locks cannot be removed by the do-it-yourselfer because their tamperproof screws require the special tools of a locksmith for disassembly.

TROUBLESHOOTING GUIDE

SYMPTOM	POSSIBLE CAUSE	PROCEDURE
Key won't fit in keyhole	Keyhole blocked by foreign material	Pick keyhole clear *(p. 10)* □○; if foreign material won't come out, remove cylinder for service *(deadbolt lock, p. 70; rim lock, p. 71; mortise lock, p. 73; for key-in-knob lock, call a locksmith)* ▪○
	Cylinder broken	Remove cylinder for service *(deadbolt lock, p. 70; rim lock, p. 71; mortise lock, p. 73; for key-in-knob lock, call a locksmith)* ▪○
Key stuck in lock	Cylinder needs lubricating	Pull key out slowly with pliers and lubricate keyhole *(p. 68)* □○
	Cylinder upside down	Turn key one-half turn and remove it □○
	Retaining plate screws of deadbolt lock or rim lock loose	Disassemble lock and tighten cylinder retaining plate screws *(deadbolt lock, p. 69; rim lock, p. 71)* ▪○
Key turns in keyhole but doesn't lock	Cylinder broken	Remove cylinder for service *(deadbolt lock, p. 70; rim lock, p. 71; key-in-knob lock, p. 72; mortise lock, p. 73)* ▪○
Key broken in lock	Key turned in lock when only partially inserted or when lock is jammed	Pick broken piece from cylinder *(p. 10)* □○; if broken piece won't come out, remove cylinder for professional service *(deadbolt lock, p. 70; rim lock, p. 71; mortise lock, p. 73; for key-in-knob lock, call a locksmith)* ▪○
Key won't turn in keyhole or turns stiffly	Cylinder or bolt needs lubricating	Lubricate keyhole or bolt *(p. 68)* □○
	Bolt binding on strike plate	Adjust strike plate *(p. 43)* ▪○
	Cylinder dirty or gummed up	Remove cylinder *(deadbolt lock, p. 70; rim lock, p. 71; key-in-knob lock, p. 72; mortise lock, p. 73)* ▪○; clean and lubricate *(p. 75)* ▪○
	Bolt assembly dirty	Remove assembly *(p. 72)* for cleaning and lubrication *(p. 75)* ▪○
	Lock case of rim or mortise lock dirty	Remove lock case of rim lock *(p. 71)* ▪○, or mortise lock *(p. 74)* ▪◐, for cleaning and lubrication *(p. 75)* □◐
	Bolt assembly broken	Replace assembly *(p. 72)* ▪○
	Cylinder frozen	Thaw cylinder *(p. 10)* □○
Bolt won't enter bolthole	Strike plate misaligned	Adjust strike plate *(p. 43)* ▪○
Doorknob loose	Knob retaining setscrew loose	Tighten setscrew *(p. 42)* □○
Doorknob of key-in-knob lock turns but bolt doesn't move	Bolt assembly broken	Replace assembly *(p. 72)* ▪○
	Knob tailpiece broken	Replace key-in-knob lock with one of the same backset measurement, following manufacturer's instructions ▪◐
Present lock inadequate	Lock is worn or of poor quality	Add an accessory deadbolt lock *(p. 68)* ▪◐▲

DEGREE OF DIFFICULTY: □ Easy ▪ Moderate ■ Complex
ESTIMATED TIME: ○ Less than 1 hour ◐ 1 to 3 hours ● Over 3 hours   ▲ Special tool required

TYPES OF DOOR LOCKS

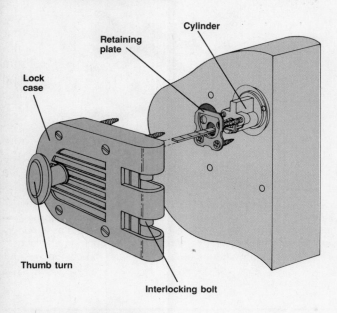

RIM LOCK (AUXILIARY LOCK)
A rim lock is mounted on the surface of the door near its edge (rim). The bolt locks into a strike plate on the door jamb and requires no mortising for installation. Long screws must be used to install it securely. The model above uses a vertical deadbolt that engages the strike plate hinge-style; this is the most secure type of rim lock.

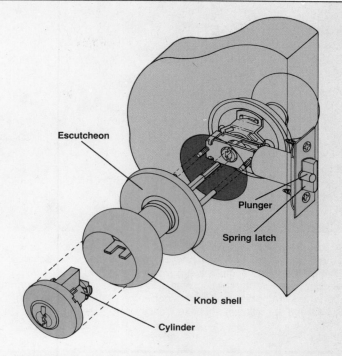

KEY-IN-KNOB LOCK
The lock cylinder is found in the exterior knob shell. The deadlatch design has a small plunger alongside the spring latch, which protects the latch assembly from being pushed back by a plastic card. Some newer models have a latch that extends a full inch into the strike—the length of a deadbolt—for added security.

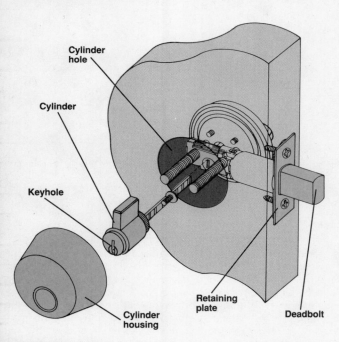

DEADBOLT LOCK
When its key or thumb-turn knob is turned, this lock forces a 1-inch bolt from the door into the strike in the jamb. Double-cylinder deadbolts require a key to open from both inside and outside the door; single-cylinder locks have a thumb turn inside (but an intruder can reach through a window to open it). Some building codes prohibit double-cylinder locks because of the danger of being locked inside in an emergency. If you have one, keep a key nearby.

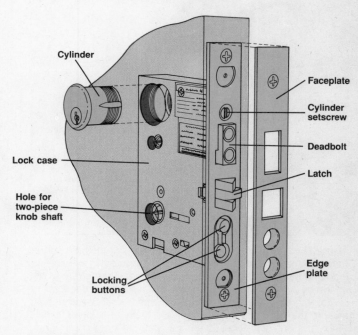

MORTISE LOCK
A mortise lock combines a latch and a deadbolt and contains its workings inside a metal case much like a precise Swiss watch. A large rectangular cavity must be made within the door to hold it—and care must be taken not to extensively weaken the door's structure when installing it. The best mortise locks are secure and attractive, but expensive. Locking buttons lock the handle without the key.

EASING A STICKING LOCK

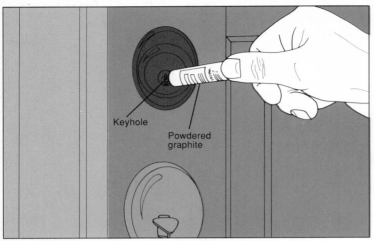

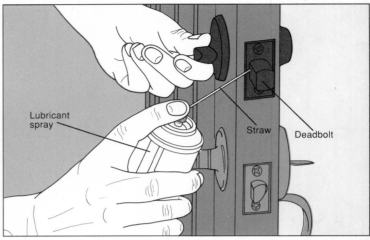

Lubricating a lock. Lubricate your lock twice a year. Choose one lubricant and stick to it; mixing lubricants may gum the lock, requiring disassembly for a thorough cleaning *(page 75)*. One of the best lubricants, particularly in dry, dusty climates, is graphite powder puffed from a tube. Press the nozzle of the container to the keyhole and into the cracks around the bolt and squeeze it once or twice *(above, left)*.

Another effective lubricant is petroleum-based lubricant spray. Fix the plastic straw in the nozzle to focus the spray into the keyhole and around the bolt *(above, right)*. Spray liberally to saturate the assembly, then use a rag to wipe away excess lubricant. After applying any lubricant, insert the key and work the bolt back and forth to help it penetrate the lock.

INSTALLING A DEADBOLT LOCK

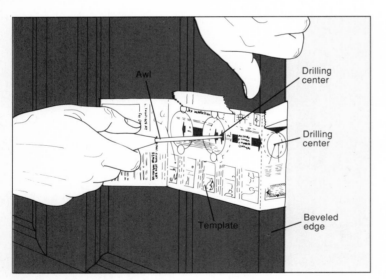

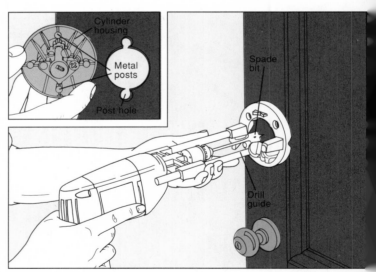

1 **Using the template.** If you are replacing your lock, be sure to measure the distance between the door edge and keyhole—the lock's backset—and buy a lock with this measurement. Use a lock with the backset of your choice if you are installing a deadbolt from scratch. Most backsets measure 2 3/8 inches or 2 3/4 inches. Also measure the thickness of your door; the majority of locks fit either a 1 3/8-inch or 1 3/4-inch door. To ensure accurate installation, most manufacturers supply paper templates with their locks to indicate the position and size of holes you will need to drill in the door. Always read the manufacturer's instructions carefully before you start. Fit the template over the high side of the door, that is, its beveled edge *(page 53)* and tape it in place. Then use an awl or a finishing nail to make 1/16-inch starter holes in the required drilling centers *(above)*, on the door face for the cylinder, and on the door edge for the bolt itself.

2 **Drilling the hole for the cylinder.** Remove the template and wedge the door wide open with shims. Fit a spade bit and drill guide, shown above, or a hole saw *(page 120)* on a power drill. Holding the bit perpendicular to the door, drill through the door face at the starter hole. Stop drilling just when the drill bit pierces through the door. Then go to the other side and finish drilling in the hole just made by the bit's tip *(above)*; drilling from both sides of the door will prevent splintering of the door's surface. Some single-cylinder tubular deadbolts, such as the one being installed here, have two metal posts that protrude from the back of the cylinder housing to fit in the door and thus stop the cylinder from being twisted out with a wrench. Drill two smaller holes above and below the cylinder hole to the depth required by the manufacturer's instructions *(inset)*.

INSTALLING A DEADBOLT LOCK (continued)

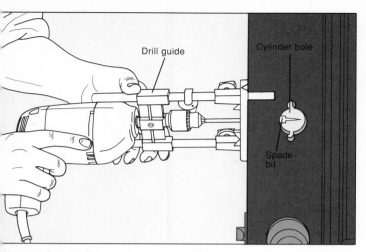

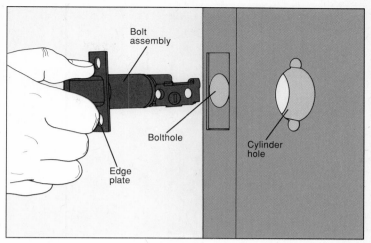

3 **Boring the bolthole.** Fit the drill with a spade bit and drill guide; the bit size will vary depending on manufacturer's instructions. In most cases it will be 1/8 inch larger than the diameter of the bolt. Position the bit in the starter hole made in the edge of the door in step , and drill a straight hole perpendicular to the door edge. Accurate drilling is essential for the lock to function properly. Brush away sawdust and wood chips left by the drilling before you continue.

4 **Inserting the bolt assembly.** Insert the bolt assembly into its hole. Hold the bolt edge plate against the door and etch its outline with a utility knife. Remove the assembly and, using a wood chisel and rubber mallet, chip a mortise deep enough for the edge plate to fit flush, usually 1/8 inch. Reinsert the bolt assembly right side up and extended, as shown above, or retracted, depending on the manufacturer's instructions. Screw the faceplate to the door.

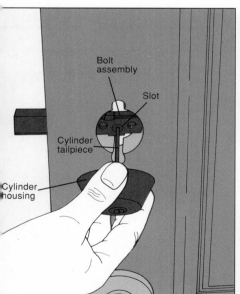

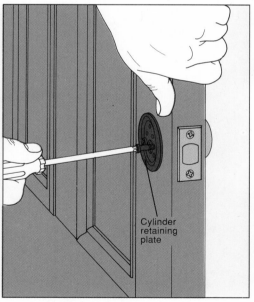

5 **Installing the cylinder housing and thumb turn.** Before completing the installation, check whether the deadbolt retracts and extends as it should by inserting the tip of a screwdriver through the slot in the bolt assembly and working it back and forth. If the deadbolt slides freely, install the cylinder housing on the outside of the door. Hold the housing so that the notched end of the keyhole points up, and push the tailpiece through the slot in the bolt assembly *(above, left)*. Position the retaining plate against the cylinder hole on the inside of the door and screw it through the door into the back of the cylinder housing *(above, center)*. Finally, screw the thumb turn over the retaining plate *(above, right)*. When you have finished, check that the lock works with the door open before installing the strike plate *(page 70)*.

INSTALLING A STRIKE PLATE

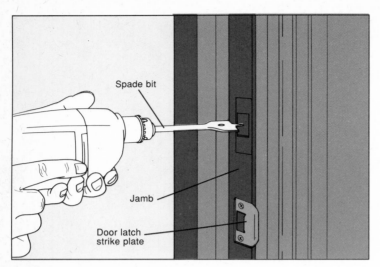

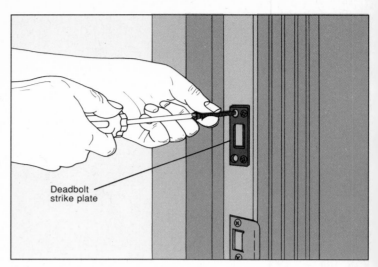

1 **Boring the strike hole.** First make a dot in the center of the deadbolt with lipstick or crayon. Then retract the deadbolt, close the door and turn the key or thumb turn to force the deadbolt against the door jamb. The smudge on the jamb indicates the center of the strike hole. Position the strike plate on the jamb with the mark in the center of the opening and trace the plate and the plate opening. Then, using a spade bit or auger bit, bore a hole slightly larger than the deadbolt at the mark on the jamb *(above)*. A typical deadbolt is 7/8 inch in diameter and extends 1 inch beyond the edge plate. In this case, drill a hole 1 inch in diameter and 1 1/8 inches deep.

2 **Securing the strike plate.** Use a wood chisel and rubber mallet to cut a mortise about 1/8 inch deep so that the plate will sit flush with the jamb. Pencil the screw positions in the mortise, drill pilot holes and screw the plate in place *(above)*. Many manufacturers provide 3-inch screws which are long enough to reach the stud behind the jamb. If your strike plate's screws are short, replace them with longer ones for added security. If the mortise is too deep, shim the strike plate with thin metal washers; place washers under the strike plate, around each screw hole if possible, and drive the screws in securely.

SERVICING A DEADBOLT LOCK

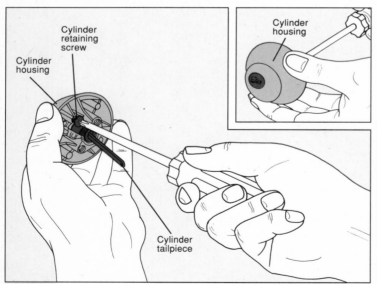

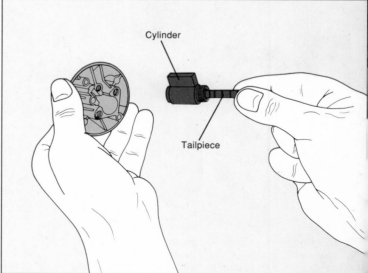

Removing the cylinder. To remove the cylinder housing from a deadbolt lock, unscrew the thumb turn and remove the two screws securing the cylinder retaining plate to the door. Some screws may have caps which must be drilled or chipped off to allow removal. Lift off the retaining plate and the cylinder housing. In some models, like the one shown here, the cylinder can be taken out of its housing. Remove the cylinder retaining screw from the back of the housing *(above, left)* and pull out the cylinder by its tailpiece *(above, right)*. Take it to a locksmith for service.

SERVICING A RIM LOCK

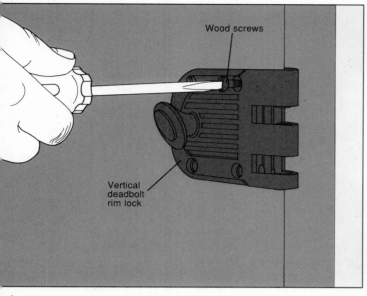

Wood screws

Vertical
deadbolt
rim lock

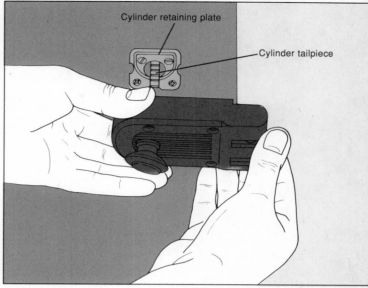

Cylinder retaining plate

Cylinder tailpiece

1 Removing the lock case. Rim locks may have either horizontal or vertical deadbolts. To give the lock case of either type a thorough cleaning *(page 75)* or to remove the cylinder for servicing, you must first unscrew the lock from the door. If your rim lock was installed with carriage bolts for increased security, you may need a locksmith to remove the case from the door. Otherwise, remove the three, four or five screws that secure the lock case in position *(above, left)*. Beneath it is the cylinder retaining plate with its tailpiece protruding through the center *(above, right)*. Do not risk damaging the inner workings of the lock by opening the lock case.

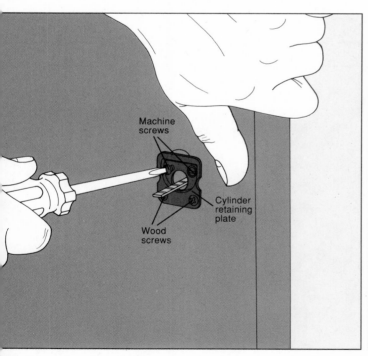

Machine
screws

Cylinder
retaining
plate

Wood
screws

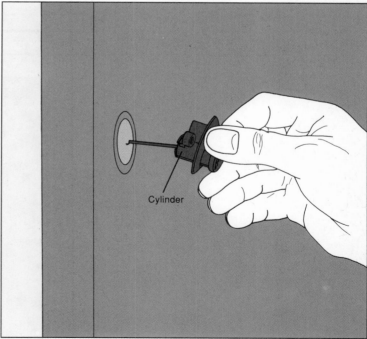

Cylinder

2 Removing the cylinder. If your lock isn't responding to the turn of its key, try tightening the cylinder retaining plate screws with a screwdriver. To free the cylinder, remove the two machine screws that pass through the retaining plate and door into the cylinder on the other side *(above, left)*. As the last screw is taken out, support the cylinder with one hand to prevent it from falling *(above, right)*. In some locks, the retaining plate is fastened to the door with two wood screws. In this case, the plate will remain on the door when the machine screws are removed. Clean the cylinder *(page 75)*, or take it to a locksmith for rekeying or replacement. To install the lock, reverse the steps you took to disassemble it.

SERVICING A KEY-IN-KNOB LOCK

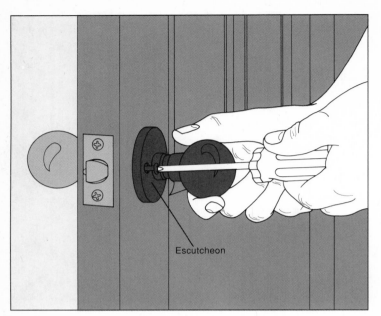

Escutcheon

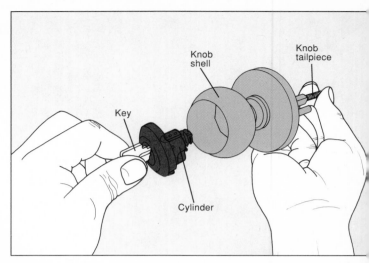

Knob shell

Knob tailpiece

Key

Cylinder

1 **Removing the knobs.** The cylinder housing of a key-in-knob lock is the exterior knob itself. You must remove the doorknobs from the door before you can free the cylinder. On the popular model shown above, unfasten the screws on the inside escutcheon *(above)*. With these screws removed, the inside and outside knob assembly can be pulled apart. Some key-in-knob locks require that you first remove the inside knob by depressing a release catch on the knob's neck and pulling the knob off its shaft *(page 43)* to reveal the screw.

2 **Removing the cylinder.** With one hand, insert the key in the outside knob and hold it with the notched edge up. With the other hand, hold on to the tailpiece. Pull on the tailpiece while you turn the key about 45 degrees counterclockwise. Withdraw the key; the cylinder and knob face will separate from the knob shell. Take the cylinder to a locksmith for service.

To replace the cylinder in the knob, first insert the key in the keyhole with its notched edge pointing up. Turn the key counterclockwise as before. Fit the top of the cylinder between the prongs of the bracket inside the knob's shell and press it into place. Turn the key back to the upright position until you hear a snap. Remove the key. Now reassemble the lock, reversing the steps you took to disassemble it.

REPLACING A BOLT ASSEMBLY

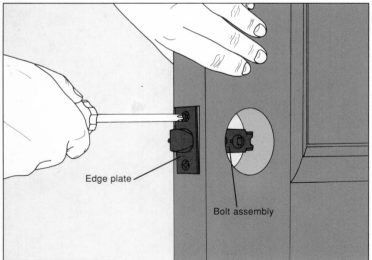

Edge plate

Bolt assembly

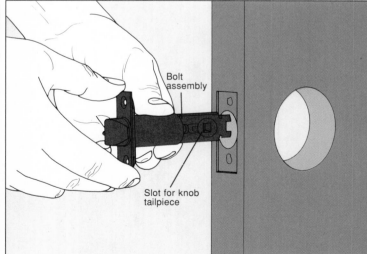

Bolt assembly

Slot for knob tailpiece

1 **Removing a bolt assembly.** To remove a key-in-knob dead-latch, first remove the doorknobs *(top, left)*. Then unscrew the edge plate from the door *(above, left)*, and pull the deadlatch free. If you are removing the bolt assembly of a deadbolt lock, reverse the actions taken to install the cylinder housing *(page 69, step 5)* and then unscrew the edge plate. Contractors sometimes use bolt assemblies in metal doors which are of the "drive-in" type, with no retaining

screws. This kind must be pushed out with a screwdriver blade inserted into the knob opening and forced behind the latch. Take a broken bolt assembly to a locksmith and buy an exact duplicate. Clean and lubricate it as you would a lock case *(page 75)*. Use a cotton swab to wipe dirt from the assembly. When replacing it in the door, reverse the steps you took for removal. Make sure the assembly is right side up, or the door will not close.

REMOVING THE CYLINDER FROM A MORTISE LOCK

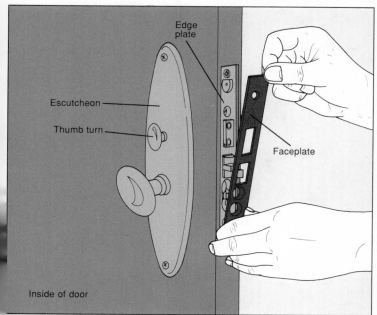

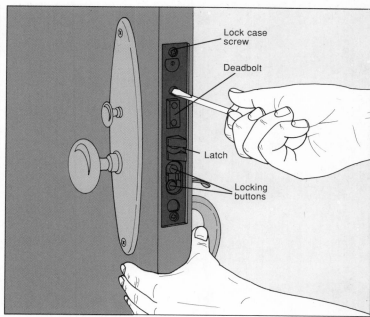

1 Freeing the cylinder. Before removing a cylinder for repair or replacement, check to see if the lock case edge plate is hidden by a decorative faceplate. If it is, remove its screws and lift it off *(above, left)*. The cylinder is held in the door by a setscrew. Use a screwdriver to free the cylinder by loosening the setscrew, usually three or four turns counterclockwise *(above, right)*. Do not remove it. Some models may have a second setscrew on the inside edge of the lock case that connects to the thumb turn; do not loosen this screw.

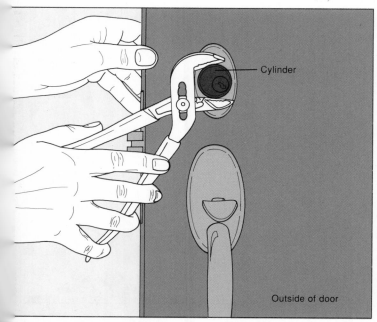

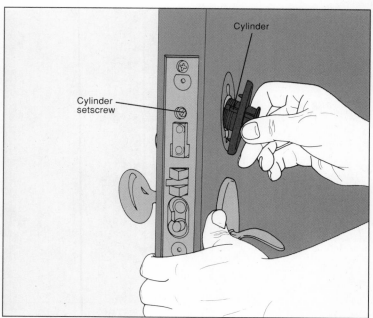

2 Removing the cylinder. Loosen the top and bottom lock case screws to give the cylinder some play. Then, using channel-joint pliers padded with masking tape to protect the cylinder's finish, gently grip the rim of the cylinder and turn it counterclockwise to loosen *(above, left)*. In some locks, the cylinder may have a rotating collar that prevents it from being loosened in this way; instead insert the key in the keyway and turn the cylinder. Do not use excessive force, or the key may break off in the cylinder. Remove the cylinder by unscrewing it by hand *(above, right)*. Count the number of rotations (usually five or six) for proper reassembly later.

To replace a cylinder after servicing, insert it in the door with the keyhole's notched edges pointing up. Taking care to keep the threads of the cylinder in line with those in its lock case, screw the cylinder back into the door; rotate it by hand the same number of times required for removal earlier. Then retighten the setscrew and the top and bottom lock case screws. Reinstall the faceplate, if the lock has one.

REMOVING THE LOCK CASE FROM A MORTISE LOCK

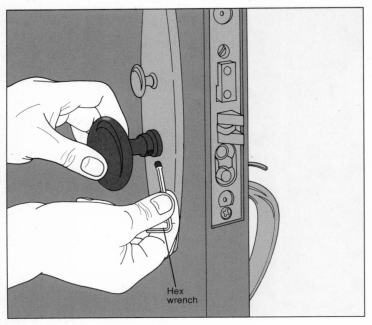

1 **Removing the inside doorknob.** To remove a lock for cleaning or repair, first remove its cylinder from the lock case *(page 73)*. Then, using a screwdriver or hex wrench, loosen the two knob setscrews two or three turns or remove them *(above)*. If the screws are exceptionally tight, insert the short end of the wrench into the screw head, using the long arm for greater leverage; you will need to remove and reinsert the wrench several times. Turn the knob counterclockwise to remove it from its threaded shaft.

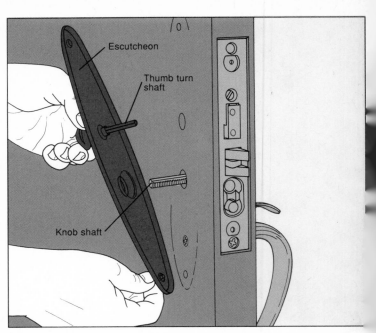

2 **Removing the escutcheon and thumb turn.** Use a screwdriver to remove the screws at the top and bottom of the escutcheon on the inside of the door, and lift it off. The thumb turn and its shaft are attached to the escutcheon and come away with it.

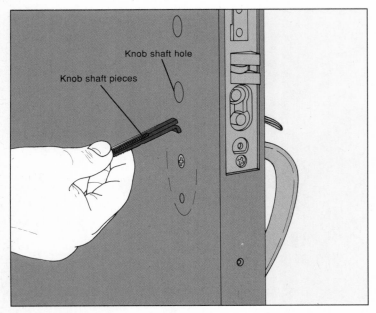

3 **Removing the knob shaft.** If your mortise lock has a knob on the inside and a handle on the outside, the knob shaft is likely to consist of a straight piece and a hooked piece; together they form a threaded square shaft. Pry the ends apart with the tip of a screwdriver and slide the straight piece out. Then unhook the bottom piece and pull it free. Place them together, with the threaded edges on the outside *(above)*, to ensure proper reassembly later. If your lock has knobs on both the exterior and the interior, the shaft will be a simple square one. Pull it free from the door, and go to step 5.

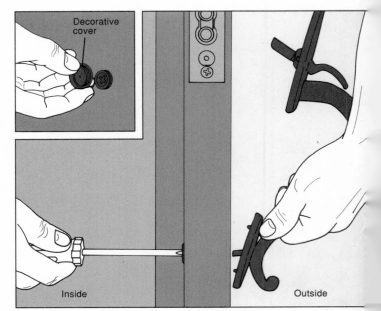

4 **Removing the exterior door handle.** The outside handle is held by two screws that pass through the door from the inside. With a screwdriver, remove the screw that secures the top of the handle. The head of the bottom screw is often hidden by a decorative cover. Using channel-joint pliers padded with masking tape, loosen the cover, then take it off by hand *(inset)*. Finish by removing the bottom screw while you support the handle on the outside *(above)*.

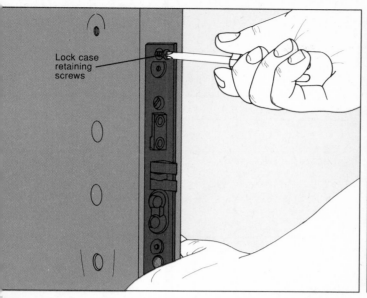

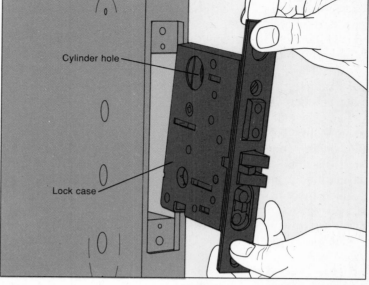

Freeing the lock case. If there is any paint buildup on the edge of the door around the lock case, use a utility knife to break the seal and scrape it off. If necessary, first apply paint remover sparingly to soften the paint. The lock case is retained in its mortise by two screws at the top and bottom of the lock edge plate. Use a screwdriver to remove first the bottom screw, then the top one *(above, left)*, and lift out the entire lock case *(above, right)*. Do not risk damaging the delicate mechanisms inside the lock case by trying to remove its cover. Clean the lock case thoroughly if necessary *(below)*, or take it to a locksmith for service. To reassemble a mortise lock, reverse the steps taken for the removal of the lock case and finish by replacing the cylinder *(page 73)*.

CLEANING AND LUBRICATING A LOCK CASE

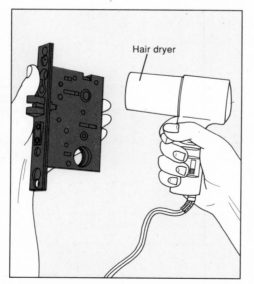

1 Washing the lock case. Working in a well-ventilated area and wearing rubber gloves, wash dirty lock parts such as bolt assemblies, cylinders and lock cases in a shallow basin filled with mineral spirits or turpentine. Do not open lock cases; instead, flush solvent into the openings *(above)*. Clean the bolt assemblies of key-in-knob and deadbolt locks with a cotton swab.

2 Drying the lock case. Set clean lock parts on a newspaper to drain for an hour or so. Dispose safely of all dirty solvents, cleaning rags and papers *(page 9)*. Cap solvent containers and store them. To speed drying of the lock case, use a hair dryer set at low heat *(above)*.

3 Lubricating the lock case. Generously apply light machine oil through the holes scattered over the surface of the case cover plates *(above)*. Also oil the surface of a deadlatch or deadbolt assembly and lubricate the cylinder *(page 68)*. In dry, dusty environments, use powdered graphite.

PANES AND SCREENS

Fixing any broken window used to be a fairly standard procedure involving a piece of glass, glazier's points and putty. But new developments in window construction—such as double-glazed aluminum casements and plastic panes—require that you know more about your windows before attempting repairs. These innovations also afford you more alternatives; for example, a heat-stealing single-pane door can be fitted with an energy-efficient double pane (*page 82*).

The age-old problem with window panes remains the same—they break. Antique leaded-glass panes often loosen and rattle. Modern panes exhibit some modern problems as well—a double pane may fog if moisture gets between its layers, and a plastic pane yellows or crazes over time. The Troubleshooting Guide at right lists typical problems and directs you to corrective procedures in this chapter. The tools you need to work on windows are few and simple (*Tools and Techniques, page 118*). The Glazing Alternatives chart below lists the types of window fittings available, and their features and uses. The National Glazing Code requires that shatter-resistant panes be used in certain applications, such as doors. Check with a professional glazier or window dealer before replacing a pane. If you plan to install a double or triple pane, order the unit in advance; it may have to be built to size.

You can cut your own glass or plastic single pane (*page 77*). When cutting glass, wear work gloves and safety goggles. Practice cutting a scrap piece first, and work on a level surface padded with layers of newspaper or a piece of thin carpet. Cutting a plastic pane is safer, but take care not to scratch its relatively soft surface. Panes in modern windows—especially metal ones—are installed with specialized sealants, gaskets, clips or moldings. When you buy a new pane, consult with the dealer to choose installation materials compatible with both the pane and the window—bring a sample of the old materials with you as reference.

Window screens are easy to repair and replace. Fiberglass screening is easy to install, but tends to sag. Aluminum screening is more expensive but stronger, though it eventually oxidizes in humid climates. Both types of screening are replaced the same way (*page 84*).

TROUBLESHOOTING GUIDE

SYMPTOM	PROCEDURE
Single-pane window cracked or broken	Cut glass or acrylic (*p. 77*) ▣○▲ and reglaze (*wood window, p. 78* ▣●; *metal window, p. 79* ▣○; *leaded window, p. 80* ▣●; *jalousie window, p. 30* □○); replace single pane with an insulating unit (*p. 83*) ▣●▲
Glass pane rattles	Replace deteriorated glazing compound (*wood window, p. 78; leaded window, p. 82; steel window, p. 81*) ▣○ or worn gasket (*p. 81*) ▣○
Double- or triple-pane window cracked or broken	Reglaze (*p. 82*) ▣○
Double- or triple-pane window foggy	Reglaze (*p. 82*) ▣○
Acrylic pane cracked or yellow	Cut glass or acrylic (*p. 77*) ▣○ and reglaze (*wood window, p. 78* ▣○; *metal window, p. 82* ▣○)
Screen torn	Patch (*p. 84*) □○ or replace screen (*wood window or door, p. 84; metal window or door, p. 85* ▲) ▣○

DEGREE OF DIFFICULTY: □ Easy ▣ Moderate ▣ Complex
ESTIMATED TIME: ○ Less than 1 hour ● 1 to 3 hours ▲ Special tool required

GLAZING ALTERNATIVES

TYPE	CHARACTERISTICS	APPLICATIONS
Float glass	Untreated and least expensive.	May be single-strength for small windows or double-strength for large windows, storm windows and storm doors.
Laminated glass	Bonded to an internal core of polyvinyl chloride film. Broken pane remains in one piece.	Safety glass for doors, skylights, bathrooms and solariums.
Tempered glass	Strengthened by heating and cooling. If broken, shatters into small, blunt-edged pieces.	Safety glass for doors, most commonly in bathrooms and solariums.
Wired glass	Wire mesh is embedded in the glass. Cut and installed like regular glass; wire must be snipped after glass is cut.	Basements and other areas with high risk of damage.
Double-pane or triple-pane glass	Panes of glass are separated by a spacer bar to form an insulating airspace.	Any door or window requiring control of heat loss or gain.
Low emissivity (low e) glass	Metal coating is baked onto glass surface; applied to single or multiple panes to reduce heat transfer.	Any door or window requiring control of heat loss or gain.
Acrylic	Lightweight, tendency to yellow, scratches more easily than glass. Installed like regular glass, using elastic-type glazing compound.	Safety pane for storm and shower doors, and for skylights.

CUTTING A RECTANGULAR WINDOW PANE

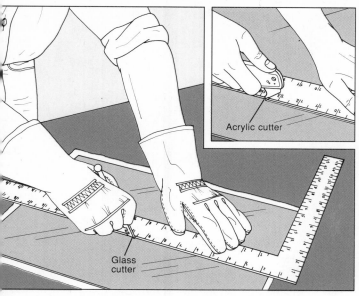

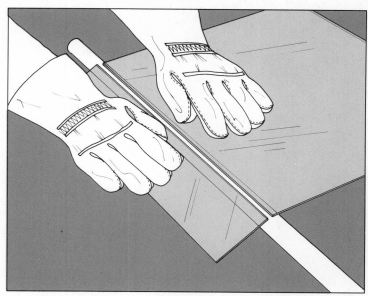

Acrylic cutter

Glass cutter

1 **Scoring a straight line.** Lay the glass on a surface padded with newspaper or an old piece of carpet. Wearing gloves and using a straightedge as a guide, score the glass once with a glass cutter that has a carbide cutting wheel. Dip the wheel in kerosene or light machine oil, then grasp the cutter between the index and middle fingers as shown. Starting at the far edge of the glass, pull the cutter toward you in one steady stroke *(above)*. Apply even pressure until you reach the end of the cut; do not allow the cutter to slide away from the straightedge. Use an acrylic cutter to cut an acrylic pane *(inset)*; retrace the line several times to deepen the cut.

2 **Dividing the pane.** Deepen the score line by tapping along the line from underneath *(below, step 2)*. Then place a wood dowel, broomstick or other thin rod at least as long as the score line directly under the line. Press down firmly on both sides of the glass to snap it *(above)*. On a small piece of glass or stained glass, position your thumbs on top—one on each side of the score line—and your fingers underneath. Push up with your fingers while you twist your thumbs apart. Use the edge of a worktable to break an acrylic pane after it has been scored.

CUTTING A CURVED PANE OF GLASS

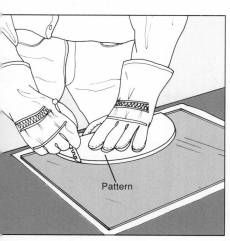

Pattern

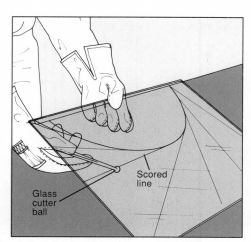

Scored line

Glass cutter ball

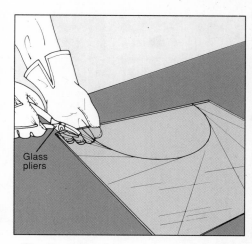

Glass pliers

1 **Scoring a curved line.** Trace the shape of a curved pane onto a piece of cardboard and trim it with scissors to make a pattern. Using the pattern as a guide, score the glass as described in step 1, above, drawing the glass cutter closely and steadily around the edge of the pattern *(above)* to score a well-fitting pane.

2 **Deepening the score lines.** Score several straight lines radiating from the curve to the edge of the glass. Then deepen each score by lifting the glass and tapping lightly along the line from underneath with the ball end of the cutter *(above)*.

3 **Snapping the curve.** Use glass pliers to snap off the scored segments *(above)*. If any jagged edges remain along the curve, nip away about 1/16 inch at a time with glass pliers until the edge is uniform. Smooth any roughness with fine sandpaper.

REPAIRING A BROKEN WINDOW IN A WOOD SASH

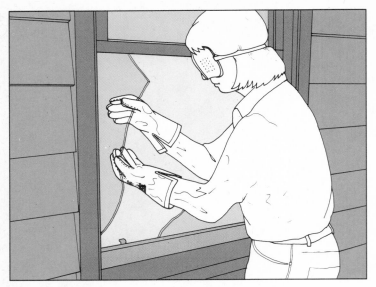

1 Removing the glass fragments. Wearing heavy work gloves and safety glasses, start at the top of the window to remove shards of glass *(above)*. Pull each shard straight out of the sash; gently wiggle stubborn fragments free. Place the fragments in a cardboard box for disposal. Remove glass from muntins—strips that divide the panes of a window—with care. Muntins are delicate, and their replacement requires a carpenter's skills.

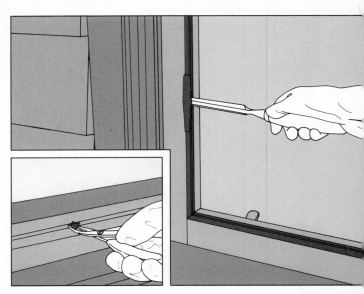

2 Removing the old glazing compound. Using an old chisel or a narrow, stiff putty knife, pry old glazing compound out of the sash *(above)*. Hardened glazing compound may first require softening. To soften unpainted putty, coat it with linseed oil and let it saturate for 30 minutes. Soften painted compound using a soldering iron with a 1/4- to 1/2-inch tip; be careful not to burn the surrounding wood. Once the glazing compound has been removed, pull out the glazier's points with long-nose pliers *(inset)*.

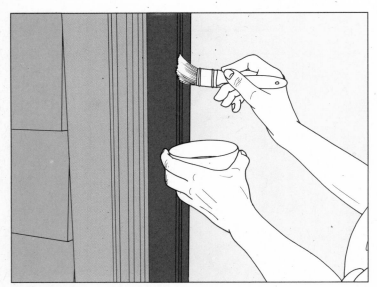

3 Preparing the channel. Before installing a new pane, clean the sash channel by carefully brushing it with a wire brush. Remove splinters with medium-grit sandpaper. If you are using putty, prime the channel with linseed oil, as shown. Follow manufacturer's instructions for elastic-type glazing compound. To fit a replacement pane, measure the opening inside the window frame and subtract 1/8 inch from the length and width for glass expansion. Have the replacement pane cut or cut it yourself *(page 77)*.

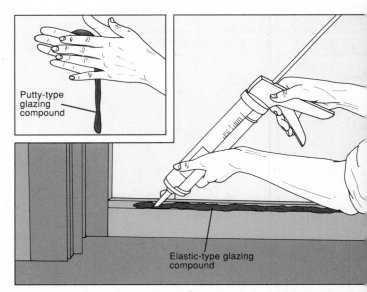

Putty-type glazing compound

Elastic-type glazing compound

4 Preparing the "bed." Make a "bed" for the glass by lining the sash channel with a thin bead of glazing compound. If you are using an elastic-type glazing compound in a tube applicator, apply the compound in a uniform 3/8-inch bead using a caulking gun *(above)*. Glazing putty, however, generally comes in a tin; remove it from the container and roll into a snake-like shape between the palms of your hands *(inset)*. Then press it into the channel around the edge of the sash.

5 **Installing the glass.** Lift the pane and set it in place, as shown. Since a properly cut pane will be approximately 1/4 inch smaller than the frame, position it with equal space on each side. Press glazier's points into the sash flush against the glass—two to a side on a small window and about every 6 inches on a larger one. Then use a stiff putty knife *(inset)* or a mallet and an old screwdriver to insert them halfway into the sash.

6 **Covering the glazier's points.** Apply glazing compound to the joint between pane and frame in the same manner as in step 4. If you are using a tube applicator, cut the nozzle opening a little larger for a larger bead. For a neat appearance, dip a putty knife in water or light machine oil and draw it over the bead to create a bevel of approximately 45 degrees *(above)*. Seal the corners well and trim off excess compound inside and out. When the glazing compound is dry—it no longer shows a thumbprint—paint or varnish it *(page 121)*.

REPAIRING A BROKEN WINDOW IN A METAL SASH

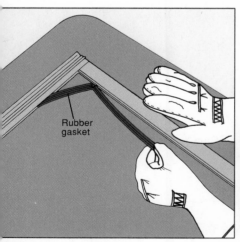

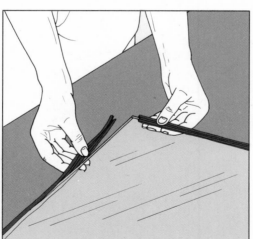

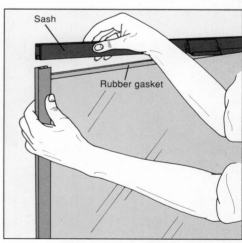

Replacing a broken pane. Remove window fragments from the metal sash *(page 78)* and lay the sash on a work table. Many metal storm sashes can be reglazed simply by prying out the rubber strip or spline that secures the pane to the sash, inserting the new pane and pressing the spline back in under the sash with your thumbs. Other metal sashes, such as the sliding window shown here, must be disassembled to fit the new pane. Measure the length and width of the opening from the inside edges of the frame. Then pull out the rubber gasket *(above, left)*, and measure its width. For a glass pane, add twice the gasket width to the frame's inside length and width; for plastic use the same measurements

less 1/8 inch each. Buy a pane cut to size or buy and cut your own *(page 77)*. To disassemble the sash, remove any framing screws that hold the sash pieces together and pull them apart. Replace a dried or cracked gasket with a new gasket cut to the length of the pane's perimeter. Fit the gasket around the edge of the window *(above, center)*, snipping it partway at each corner. Reassemble the sash by reversing the dissassembly steps *(above, right)*. Replace a pane in a steel casement window as described for a wood sash *(page 78)*, but use spring clips and prepare the channel with rustproof paint before bedding the pane with elastic-type glazing compound.

REPAIRING A LEADED WINDOW

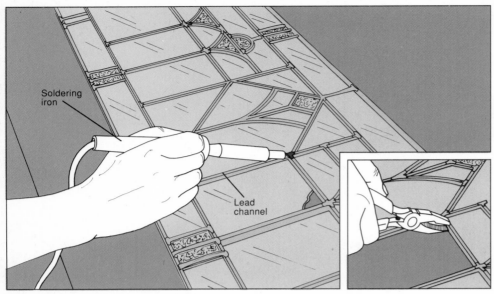

1 Removing the damaged pane. Remove the window and glazing compound from the sash *(page 78)*. Check a metal window for spring clips, and remove them. If the glass is secured by molding, use a stiff putty knife to pry the molding away. Melt solder at the joints with a narrow-tipped soldering iron *(above)*, then use glass pliers or a wide putty knife to lift the lead flanges around the perimeter of the broken piece *(inset)*. Wearing gloves and safety glasses, remove any glass fragments from the window. On difficult-to-remove pieces, score a crisscross pattern with a glass cutter *(page 77)*, fracture the glass with the ball end of the cutter and wiggle the fragments loose. Use a small wire brush to clean the lead channel.

2 Replacing the glass. Place a piece of cardboard under the space in the window and trace its shape to make a template, then add 1/8 inch to the width and length and cut it out. Trace the template onto replacement glass, then cut the pane *(page 78)*. Slide the new pane into position *(above)* you may have to wiggle the glass as you push it in.

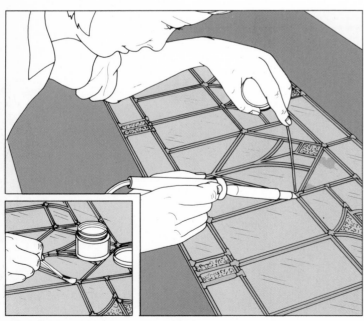

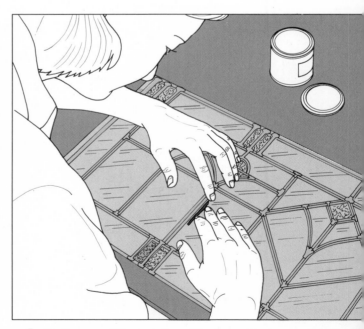

3 Resoldering the joints. Press the upper flange of the lead channel back into position, forming a rim over the glass. Use a soldering iron to resecure the joints. Heat the iron and apply a drop of flux to the joint *(inset)*. Then hold the iron over the joint, coat it with solder and let a small amount melt onto the lead *(above)*. If the solder does not adhere, roughen the lead with the point of a nail or knife, add more flux, then resolder.

4 Sealing a rattling section. After the solder has cooled, fill the spaces between the lead and glass with glazing compound. Roll out a very thin bead of putty *(page 78)* and, using your finger, push it between the lead and the glass on all sides, front and back. Trim excess compound using a utility knife or the point of a nail. Finally sprinkle whiting over the surface of the glass to pick up the oil residue then brush the surface clean.

INSULATING WINDOWS

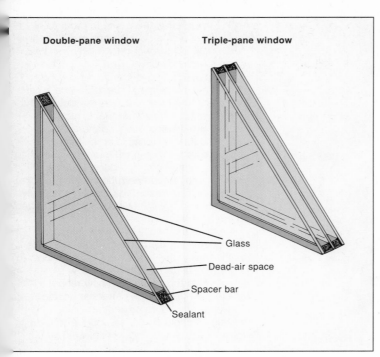

Double-pane window

Triple-pane window

Glass

Dead-air space

Spacer bar

Sealant

An insulating window is composed of two—or sometimes three—parallel sheets of glass. The sheets are separated by metal or plastic spacer bars around their edges. An elastic sealant around the perimeter of the pane holds the glass and spacers in place, as well as sealing the air space betweeen the glass sheets. It is this dead-air space that works as an insulator, preventing heat from passing through the pane.

The efficiency of an insulating window is directly related to the width of the dead-air space. The insulation value of the space increases up to about 5/8 inch, then decreases as the space gets wider.

The spacer bars in an insulating window often contain a dessicant—chemical granules that absorb moisture—to prevent condensation between the glass sheets. If the edge seal breaks, however, excess moisture will cause internal fogging, and the pane will have to be replaced. Twisting or racking of the pane are major causes of edge-seal failure and glass breakage; an insulating window must be installed perfectly flat and square, with room to expand.

REPLACING A BROKEN INSULATING WINDOW

Replacing a broken insulating window. Most insulating units are held in place by a snap-on glazing bead or by wood molding screwed, nailed or glued to the frame. To determine the size of a replacement unit, measure between the moldings and add an inch to each measurement. If your insulating window is secured by wood molding as shown at left, slip a utility knife between the molding and the window to cut the sealant *(inset)*. Then unscrew the molding or pry it free with a stiff putty knife. (In some cases, the frame must be disassembled to reglaze the window; remove the sash and look for screws or clips holding the corners of the sash together.) If the window is in one piece, lift it out of the frame *(left)*; wear work gloves and get help if it is heavy.

If the glass is broken, the seal around the edge may continue to hold the pieces together. Otherwise, remove the broken pieces carefully *(page 78)*, then remove the edges from the sash. Scrape old glazing compound from the sash and molding. Place the new window in the sash and, if it had a sealant, apply a new bead that is compatible with the edge seal; check with the dealer. Resecure the molding to the sash, using wood screws spaced 8 to 10 inches apart. Make sure the screws do not touch the window.

FITTING A SINGLE-PANE DOOR WITH AN INSULATING WINDOW

Window opening

Door

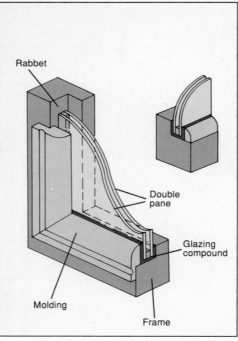

Rabbet

Double pane

Glazing compound

Molding

Frame

1 Preparing the door. In order to be fitted with a double-pane insulating window, an exterior door must have solid wood stiles and rails at least 1 3/4 inch thick. Check that the hinges are strong and tight; correct any problems *(page 123)*. Use a carpenter's square to make sure the door frame is square *(far left)*; a door that is racked or warped will break a double-pane unit.

The double pane sits in an L-shaped groove called a rabbet cut into the edge of the door frame *(left)*. The pane edges are cushioned by neoprene rubber setting blocks, sealed with an elastic-type glazing compound and held in place by a wood molding screwed to the door frame.

Measure the height and width of the window opening in the door and add 1 inch to each—this is the size double-pane window to order. It is better to order a window slightly too big than too small—the new rabbet will be cut to fit the window. After the double pane has arrived, remove the molding and glazing compound from around the window *(page 78)* and, wearing work gloves, lift out the old pane.

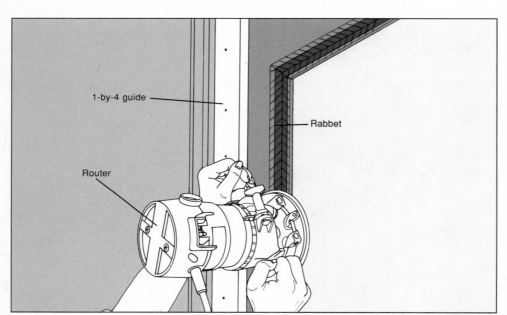

1-by-4 guide

Rabbet

Router

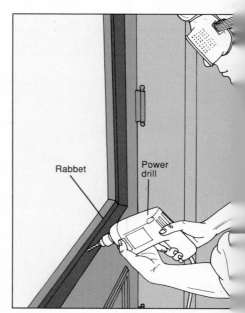

Rabbet

Power drill

2 Enlarging the rabbet. To cut the new rabbet, use a router fitted with a rabbet bit *(page 121)*. First, measure the exact width of the double pane, add 1/2 inch for setting blocks and for expansion, and subtract the width of the existing window opening. Divide the result in half to determine the width to cut each side rabbet. Calculate the width of the top and bottom rabbets the same way. Choose rabbet bits of the right size to cut these widths. Then measure the exact thickness of the double pane, and add 1/4 inch for glazing compound and 1/2 inch or more as needed for the finish molding. This is the depth you should cut the rabbet. Use a straightedge to mark a line for the edge position of each side rabbet on the door frame. Nail or clamp a perfectly straight 1-by-4 parallel to the rabbet line to guide the router. Set the router bit to cut 3/8 inch deep, turn on the motor and move the bit into the wood, running the baseplate firmly along the guide *(above)*. Deepen the rabbet in increments of 3/8-inch or less to its final depth. Cut the other side rabbet and the top and bottom rabbets the same way. The router bit will leave the corners rounded; cut them square with a sharp wood chisel.

3 Preparing the rabbet. Using a pow[er] drill, make drainage holes about 1/4 inch in diameter at 6-inch intervals through the side edge of the rabbet *(above)*. Angle the holes down toward the outside. Brush sawdust out of the rabbet. Lay four 2-inch rubber setting blocks, 1/8 inch thick an[d] 1/8 inch wider than the double pane, at equ[al] intervals along the bottom edge of the rabb[et].

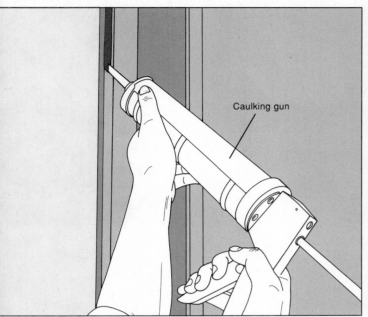

4 Installing the window. Choose an elastic-type glazing compound compatible with the compound used to construct the window; check with the window dealer. Using a caulking gun, apply a 1/4-inch bead of compound along the back edge of the rabbet *(above, left)*, leaving no spaces. With a helper, lift the window into the bottom rabbet *(above, right)* and, resting its bottom edge on the setting blocks, push its top edge into the top rabbet. Center the window and gently press its edges into the glazing compound.

5 Trimming the window. Slip setting blocks around the perimeter of the window, about every 8 inches *(above, left)*. Fill spaces between the blocks with glazing compound. Measure and cut molding trim to fit around the window, and set it aside. Apply a bead of glazing compound to the joint between window edge and rabbet all around, and install the molding over it. Tack the molding in place with finishing nails, then screw it to the door frame every 8 inches. Be sure that nails or screws do not contact the glass. Test the operation of the door; if it sags, replace weak hinges with stronger ones, or replug worn screw holes and install longer screws *(page 123)*.

PATCHING A SCREEN

Patching a fiberglass screen. Repair tiny holes in a fiberglass screen by applying a few drops of acetone-based glue. To repair a larger hole, make a patch from left-over screening that is large enough to cover the hole. Coat the edges of the patch and the area around the hole with a thin coat of the glue *(above)*, and press the patch in place. Wipe off excess glue with a clean rag.

Patching an aluminum screen. Tiny holes in aluminum screens can be sealed with a few dr[...] of waterproof glue. To repair a larger hole, first use scissors to cut the hole square. Then cut a patch of matching screening about 2 inches wider than the hole. Pull several strands of wire ou[...] of each edge of the patch and bend the remaining wires down on all four sides *(above, left)*. Position the patch evenly over the hole and work the wires through the screening. Turn the screen over, pull the patch tight and bend the wires down against the screen *(above, right)*.

REPLACING SCREENING ON A WOOD DOOR

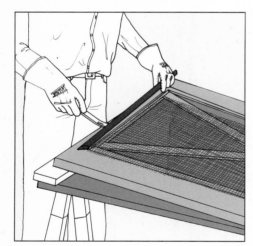

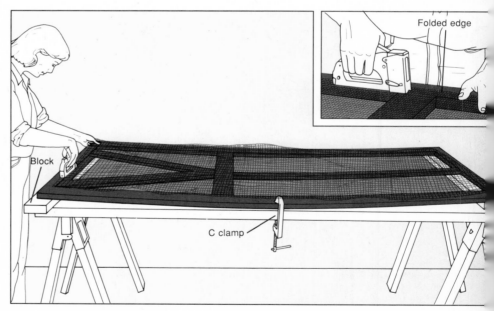

1 Removing molding and screening. Unscrew the door hinges from the jamb and remove the door. Lay it on a flat work table. Use a utility bar to lift the molding around the screening; start in the middle and work toward the corners. Then, with an old screwdriver, pry loose the tacks or staples that hold the screen to the door. Wearing gloves if working with metal screening, pull the screening off the frame. Place a block under each end of the door and attach C clamps to the frame at its midpoint. Bow the door by tightening the clamps.

2 Stapling new screening to the frame. Cut new screening 4 inches wider and longer than the opening in the door. Lay the screening on top of the door, aligning the weave with the frame. Using a staple gun, staple the screening to the frame at one end *(above[...]* driving staples 3 inches apart at a right angle to the frame. On fiberglass screening, fold the edge for extra strength before stapling *(inset)*. Staple the screening at the other end the same way, keeping it taut and straight. Release the clamps to pull the screening tight, and staple it along one side and then the other. Trim excess screening with scissors or a utility knife, and replace the molding.

REPLACING SCREENING IN A METAL FRAME

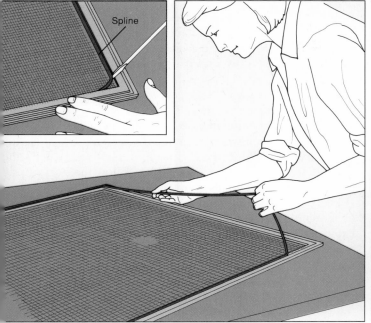

Spline

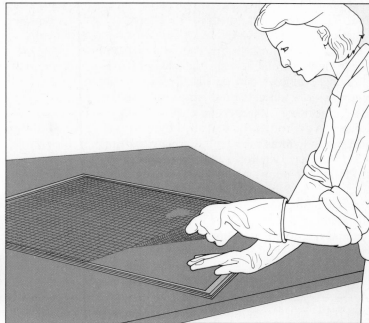

1 Removing the spline. Metal screen doors and windows use a rubber or plastic strip called a spline to secure the screening to the frame. Remove the door from its hinges or slide the storm window free of its frame and lay it on a flat surface. To remove the spline, use an old screwdriver to dig up one corner *(inset)*. Pull the spline gently out of its channel; do not tear or stretch it *(above, left)*.

If the spline is cracked or stiff, take it to a hardware store and buy a roll of matching spline. Cut the new spline a bit longer than the old one. Wearing work gloves, pull the old screening free from the spline channel *(above, right)*. Lay the new screening over the frame and cut it so that it extends 1 inch beyond the channel. Trim the corners of the screening diagonally so they don't bunch up in the corners of the channel.

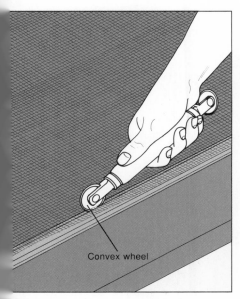

Convex wheel

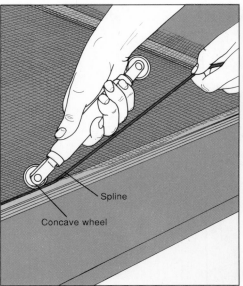

Spline

Concave wheel

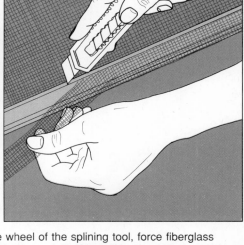

2 Creasing metal screening. If rescreening with fiberglass, go to step 3. The edges of aluminum screening must be bent and pushed into the channel. Roll the convex wheel of a splining tool back and forth along the edges of the screen, creasing it into the channel *(above)*. Repeat on all sides.

3 Installing the spline. Using the concave wheel of the splining tool, force fiberglass screen and spline together into the channel *(above, left)*. If installing aluminum screening, force the spline into the channel over the screening you creased in step 2. If the frame is long and narrow, cut the spline and install the two short sides first. If it is nearly square, install the spline in one piece. The action of the spline pushing the screen into the channel should tighten the screen. Cut off excess spline, then use a utility knife to trim the screen close to the spline *(above, right)*.

REPLACEMENT WINDOWS AND DOORS

Over time, a window or door may become so damaged or inefficient that replacement of the entire unit is the simplest, least costly repair. A prehung window or door, which comes complete with finish frame, can be inserted in one piece into the rough opening left by the old window or door. Some prehung windows can be installed in the jambs of the old window; in a sense, the old jambs become the new frame.The new unit doesn't have to be custom made—the addition of boards to the rough frame, called blocking *(page 90)*, and the insertion of shims between the rough and finish frames *(page 92)*, will make up for a unit that is a bit too small.

Prehung windows and doors are made in hundreds of styles and sizes. They may be wood, aluminum, steel or even vinyl. Each manufacturer's product comes with instructions for installation; the procedures in this chapter cover taking out a standard double-hung window and replacing it with a typical double-hung wood replacement unit. The steps for replacing an exterior door *(page 98)* are nearly the same.

Installing a prehung door or window requires careful planning. First, check your local building code. Before ordering a prehung unit, consult a reputable window and door dealer for advice. Shop around for the unit closest to the size and style you need—a window, especially, should be well matched to others in the house. Measure the opening precisely, following the guidelines on page 88. Expect installation to take at least a day, and be prepared to install plastic sheeting or a plywood panel over the opening in case it takes longer *(page 10)*. Work with a helper, even when installing a small window; it is often necessary to post one worker inside the house and the other outside. If you must work on a ladder, follow the safety tips in the Tools & Techniques chapter *(page 118)*.

The exterior siding and sheathing of a house may be cut away with a circular saw to fit the brickmold of a window or exterior door *(page 91)*, or to accommodate a longer replacement window. If modifications must be made to a brick or stone house, consult a mason.

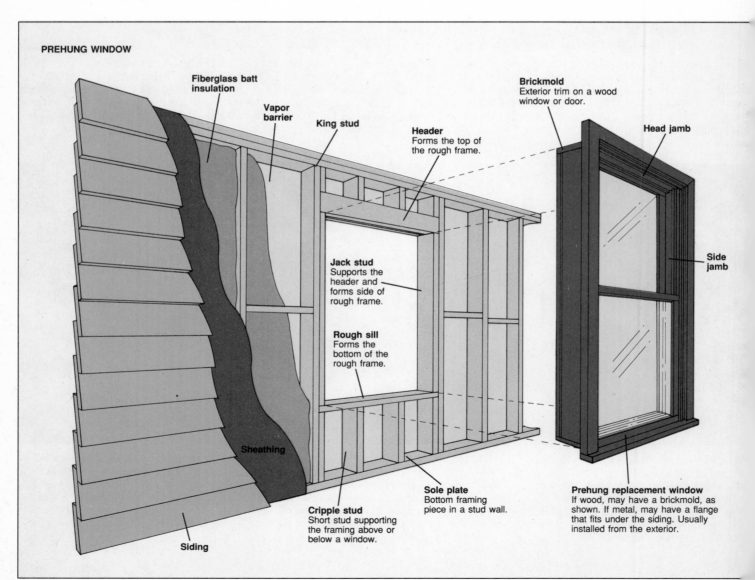

PREHUNG WINDOW

Fiberglass batt insulation

Vapor barrier

King stud

Header
Forms the top of the rough frame.

Brickmold
Exterior trim on a wood window or door.

Head jamb

Jack stud
Supports the header and forms side of rough frame.

Rough sill
Forms the bottom of the rough frame.

Side jamb

Sheathing

Siding

Cripple stud
Short stud supporting the framing above or below a window.

Sole plate
Bottom framing piece in a stud wall.

Prehung replacement window
If wood, may have a brickmold, as shown. If metal, may have a flange that fits under the siding. Usually installed from the exterior.

TROUBLESHOOTING GUIDE

SYMPTOM	POSSIBLE CAUSE	PROCEDURE
Window or door finish frame damaged beyond repair	Age; poor maintenance	Remove old window (p. 89) ▭◐ or door (p. 98) ▭◐; block if necessary (rough frame, p. 90 ▭◐; finish frame, p. 91 ▭◐) and install prehung unit (window, p. 91 ■●; door, p. 98 ■●)
Window or door finish sill rotted	Water pooling at threshold; gutter or downspout faulty; weather stripping faulty	Inspect and repair gutter and downspout; if rot is minor, remove rot and patch with epoxy (p. 123) ▭○ and replace weather stripping (p. 112) ▭○; if rot is extensive, replace sill (window, p. 17 ▭◐; door, p. 61 ▭◐)
Window or door rough sill rotted	Chronic dampness; window or door frame rot spread to rough framing	If minor, remove rot and patch with epoxy (p. 123) ▭○; under a window, replace rough sill (p. 94) ▭◐, or rebuild under sill (p. 94) ■●; under a door, call for professional service.
Window cripple studs or sole plate rotted	Window frame rot spread to wall framing	Remove and replace affected cripple studs and sole plate (p. 94) ■●; if jack studs are affected, call for professional service

DEGREE OF DIFFICULTY: ☐ Easy ▭ Moderate ■ Complex
ESTIMATED TIME: ○ Less than 1 hour ◐ 1 to 3 hours ● Over 3 hours

▲ Special tool required

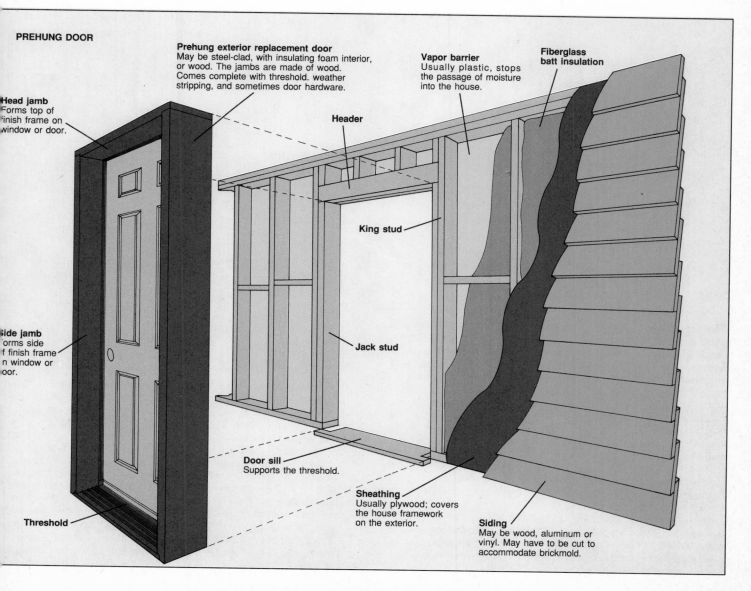

PREHUNG DOOR

Prehung exterior replacement door
May be steel-clad, with insulating foam interior, or wood. The jambs are made of wood. Comes complete with threshold. weather stripping, and sometimes door hardware.

Vapor barrier
Usually plastic, stops the passage of moisture into the house.

Fiberglass batt insulation

Head jamb
Forms top of finish frame on window or door.

Header

King stud

Side jamb
Forms side of finish frame on window or door.

Jack stud

Threshold

Door sill
Supports the threshold.

Sheathing
Usually plywood; covers the house framework on the exterior.

Siding
May be wood, aluminum or vinyl. May have to be cut to accommodate brickmold.

MEASURING FOR A PREHUNG WINDOW OR DOOR

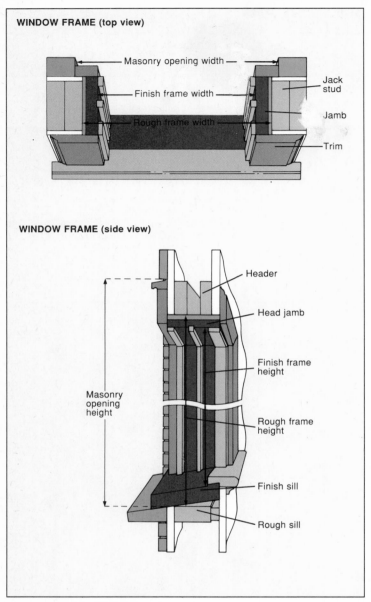

WINDOW FRAME (top view)

- Masonry opening width
- Finish frame width
- Rough frame width
- Jack stud
- Jamb
- Trim

WINDOW FRAME (side view)

- Header
- Head jamb
- Finish frame height
- Masonry opening height
- Rough frame height
- Finish sill
- Rough sill

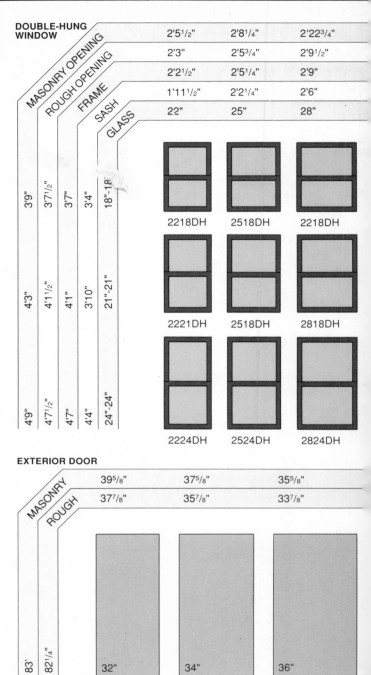

Measuring for a replacement unit. Most prehung windows and doors are built to be installed in the rough frame. To measure the rough opening for a window or door, remove the interior trim *(page 89)* and measure its height between the rough sill and the header, and its width between the jack studs *(above)*. Measure each dimension at three different places; note the smallest measurements for height and width. To measure for a window or door in a brick or stone house, measure the masonry opening as well; go outside and measure the height between the stone or brick lintel (which serves as the header in a masonry house) and the rough sill, and the width between the side edges of the masonry opening. For an exterior door, if you can't reach the rough sill, measure to the finish sill and add 1/2 inch. Consult the specification sheets of several window or door manufacturers *(right)* and choose the prehung unit that matches your measurements as closely as possible.

Some prehung windows and doors fit into the jambs of the old unit, particularly metal window or door kits that are used to replace an old wood window or door. For this type of installation, measure from the head jamb to the finish sill and between the side jambs in several places, and note the smallest width and height.

Reading a specification sheet. To help you order a prehung door or window of the right size, manufacturers supply specification sheets to their distributors and to the consumer, listing measurements for the units they make. Study the typical specification sheets for a double-hung window and an exterior door, shown above. The numbers across the top indicate the width of the unit and the openings needed for it; the numbers down the side indicate height. The diagrams in the center represent the unit type, with its order number. Match the measurements of your rough opening to rough opening measurements on the sheet. Notice that the measurements for the frame are 1/2 inch less than those for the rough opening; this allows for shimming when you install the prehung unit. If you cannot find a prehung window or door that fits your rough opening, choose one that is 1 1/2 to 2 inches smaller; you can reduce the size of the rough opening by blocking it with 1-by-4 boards *(page 90)*.

EMOVING AN OLD WINDOW

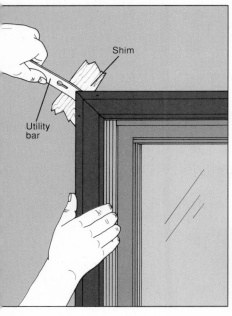

Shim

Utility bar

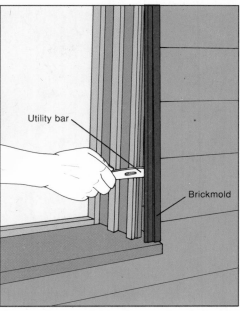

Utility bar

Brickmold

1 **Removing trim.** With a utility knife, slice through any paint sealing the trim to the wall and jambs. Slip a utility bar between trim and wall at a nail location and, inserting a shim to protect the wall, carefully pry up the trim about 1/4 inch. Repeat at each nail location on each side trim piece. When the side trim is separated from the wall, work on the top corners. If the corners are blind-nailed together, use a utility bar to lift each corner in one piece *(far left)*. If necessary, first use a hacksaw to cut the face nails *(page 49)*. To take out the window from the inside, remove the exterior trim, or brickmold *(near left)*, as you did the interior trim. Pull nails from reuseable trim *(page 48)*. To install a prehung unit in the rough frame, remove the stool and apron *(page 17)* or the door sill *(page 61)*. For a metal flange-mounted window, continue to step 2. For a wood window or a door, go to step 3.

Edge of flange

Saber saw

Nail set

2 **Freeing a metal flange-mounted window.** Many metal windows have flanges that fit between the siding and the sheathing. Since the nails that secure the flanges to the sheathing are hid- n beneath the siding, you must saw the window free. If the new ehung window doesn't have flanges, cut through the flanges of the window, using a saber saw fitted with a metal-cutting blade. First l a pilot hole at the bottom of each side flange of the window. earing safety goggles, put the tip of the blade into one of the pilot es and move up the side of the window, cutting close to the siding pove). Cut through the other side and then along the top and bottom the window. If the prehung unit is flange-mounted, use a circular w *(page 91)* to cut through the siding 1 3/4 inch from its edges, ving the flanges of the old window intact.

3 **Removing the window.** To install a prehung window in the finish frame remove the stops, parting strips and sashes *(page 15)*, leaving the frame in place, and block it *(page 91)* if necessary. A window and finish frame you don't intend to reuse can be removed by collapsing the jambs *(page 90)*. To take out a window and its finish frame without damaging them, inspect the jambs and sill for screws or nails; unscrew screws and punch nails through *(inset)*, or cut them with a hacksaw. Lock the window and tape the glass with nylon filament tape for safety. With a helper, lift out the old unit from the outside *(above)*. Pull out nails protruding from the rough frame and sweep away debris before installing the new unit *(page 91)*. A high window can be removed from inside; first pry off the brickmold *(step 1)*. Examine the rough sill for rot and, if minor, patch with epoxy *(page 123)*. If the rot is extensive, you may have to replace the rough sill or rebuild the wood framing below the window *(page 94)* before installing the prehung window.

COLLAPSING THE FINISH FRAME

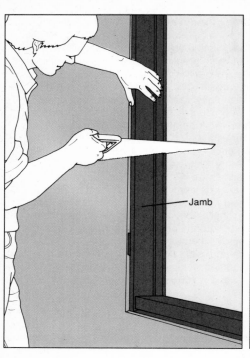 

Jamb

Pry bar

Demolishing the jambs. If the window is too fragile to take it out intact *(page 89)*, and you do not intend to use the finish frame, collapse the jambs. If you plan to reuse the trim, first detach it carefully *(page 89)*. On a double-hung window, pry off the interior stops and parting strips *(page 15)*, then remove the window sashes. Unfasten the hinges and operator of a casement or awning window. Using a crosscut saw, cut through a side jamb near the middle *(far left)*. Pull the upper jamb segment loose and work the head jamb free with a pry bar *(near left)*. Saw through the other jamb and the sill *(page 17)* and pry them free. Discard the broken pieces of jamb, sill and shims, and pull out nails protruding from the rough frame. Sweep away debris from the rough frame and block the frame *(below)* or install the new unit *(page 91)*.

BLOCKING THE FRAME

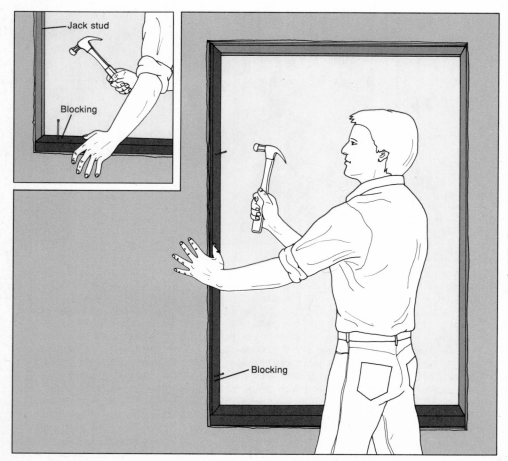

Jack stud

Blocking

Blocking

Blocking a rough frame. Remove the old window in one piece *(page 89)* or by collapsing the finish frame *(above)*. Measure the height and width of the rough frame and subtract the height and width of the prehung window (plus 1/2 inch for shimming); the result is the thickness of the blocking you need. For example, if the width difference is 1 1/2 inch, add a 3/4-inch-thick board to each side jamb—1-by-4s will do. Block the jack studs equally on both sides. Do not block the header more than 1 inch, to keep the top of the window in alignment with other windows in the room. Do not add more than 2 1/2 inches to the rough sill or jack studs, or retrimming *(page 100)* will not cover the extra width. To make the blocking for the rough frame, use a crosscut saw to cut the boards to length. Block the rough sill first *(inset)*, then block the header, and finish by blocking the jack studs. Use a hammer to drive nails through the blocking into the rough frame *(left)* at intervals of 12 inches.

BLOCKING THE FRAME (continued)

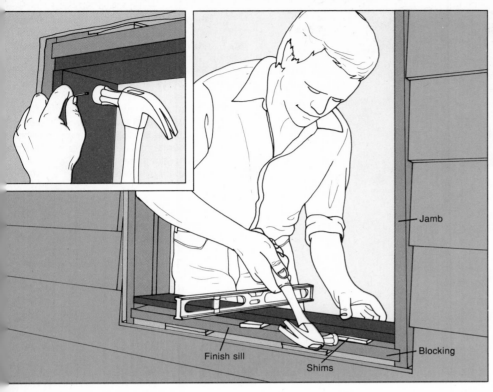

Jamb

Finish sill

Shims

Blocking

Blocking a finish frame. After removing the stops, parting strips, sashes *(page 15)* and balance system *(page 13)*, measure the finish frame for blocking as you would a rough frame *(page 90)*. If the finish sill is angled, level the sill blocking by inserting shims beneath its outside edge *(left)*, tapping them in with a hammer until a carpenter's square shows that the blocking is level. Nail the blocking to the finish sill through the shims. Block the head jamb, then the side jambs, as you would for a rough frame *(page 90)*.

INSTALLING A PREHUNG WINDOW

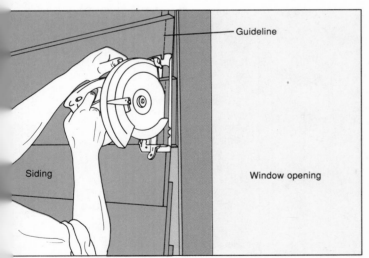

Guideline

Siding

Window opening

Drip cap

Siding

1 Cutting the siding. If the new window has a wood brickmold or a metal flange, you may need to cut away a strip of siding around the frame to fit the window against the sheathing. With helper, lift the replacement unit into the window opening and center Trace the edge of the brickmold or flange on the siding and remove window. Fit a circular saw with a metal-ctting blade for aluminum ding; use a crosscut blade for wood or vinyl siding. Set the depth of e blade to the thickness of the siding. Wearing safety goggles, cut out 1/8 inch outside the guideline, moving the circular saw up the t side and around the frame *(above)*.

2 Installing a drip cap. Windows and doors with a brickmold that are set into houses with siding will need a drip cap to keep rain from leaking through the space between the head jamb and rough frame. Measure the thickness of the brickmold and the width of the window opening and buy a drip cap or piece of flashing to fit, cutting it to the correct length yourself with tin snips. Slip the edge of the drip cap between the siding and sheathing above the window opening, as shown.

INSTALLING A PREHUNG WINDOW (continued)

3 **Installing the window.** Before installing a window, apply a plastic vapor barrier around its finish frame. Cut a piece of vinyl sheeting long enough to wrap around the jambs and sill. Its width should be about double that of the jambs. Staple the plastic to all four sides of the window frame *(inset)*; when the window is installed, the free edge will be stapled to the interior wall covering *(step 6)*. If you are installing a metal window with a thermal break (a strip of wood or plastic running along the center of the jambs), staple the vapor barrier to it. As an alternative to vinyl sheeting, inject polyurethane foam after installing the window *(page 110)*. Working from the outside with a helper, lift the window into place and slip the brickmold under the drip cap. Butt the head jamb against the header and check with a carpenter's level which top corner is lower. Tack the brickmold of the lower corner to the sheathing temporarily with a finishing nail *(left)*; lower the other corner until it is level with the first, and tack it in place as well.

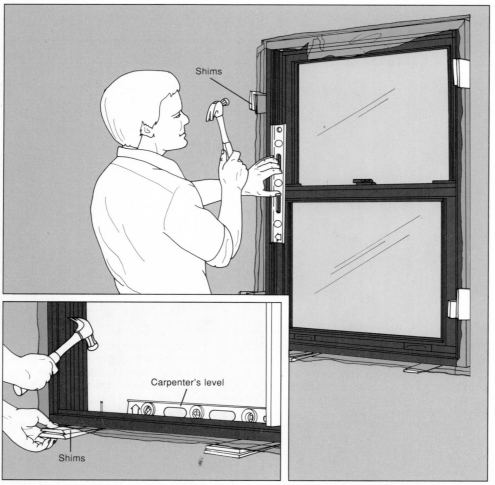

4 **Shimming the window.** Working from inside, shim with cedar shingles between the finish frame and the rough frame to level and plumb the window. First, shim the finish sill; insert the thin ends of the shingles under the sill near each end and tap the thick ends with a hammer. Set a carpenter's level on the sill to check that the sill is level. Drill pilot holes through the sill and shims and drive finishing nails through the holes into the rough sill *(inset)*, leaving the nail heads exposed. To shim the side jambs, insert the thick end of a shingle into the gap between the jamb and jack stud near a top corner. Then wedge the thin end of a second shim against it until snug. Fit a similar set of shims near the bottom, and at the middle if the window is taller than 4 feet. Insert shims on the other side, and at the top. Tap in the shims with a hammer *(left)*, while checking for plumb with a level along the sides of the jambs and along their faces. If you notice the jambs bowing in even slightly, pull out the shims partway. Drill holes and drive finishing nails as for the sill. When the window is square, level and plumb, countersink the nails *(page 48)*. Use a utility knife to score the shims flush with the frame and break them off by hand. Reinstall the stool, apron and trim. If you blocked the frame *(page 91)*, cut a new stool and apron *(page 99)* and trim *(page 100)*.

Jamb extension

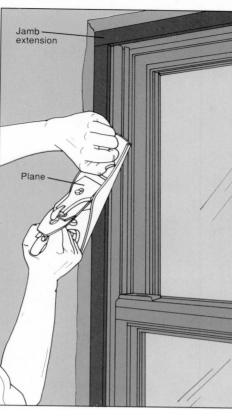

Jamb extension

Plane

5 **Extending the jambs.** If the front edges of the window jambs are not flush with the interior wall, extend the jambs by adding strips of wood. Measure the length and thickness of each jamb. If you are not planning to add a stool *(page 99)*, also measure for a sill extension. To determine the depth of the jamb extensions, measure the distance between the jamb faces and the wall surface in several places and subtract 1/8 inch from the largest measurement. Cut strips of the correct size from dimensional lumber. If you plan to varnish or stain the wood *(page 124)*, make sure it matches the new window. Fasten the smooth milled side of the jamb extensions against the jambs with carpenter's glue and finishing nails *(far left)*, and countersink the heads *(page 48)*. Using a bench plane *(near left)* or a block plane, smooth the surface of the jamb extensions to match any variations in the wall surface. Older walls are seldom flat; the shaping of jamb extensions allows the trim to fit against the interior wall. Forcing jamb extensions or trim to fit can twist the window or door frame or break the trim.

Insulation

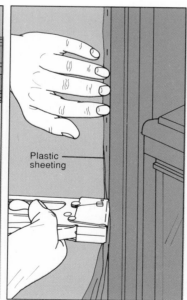

Plastic sheeting

Caulking gun

Insulating the frame. Insulate the gap between the jambs and the rough frame with strips of fiberglass batt. (Wear a respirator, work gloves, long sleeves and safety goggles when working with fiberglass.) Cut the insulation into strips with a utility knife and [us]e a putty knife to push it between the plastic vapor barrier and the [rou]gh frame, loosely filling the gaps between the shims *(above, left)*. [Th]en fold the vapor barrier over the insulation and staple it to the raw [edg]e of the interior wall *(above, right)*. Cut away excess plastic with [a u]tility knife.

7 **Caulking around the window.** Choose an exterior sealant *(page 110)* and cut a small hole in the tip of the tube at a 45-degree angle. Using a caulking gun, lay a fine bead of sealant along the joint between brickmold and jambs. Then cut the tip for a wider bead and apply sealant along the joint between brickmold and siding *(above)* or exterior masonry.

REBUILDING BELOW THE SILL

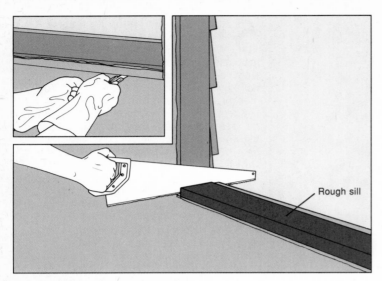

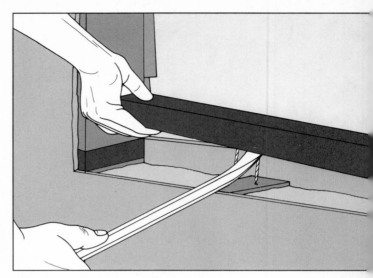

Rough sill

1 **Cutting the rough sill.** After removing a window for replacement *(page 89)*, examine the rough sill for rot. Patch small spots with epoxy *(page 123)*; if most of the sill is soft and spongy, replace it. Draw a horizontal line 1 1/2 inch below the top of the rough sill, and cut away the wall across the front edge of the sill, using a utility knife for drywall *(inset)* or a cold chisel for plaster *(step 4)*. Saw through the sill with a crosscut saw at each end, flush with the jack studs *(above)*.

2 **Prying up the rough sill.** Use a pry bar to pry up the sill *(above)*, lifting carefully to minimize damage to the interior wall surface. Twist the sill free of any nails securing it to the sheathing. Pull out exposed nails, or cut them off with a hacksaw. Rot may have spread to the wood framing below the window. Telltale signs are the smell of mildew and discoloration of the interior wall surface. Inspect the tops of the cripple studs. If the cripple studs look healthy, install a new rough sill *(step 9)*, patch the wall *(page 97)* and install the replacement window *(page 91)*. If the cripple studs are rotted, replace them. The frame may have a double rough sill; if it too is rotted, remove it as you did the first and examine the cripple studs.

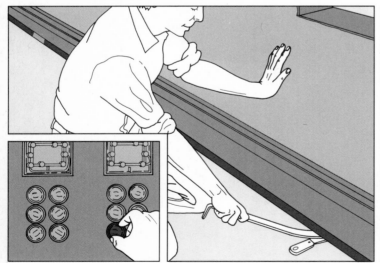

3 **Removing the baseboard and shoe molding.** Using a utility knife, slice through any paint sealing the trim to the wall, or the shoe molding to the baseboard. Check a corner of the room where the trim beneath the window begins. If the end of the trim to be removed is tucked behind the adjacent trim, you must remove the adjacent trim first. Near one corner, push the blade of a putty knife between the shoe molding and the floor. Gently insert the end of a pry bar between the knife and the shoe molding and ease the molding up *(above, left)*. Continue along the length of the molding. If a hard-to-match shoe molding breaks, save the pieces; they can be glued back

together. Near one end of the baseboard, insert a putty knife blade between baseboard and wall. Push in a wood shim behind the knife and work the end of a pry bar between them *(above, right)*. Pry out the baseboard 1/2 inch and wedge a second shim behind it about 2 feet away. Insert the putty knife in front of the second shim, work the pry bar between them and continue prying off the baseboard. After removing the molding, use a nail puller to work nails out from the back *(page 48, step 2)*. Before cutting into the wall, disconnect electrical power to the room at the fuse box *(inset)* or circuit-breaker panel.

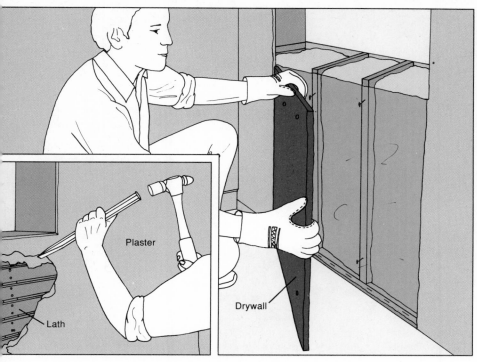

Plaster

Lath

Drywall

4 **Cutting away the wall.** Using a level, draw a vertical line from each lower corner of the rough frame to the floor. If there are any electrical outlets in the wall, make small exploratory holes below the window to check cable positions before cutting. To cut drywall, score along the lines with a utility knife, then cut through the drywall with the knife or a keyhole saw. Lift away the cut drywall, as shown. You may have to break the drywall to free it from the nails or screws that fasten it to the studs. Some fasteners may come out with the drywall; others may remain in the studs. If the drywall is glued to the studs, chip it off with a cold chisel. If the wall contains fiberglass insulation, wear a respirator, work gloves, long sleeves and safety goggles to cut away the vapor barrier that covers the insulation, and pull out the batts. To chip away a plaster wall, use a cold chisel and ball-peen hammer *(inset)*, and a sharp wood chisel and mallet to cut the lath.

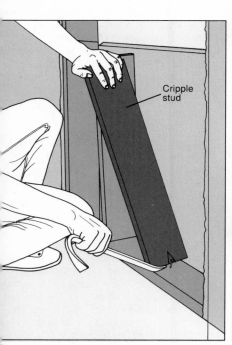

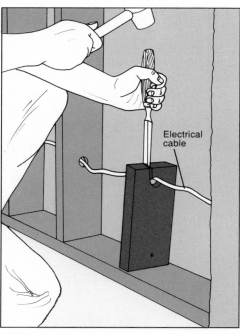

Cripple stud

Electrical cable

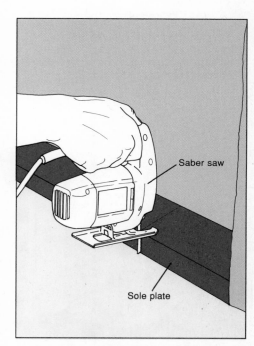

Saber saw

Sole plate

5 **Removing rotted cripple studs.** If a jack stud below the window is rotted, call a building inspector or contractor before you proceed. A cripple stud is nailed to the sole plate and sometimes to the exterior sheathing as well. To remove a rotted cripple stud, insert a pry between it and the sole plate and twist it free of the nails *(above, left)*. Use a nail puller to any nail shafts protruding from the sheathing.
To remove a cripple stud with an electrical cable or pipe running through it, shut off power to cable's electrical circuit *(step 3)*. Using a saber saw, cut through the stud an inch above the le or pipe. If necessary, finish the job with a sharp wood chisel and rubber mallet. Pull the part of the stud free. Then use the chisel to split the wood where the cable or pipe passes ugh *(above, right)*. Twist out the stud as above, without damaging the cable or pipe.

6 **Removing a damaged sole plate.** If the sole plate is healthy, go to step 8. To cut out a rotted section of sole plate, cut through the plate with a saber saw 2 inches outside the damaged area at each end *(above)*. Use a sharp wood chisel and rubber mallet to cut through the last bit that the saber saw can't reach. Use a pry bar to lift out the damaged section and a nail puller to pull or cut any protruding nails.

REBUILDING BELOW THE SILL (continued)

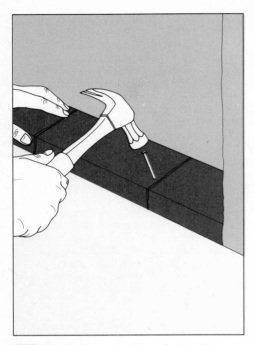

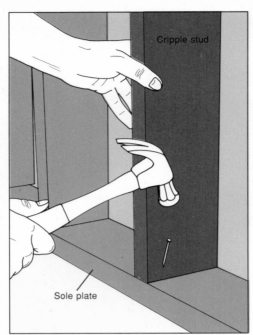

Cripple stud

Sole plate

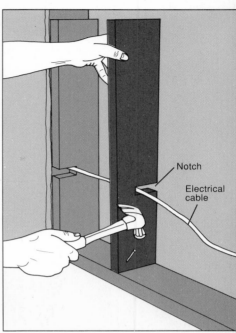

Notch

Electrical cable

7 Replacing a section of sole plate.
Measure the length of the gap between the cut ends of the sole plate and use a circular saw *(page 121)* to cut a matching board to size. Fit the new piece of sole plate into the gap and toenail it to the ends of the existing sole plate, as shown. If the floor beneath the sole plate is wood, drive several nails through the face of the plate as well.

8 Replacing cripple studs. The length of the new cripple studs will determine the height of the new rough sill. If the replacement window is longer than the old window, you must replace all the old cripple studs with shorter ones. Measure for the length of new cripple studs from the sole plate to 1 1/2 inch below the planned rough sill height; if you are replacing a double rough sill, measure to 3 inches below its planned height. If you are rebuilding the sill to its original height, measure to the bottom of the old sill position. Use a circular saw *(page 121)* to cut the studs to size. Nail one cripple stud against the jack stud at each side. Position the others 16 inches apart, center to center, and toenail them to the sole plate *(above, left)*. If a cable or pipe runs through the wall, use a saber saw to notch each stud at the appropriate height. Alternate the notch positions, as you install the studs *(above, right)*.

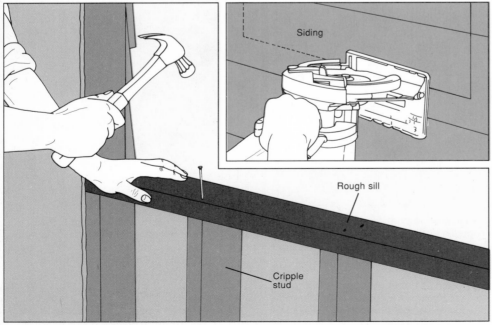

Siding

Rough sill

Cripple stud

9 Replacing the rough sill. Measure the width of the window opening and use a crosscut saw or a circular saw *(page 121)* to cut the new sill to size. Fit the rough sill snugly between the jack studs and nail it to the top of each cripple stud *(left)*. Then toenail the sill to the jack studs. If replacing a double rough sill, cut a second identical piece and nail it on top of the first. With the rough sill in place, refinish the inside wall *(page 97)*. If you lowered the sill height for a longer window, use a circular saw to cut the exterior siding and sheathing down to the new level: Measure the distance between the top of the rough sill and the top edge of the exterior wall. Go outside and, using a level, draw a vertical line extending this distance down from each bottom corner of the opening. Draw a horizontal line joining their ends. Wearing goggles, use a circular saw with the appropriate blade *(page 91)* to cut through the siding and sheathing *(inset)*.

REFINISHING THE INSIDE WALL

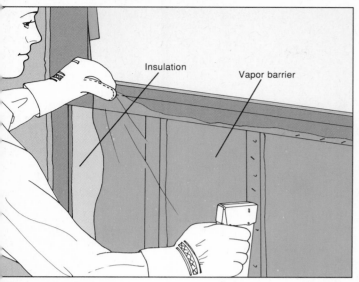

1 **Installing insulation and a vapor barrier.** Wear a respirator, goggles, work gloves and long sleeves when working with fiberglass insulation. Cut batts to fit between the cripple studs: Place batt on the floor and compress it with a board along the line to be cut. Using the board as a guide, slice through the fiberglass with a utility knife; it may take several passes. Fit the insulation between the studs. Cut plastic sheeting to make a vapor barrier large enough to cover the area under the sill. Staple the plastic to the faces of the studs and rough sill *(above)*.

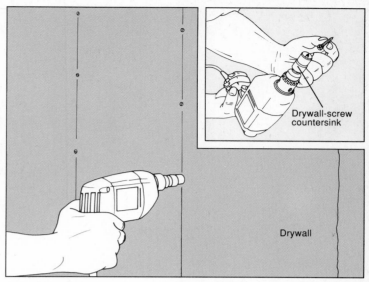

2 **Installing new drywall.** Measure the opening and draw its outline on a piece of drywall. Using a straightedge, score each line with a utility knife, then snap the drywall along the scored line and cut through the paper backing. Mark lines indicating the positions of the cripple studs on the panel. Place the drywall over the opening and use a Phillips screwdriver or a variable-speed power drill fitted with a drywall-screw countersink *(inset)* to secure the panel to the cripple studs with drywall screws. Beginning near the center of the panel, drive screws into the cripple studs at 6-inch intervals *(above)*. Replace plaster and lath with drywall of the same thickness as the plaster and lath combined.

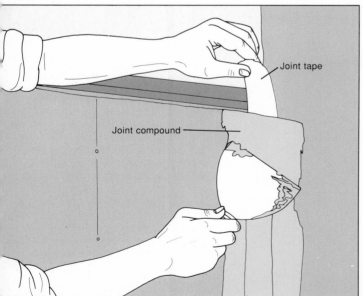

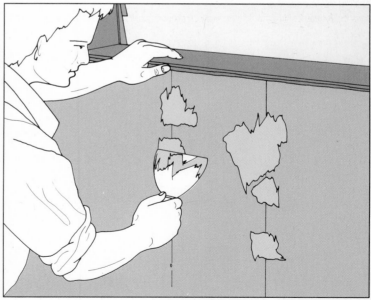

3 **Adding joint compound.** Moisten a drywall joint with a wet sponge and spread a layer of joint compound along it with a putty knife. Press joint tape into the wet compound with a wide-blade putty knife. Then spread a second layer of compound over the tape, as shown. Cover the screws with a layer of compound at the same time *(above, right)*. Feather the edges of the compound so that it tapers smoothly into the wall surface and let it dry for 24 hours. Then lightly sand the dried joint compound with medium-grit sandpaper on a sanding block and brush away dust. Add another layer or two of joint compound, feathering, drying and sanding lightly after each application. When the compound is dry, apply primer to the drywall patch. After painting or papering the wall, reinstall the baseboard and shoe molding, and the stool, apron and trim, driving slightly larger finishing nails through the old nail holes where possible. If the old holes are too large, fill them with wood putty or spackling compound and drive the nails elsewhere. If the old trim pieces broke on removal, or the gap between the jambs and the wall surface was increased by blocking, add a new stool and apron *(page 99)* and retrim *(page 100)*.

INSTALLING A PREHUNG DOOR

1-by-2 board

1 **Positioning a prehung door.** Read the manufacturer's instructions that come with the prehung door. Also familiarize yourself with the procedure for installing a prehung window *(page 91)*; many of the steps are the same for a door.

Most prehung interior doors are installed in much the same way as the exterior door shown at left. Many, however, lack a threshold and don't require weatherproofing in the form of a vapor barrier, caulk and drip cap. Prepare the door opening by removing the trim *(page 89)*. Then take down the old door *(page 45)*; if the door has fixed hinges, wedge it open and unscrew the hinge plates from the door jamb. Remove door hardware for reinstallation. Collapse the jambs *(page 90)* and saw through the door sill *(page 61)* to remove them. Block a too-large rough opening *(page 91)*. Staple a plastic vapor barrier to the side jambs and head jambs of the new unit *(page 92)*. If you are installing an exterior door with a brickmold, trim the siding with a circular saw *(page 91)* if necessary. If you are installing an exterior door without a brickmold *(left)*, nail a 1-by-2 across the top of the opening on the inside to stabilize the door temporarily while you shim it. Run two thick beads of waterproof exterior adhesive across the rough sill. Then, working from the outside with a helper, place the threshold in the rough frame and tip the door into place, resting its top end against the 1-by-2 as shown.

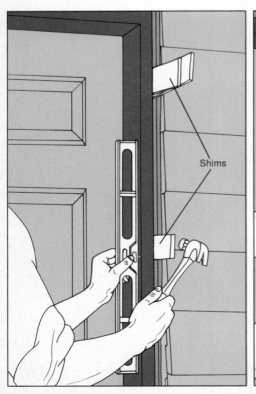

Shims

2 **Leveling and securing a prehung door.** On an exterior door with a brickmold, shim from the interior. Shim a door without a brickmold, such as the one shown, from the exterior. Check that the threshold is level by laying a carpenter's level along it. If necessary, use a pry bar to lift the threshold just enough to slip 1/8-inch shims under the lower side. Shim along the side jambs and head jamb with pairs of shims as described for shimming a window *(page 92)*, inserting shims at about 20-inch intervals. Adjust the shims with light hammer taps *(far left)*. Use a reversible power drill to make a pilot hole through the threshold and the jambs at each set of shims. Fit the drill with a Phillips screwdriver bit and drive 3-inch drywall screws into the pilot holes *(near left)*. Loosen and tighten the screws for final adjustment of the shims. After each adjustment check that the door opens and closes properly. Score the protruding ends of the shims with a utility knife and snap them off. Install a drip cap *(page 91)* and caulk around the exterior of the door as you would a window *(page 93)*. Finish the job by reinstalling the trim around the door.

BUILDING A STOOL AND APRON

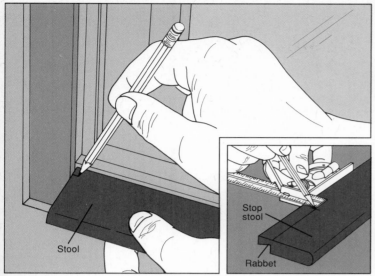

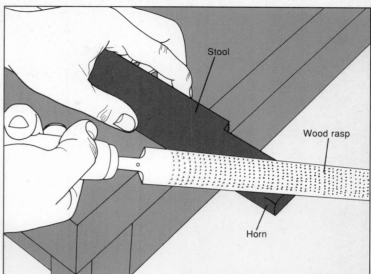

1 Measuring and marking the stool. Measure for the stool, apron and trim *(page 100)* at the same time and buy them at a building supply store. Get stool material with a bullnose or fancier milled edge, and of the same wood as the window frame if applying a natural finish. Depending on the window's finish sill, choose either a straight stool *(above)* to butt against the finish sill, or a stop stool *(inset)* which is rabbeted to overlap an angled finish sill. To determine its length, measure between the marks on the wall where the outside edges of the side window trim were, and add 1 inch. To determine the width of a straight stool, measure from the inside edge of the finish sill to the wall surface and add 3/4 inch. For a stop stool, measure from the inside edge of the sill to the outside edge of the interior stop, and add the thickness of the trim plus 3/4 inch. To determine the width of the horn on a straight stool, subtract the distance between the wall

surface and the finish sill from the width of the stool itself *(above, left)*. To determine the length of the horn on a straight stool, measure from the inside edge of the jamb to the outside edge of the side trim and add 1/2 inch. For a stop stool, measure the width of the horn by subtracting the distance between the wall surface and the sash minus 1/16 inch, from the width of the stool. Mark the lines for the horns on the surface of the stool *(inset)*. The length will be the same as for a straight stool. Clamp the stool to a work table with C clamps padded with wood shims, and use a backsaw to cut out the horns.

If you wish to finish the stool's horns with mitered returns, go to step 2; otherwise smooth the ends of the stool's horns with careful, even strokes of a wood rasp. Stroke in one direction along the grain *(above, right)*. Then sand the edge with progressively finer sandpaper to prepare for finishing.

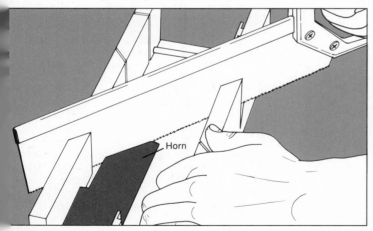

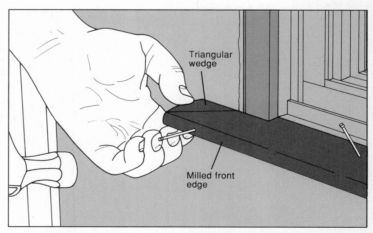

2 Making a mitered return. To precisely match the horn end to a stool's milled front edge, finish the ends with mitered returns. Use a backsaw and a miter box to cut the end of each horn inward at 45 degrees, as shown. Then mark the width of the horn on the milled edge of a piece of scrap stool. Place the scrap in the miter box and make a triangular wedge by cutting at a 45-degree angle at the mark. Make a second wedge the same way. Use carpenter's glue to glue the mitered edge of each wedge to that of the horn; the milled edge of the wedge will look like a continuation of the stool's milled front edge. Nail each wedge to the stool with a small finishing nail through the back.

3 Attaching the stool. Butt a straight stool against the finish sill, their top surfaces flush. Use finishing nails to toenail every 12 inches through the face of the stool into the finish sill and rough sill below it. Use a power drill to make pilot holes through the horns of the stool into the wall and rough frame. Then secure each horn with a finishing nail, as shown. Similarly, nail through the face of a stop stool into the finish stool below it. A stop stool's horns need not be nailed. Countersink the nails, apply putty or spackling compound *(page 48)*, and sand lightly.

BUILDING A STOOL AND APRON (continued)

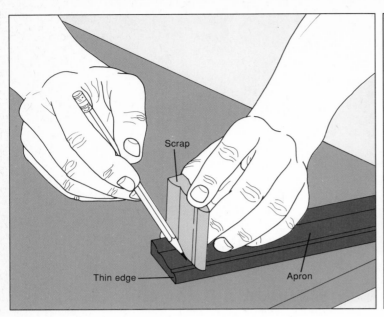

Scrap

Thin edge

Apron

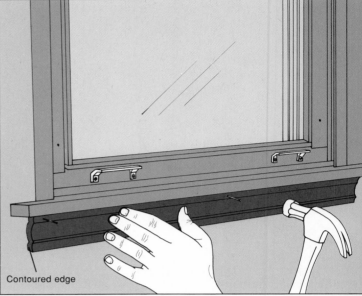

Contoured edge

4 **Making the apron.** Make an apron from the same molding to be used for the side and head trim, if desired. Measure between the outer edges of the marks on the wall left by the old trim, and use a backsaw to cut the apron to this length. For a decoratively contoured edge, place a scrap piece of the trim against the face of the apron and carefully trace the contours *(above, left)*. Using a coping saw, cut along the curved line, keeping the saw blade at a 90-degree angle to the molding. Sand the rough edges smooth. Secure the apron to the rough sill with finishing nails driven in at 12-inch intervals along the top and bottom edges of the apron *(above, right)*.

RETRIMMING A WINDOW OR DOOR

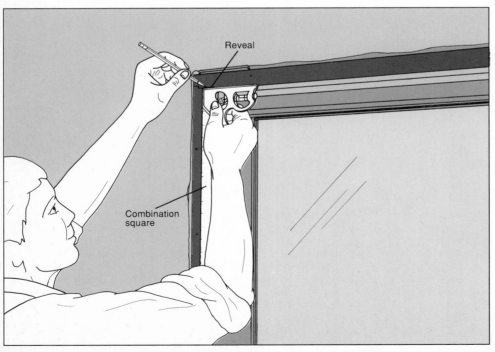

Reveal

Combination square

1 **Measuring and marking the trim.** To determine the width of trim you need to install, measure from the inside edge of each jamb to the outside edge of the marks on the wall left by the old trim. Buy enough trim molding of this width to retrim around the interior of the window or door. Allow extra length for cutting mitered corners. Using a combination square, draw a line along the face of the head and side jambs 1/8 inch from their inside edges *(above)*. This marks the "reveal"—the amount of jamb that should show along the edge of the trim. For the side trim, measure between the top of the stool and the head jamb and add 1/8 inch. Mark this measurement on the underside of the strips of trim at the thin edge, starting at least the width of the trim away from the end to allow for a mitered cut outward at 45 degrees for each side trim piece.

RETRIMMING A WINDOW OR DOOR (continued)

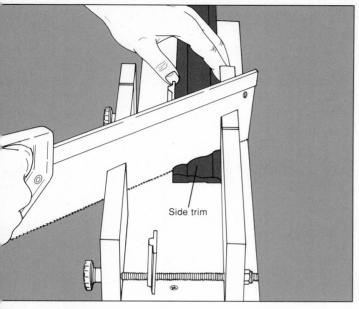

Side trim

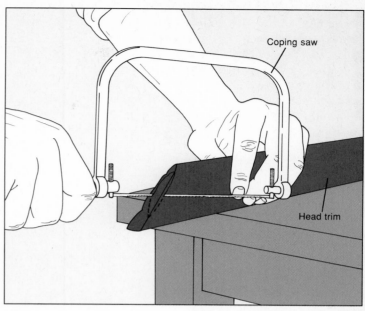

Coping saw

Head trim

2 **Mitering the trim.** Place one of the side trim pieces in the miter box and, using the measurements taken in step 1, cut a mitered corner from the thin edge outward at 45 degrees at one end *(above)*; the thin edge of the trim will be positioned nearest the corner. Make a 90-degree cut at the other end. Repeat for the other side trim piece. Position the side trim with its inner edge resting on the reveal you marked in step 1. Use finishing nails to secure the trim, nailing it first to the jamb and then, with longer finishing nails, through the wall surface into the jack studs. Leave 6 inches from the mitered corner unnailed. Install the other side trim piece the same way. Measure the distance between the side trim's top corners and mark these measurements on the thick edge of the trim stock. Use a backsaw and a miter box to cut the head trim slightly longer than these marks, fanning both ends outward at 45 degrees.

3 **Coping a mitered joint.** Before attaching the head trim, use a coping saw to cut a small crescent out of the back edge of each mitered end, leaving 1/2 inch at the top and bottom edges uncut, as shown. This will allow the finished edges of the mitered corners to fit tightly over an uneven wall surface. Fit the head trim between the side trim pieces, so that their mitered corners are even. Nail the head trim in place with finishing nails as you did the side trim, stopping 6 inches away from the ends.

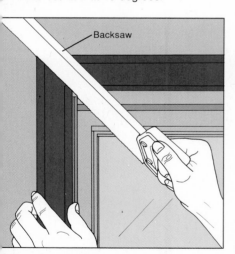

Backsaw

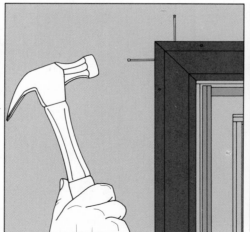

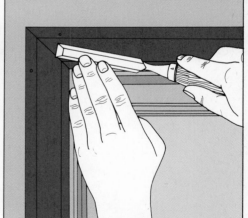

4 **Fitting the mitered corners.** If the angled edges of a mitered corner do not close tightly, cut through the corner with a backsaw to recut both edges simultaneously, as shown. Holding the two mitered edges together, nail near the end of each trim piece.

5 **Securing the mitered corners.** Lock-nail a mitered corner by tapping a finishing nail through each trim piece into the other, 1 inch from the corner *(above, left)*. Use a nail set to countersink all nail heads. Fill the holes with spackling compound or wood putty, depending on whether the wood will be painted or stained. If a trim edge protrudes, use a sharp wood chisel to shave it. Carefully follow the original contours of the trim face *(above, right)*. Then sand the corner lightly. if the exterior requires trim as well, make and install it in the same way, but first apply two coats of paint-compatible wood preservative to the trim pieces. If the rough frame was blocked, you may have to add strips of sheathing to fill the gap between the jambs and siding before installing the new trim.

GARAGE DOORS

A garage door is possibly the most neglected door in the house. As long as it continues to move up and down, few homeowners bother to inspect or maintain it.

The most common garage door is the overhead door, available in one-piece swing-up and multi- panel sectional models. A swing-up door has one or two springs on each side, and some models have a pair of overhead guide tracks. A sectional door runs on two overhead tracks and uses either extension or torsion springs. Extension springs run parallel to the overhead tracks—in pairs on a heavy door—and stretch and contract when the door is opened and closed. Each spring is fitted with a safety cable to prevent injury if an extension spring breaks. Torsion springs, located directly over the top of the closed door, wind up like a window-shade spring; their repair or adjustment requires special tools and professional expertise.

Any overhead garage door can be fitted with an automatic opener, which may be operated by a remote transmitter, a key switch located on the outside door jamb or a push button or

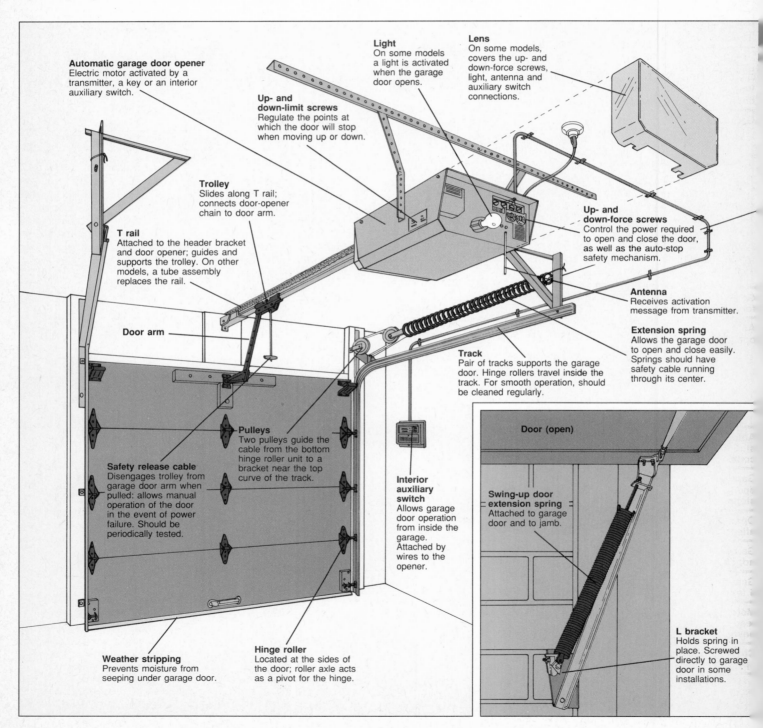

Automatic garage door opener
Electric motor activated by a transmitter, a key or an interior auxiliary switch.

Light
On some models a light is activated when the garage door opens.

Lens
On some models, covers the up- and down-force screws, light, antenna and auxiliary switch connections.

Up- and down-limit screws
Regulate the points at which the door will stop when moving up or down.

Trolley
Slides along T rail; connects door-opener chain to door arm.

T rail
Attached to the header bracket and door opener; guides and supports the trolley. On other models, a tube assembly replaces the rail.

Door arm

Up- and down-force screws
Control the power required to open and close the door, as well as the auto-stop safety mechanism.

Antenna
Receives activation message from transmitter.

Extension spring
Allows the garage door to open and close easily. Springs should have safety cable running through its center.

Track
Pair of tracks supports the garage door. Hinge rollers travel inside the track. For smooth operation, should be cleaned regularly.

Pulleys
Two pulleys guide the cable from the bottom hinge roller unit to a bracket near the top curve of the track.

Safety release cable
Disengages trolley from garage door arm when pulled: allows manual operation of the door in the event of power failure. Should be periodically tested.

Interior auxiliary switch
Allows garage door operation from inside the garage. Attached by wires to the opener.

Weather stripping
Prevents moisture from seeping under garage door.

Hinge roller
Located at the sides of the door; roller axle acts as a pivot for the hinge.

Door (open)

Swing-up door extension spring
Attached to garage door and to jamb.

L bracket
Holds spring in place. Screwed directly to garage door in some installations.

ull cord inside the garage. Most automatic openers have
uilt-in safety control devices: an auto-reverse or auto-stop
echanism stops the door if it touches anything while closing,
nd an emergency-release cord attached to the trolley allows
anual operation. The closing safety mechanism can be
djusted as described on page 104.

Weather stripping on the door protects the garage from the
ements. Lengths of specially design weather stripping (*page
08*), commonly aluminum extentions fitted with vinyl

inserts, are often nailed to the side and top door jambs. As
protection for the garage floor and the bottom of the door,
flexible tubular weather stripping (or sometimes a piece of
hose) is nailed to the bottom of the door, creating a seal for an
uneven surface.

The most common garage door problems can often be pre-
vented by regularly cleaning tracks, lubricating door hinges,
oiling extension springs (*page 105*) and checking for signs of
wear or loose parts.

TROUBLESHOOTING GUIDE

SYMPTOM	POSSIBLE CAUSE	PROCEDURE
Water enters garage under door	Threshold not level; weather stripping inadequate	Replace bottom weather stripping with heavy-duty tubular type (p. 108) ▣◐
Garage door difficult to open	Dirt clogging tracks	Clean tracks (p. 105) ☐○
	Door parts need lubrication	Lubricate parts with light machine oil (p. 105) ☐○
	Worn roller	Replace roller (p. 105) ▣◐
	Loose track	Call for service
	Dented track	Hammer out dent with mallet if minor, otherwise call for service
	Loose hinges	Tighten or replace hinges (p. 105) ▣◐
	Broken spring	Replace spring (p. 107) ■●
	Broken pulley	Replace pulley (p. 107) ■●
	Broken cable	Replace cable (p. 106) ■●
Garage door opens or closes too easily	Door not balanced	Adjust spring tension (p. 106) ▣◐
Automatic opener doesn't open or close garage door	Power cord not plugged in	Plug in power cord
	Transmitter batteries dead	Change batteries
	Antenna not receiving signal	Remove obstruction blocking transmitter signal
	Transmitter and receiver code key settings don't match	Reset transmitter and/or receive code keys
	Transmitter defective	Replace transmitter or call for service
Automatic opener does not stop garage door when it contacts object	Down-force screw set improperly	Adjust down-force screw counterclockwise (p. 104) ☐○
Garage door with automatic opener reverses direction or stops before closing fully	Object interfering with travel cycle	Remove object
	Down-force screw set improperly	Adjust down-force screw clockwise (p. 104) ☐○
Opener reverses direction after door closes fully	Down-limit screw set improperly	Adjust down-limit screw clockwise (p. 104) ☐○
Garage door opens 5 feet, but not completely	Up-limit screw set improperly	Adjust up-limit screw clockwise (p. 104) ☐○
Garage door doesn't open 5 feet	Up-force screw set improperly	Adjust up-force screw clockwise (p. 104) ☐○
Motor hums when door reaches fully opened or closed position	Up- or down-limit screw set improperly	Adjust up- or down-limit screw (p. 104) ☐○
Chain rattles when automatic opener is activated	Chain loose	Adjust chain tension (p. 104) ▣◐

DEGREE OF DIFFICULTY: ☐ Easy ▣ Moderate ■ Complex
ESTIMATED TIME: ○ Less than 1 hour ◐ 1 to 3 hours ● Over 3 hours

SERVICING THE CLOSING SAFETY MECHANISM

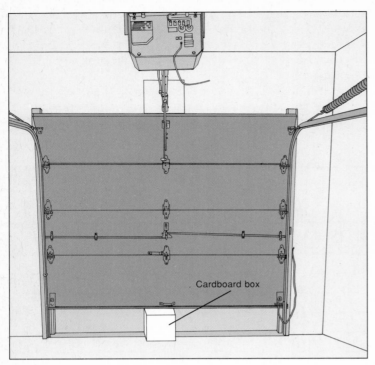

Cardboard box

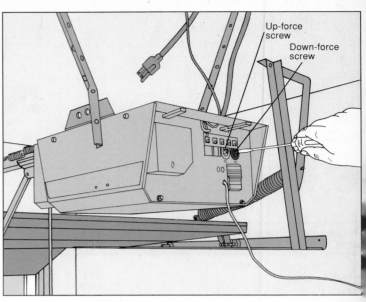

Up-force screw

Down-force screw

1 **Testing the closing safety mechanism.** For safe operation, test the mechanism every 6 months, as well as after painting the door or adjusting extension springs *(page 107)* or limit screws *(step 3)*. Open the garage door and place a cardboard box in the door's path *(above)*. Then use the transmitter, push button or key switch to close the door. When the door's bottom edge touches the box, a safety mechanism should activate by reversing the door direction on an auto-reverse model or stopping it on an auto-stop model. If the door fails either to reverse or stop, adjust the down-force screw *(step 2)*.

2 **Adjusting the down-force sensitivity.** Unplug an auto-reverse unit and locate the down-force adjustment screw. (If the screw is located inside the unit, call for professional service.) Using a screwdriver, turn the down-force screw counterclockwise 10 degrees *(above)*. Plug in the unit and repeat the cardboard-box test. Continue adjusting and testing until the door operates properly. If the door stops before reaching the fully open position—and there is no obstruction—adjust the up-force screw clockwise 10 degrees, or adjust the limit screws *(step 3)*. An auto-stop door may have just one screw; adjust it for up force or down force as labeled, or call for professional service.

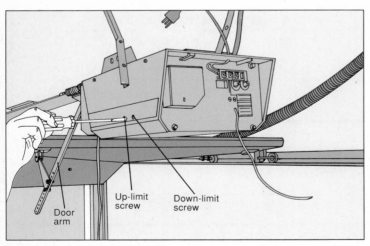

Door arm

Up-limit screw

Down-limit screw

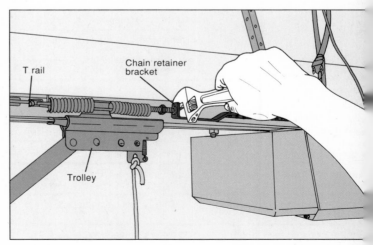

T rail

Chain retainer bracket

Trolley

3 **Adjusting the limit screws.** If the garage door opens more than 5 feet but fails to open completely, unplug the opener and locate the up-limit adjustment screw—usually on the motor unit. Turn the screw clockwise *(above)*; one full turn increases door travel by 2 inches. Plug in the opener and run it through a complete cycle to check the adjustment. When the door opens and closes completely without reversing or humming when opened or closed, it is adjusted properly. If the door does not close completely and the door arm is fully extended, unplug the opener and adjust the down-limit screw counterclockwise. Plug in the unit and check the adjustment.

4 **Adjusting the chain tension.** A chain that sags more than 1/2 inch below the T rail may cause a banging noise; tighten the chain. Using an adjustable wrench, turn the two nuts securing the chain retainer bracket to the threaded shaft on the trolley. First loosen the inner nut—closest to the trolley—and then tighten the outer nut by turning it clockwise *(above)* until the chain rests 1/2 inch above the base of the T rail; do not overtighten. Tighten the inner nut toward the chain retainer bracket until snug. On some models, the trolley moves along a tube support that contains an adjustment screw. Turn the screw clockwise to increase chain tension.

MAINTAINING A GARAGE DOOR

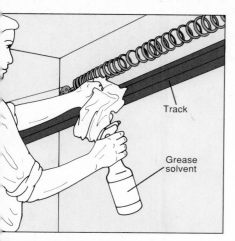

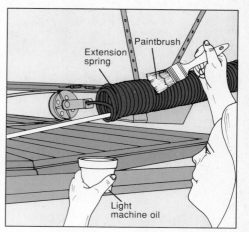

1 **Cleaning the tracks.** To keep the garage door operating smoothly, dissolve grease and dirt inside the garage or tracks with a spray solvent; wipe the same away with a cloth *(above)*. Stand on a stepladder to clean the upper reaches of the tracks. Then lubricate the rollers *(next step)* and extension springs *(step 3)*.

2 **Lubricating door parts.** As part of an annual maintenance schedule, lubricate all moving parts of a garage door with light machine oil or powdered graphite. Spray the lubricant on metal axles and into roller bearings *(above)*, and into pivot points on hinges and pulleys. If squeaks or sticking persist, replace the parts *(below)*.

3 **Oiling the extension springs.** Oiling the springs prevents rust and squeaks. Open the garage door to relax the extension springs. Standing on a stepladder, dip an old medium-width paintbrush in a container of light machine oil and coat each spring with oil.

REPLACING A WORN ROLLER

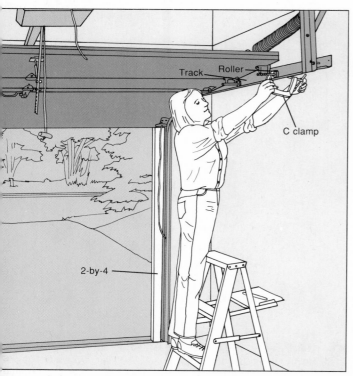

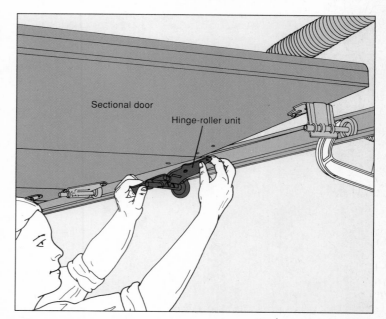

1 **Propping open the garage door.** Prop open the garage door by wedging a 2-by-4 snugly between a bottom corner of the door and the ground. As added reinforcement against accidental closure, firmly screw a C clamp to the track in front of the top roller on the garage door *(above)*.

2 **Replacing a roller on a sectional door.** Replace a hinge-roller unit by first propping open the garage door *(step 1)*, except if replacing the top unit, for which the door must be closed. (A swing-up door with tracks must be closed to replace any hinge-roller unit.) Removing and replacing only one hinge-roller unit at a time, use a screwdriver or wrench to undo the screws or bolts holding the hinge-roller unit to the door. Twist the roller out of the track *(above)*, fit the new roller in place and screw or bolt the hinge to the door. If the screw holes have become enlarged, use bigger screws or fill the holes *(page 123)* and use the original screws.

SERVICING A CABLE

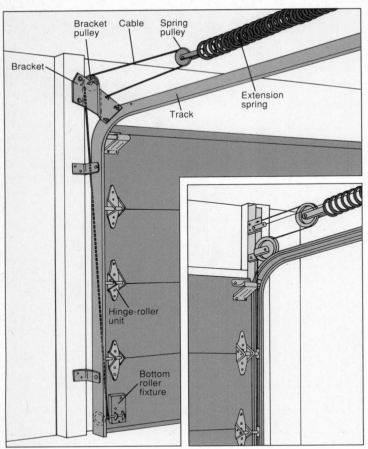

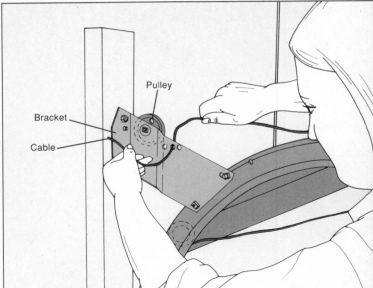

1 **Releasing the cable at the bracket end.** On models such as the one at left, the cable is knotted onto the bracket; on other models, it may be tied to a plate above the bracket *(left, inset)*. To release a cable that is attached to the bracket, prop the door open to relax the extension springs *(page 105)* and use a screwdriver to lift the cable off the bracket pulley. If the pulley is worn, replace it *(page 107)*. If the cable tension needs adjusting, go to step 3. If the cable has shiny patches or is otherwise worn, replace it. Note how the cable is threaded, then untie the knot, unthread the cable from the pulleys *(above)* and release its spring end as shown in step 2.

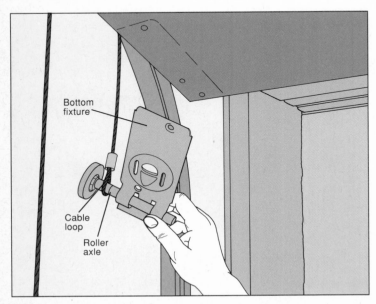

2 **Releasing the cable at the spring end.** With the door propped open, use a screwdriver or wrench to unfasten the screws or bolts attaching the bottom roller fixture to the bottom of the door. Slide the roller out of the fixture *(above)* and slip the reinforced cable loop off the roller axle. Replace the roller, if worn.

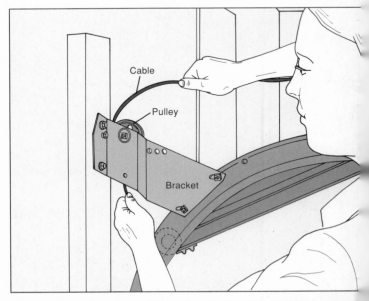

3 **Rethreading the cable and adjusting the spring tension.** Secure the cable at the spring end, then run it back to the bracket as originally threaded. Tie a knot to secure the cable to the bracket. Then adjust the spring tension: Increase tension by untying the cable knot, pulling the cable tighter to take up the slack, then retying the knot. Test the tension by opening and closing the door; it should move easily on both sides. Adjust the other spring if necessar

SERVICING A PULLEY

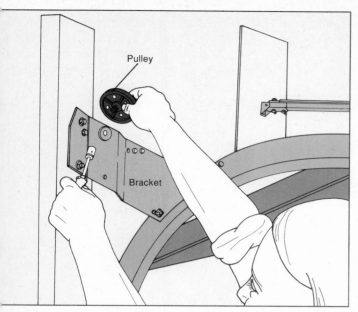

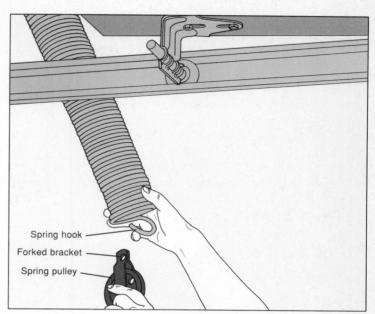

1 Replacing the bracket pulley. With the cable removed from the bracket pulley *(page 106)*, use a wrench or nut driver to release the bolt holding the pulley on the bracket *(above)*. The pulley may be held in place with a forked bracket; in that case, slip the pulley wheel out of the bracket after it has been unbolted. Replace the worn pulley with a new one, using the new bolts that came with it.

2 Replacing a spring pulley. With the cable released *(page 106)*, unhook the forked bracket of a worn spring pulley from the spring, and replace it *(above)*. If the replacement does not have a hole on the bracket, slip the spring hook into the space between the pulley and the closed end of the forked bracket. Rethread the cable *(page 106, step 3)*.

REPLACING SPRINGS

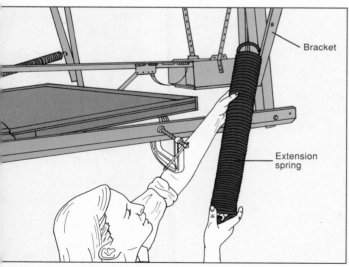

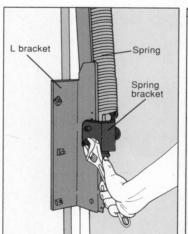

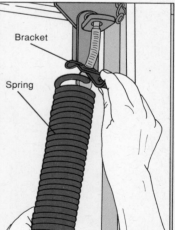

1 Replacing sectional door extension springs. If the spring coils gap more than 1/2 inch or the springs sag when the door is open, replace both springs. With the door propped open *(page 105)* detach the cable from the bracket pulley *(page 106)* and release the front end of the spring. Next, unhook the worn spring from its bracket, eye hook or hole at the back of the track *(above)*. Attach the new spring at the back of the track, thread the safety cable through it, and attach it to the spring pulley. Replace the other spring, then adjust spring tension *(page 106)*.

2 Servicing swing-up door extension springs. Prop open the door *(page 105)* and locate the end of the spring, attached to a movable bracket mounted on an L bracket or in holes on the L bracket. To adjust spring tension, remove any bolts *(above, left)*. Increase tension by moving the spring bracket up on the L bracket; decrease tension by moving it down. If the L bracket is attached to the door, increase tension by moving the spring bracket down and decrease it by moving it up. Adjust both springs. If spring coils gap 1/2 inch in the open position, replace both springs. Remove each spring at its L bracket end, then twist the other end out of its bracket *(above, right)* or hole. Install new springs and adjust the tension.

WEATHERPROOFING

Windows and doors are the most likely source of air leakage into and out of the home. Seemingly minor gaps between sashes and jambs, or doors and thresholds, add up to a major energy drain. In fact, a crack just 1/4 inch wide and 4 feet long can let in as much cold air as a fist-sized hole. Insulation—such as double-pane windows *(page 76)* or an insulating door *(page 58)*—will reduce direct heat transfer, caused when warm air contacts a cold surface. But to prevent the flow of air, all openings to the outside must be caulked with a sealant or weather-stripped.

To track down the gaps that let air into your house, tape a strip of light plastic film to a coat-hanger wire. On a windy day, move the wand slowly around each window and door, along trim edges, jamb stops, window-pane edges and sills.

Fluttering of the plastic indicates an area where air is leakin mark it with chalk. The illustration below shows typical are of infiltration and suggests remedies that are discussed in th chapter or other chapters in the book. While checking f leaks, also examine the existing weather stripping or sealar If it is stiff, cracked, worn or deformed, replace it.

The Troubleshooting Guide at right lists symptoms of a leakage and procedures for correcting them. Do not wait un winter to weatherproof your home; many weatherproofin procedures require that you open or even remove doors window sashes.

To choose the best weatherproofing material for each situ tion, consult the sealant chart on page 110 and the weath stripping guide on page 112. Sealants, available as caulk in

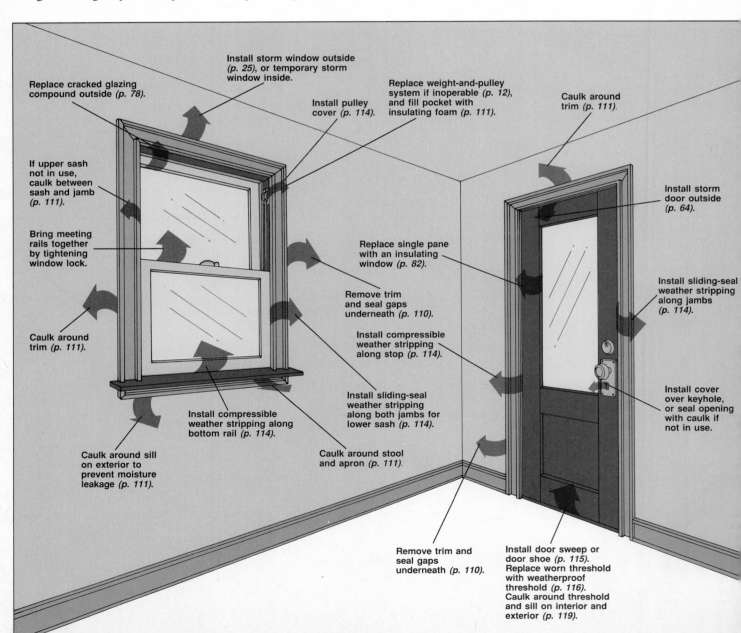

Install storm window outside *(p. 25)*, or temporary storm window inside.

Replace cracked glazing compound outside *(p. 78)*.

Install pulley cover *(p. 114)*.

Replace weight-and-pulley system if inoperable *(p. 12)*, and fill pocket with insulating foam *(p. 111)*.

Caulk around trim *(p. 111)*.

If upper sash not in use, caulk between sash and jamb *(p. 111)*.

Bring meeting rails together by tightening window lock.

Install storm door outside *(p. 64)*.

Replace single pane with an insulating window *(p. 82)*.

Install sliding-seal weather stripping along jambs *(p. 114)*.

Remove trim and seal gaps underneath *(p. 110)*.

Caulk around trim *(p. 111)*.

Install compressible weather stripping along stop *(p. 114)*.

Install cover over keyhole, or seal opening with caulk if not in use.

Install compressible weather stripping along bottom rail *(p. 114)*.

Install sliding-seal weather stripping along both jambs for lower sash *(p. 114)*.

Caulk around sill on exterior to prevent moisture leakage *(p. 111)*.

Caulk around stool and apron *(p. 111)*.

Remove trim and seal gaps underneath *(p. 110)*.

Install door sweep or door shoe *(p. 115)*. Replace worn threshold with weatherproof threshold *(p. 116)*. Caulk around threshold and sill on interior and exterior *(p. 119)*.

be, work best on fixed joints: in cracks, along trim edges, or round window sashes that do not open. Choose a flexible sealant that is resistant to cold and moisture. Read the sealant manufacturer's instructions to determine its recommended surfaces, and whether it requires a primer. When applying sealant, work in a well-ventilated room, and wear safety goggles, rubber gloves and long sleeves. Never apply an exterior sealant indoors; the fumes are too toxic.

A special type of sealant, expanding spray foam, both closes gap and insulates the space it fills. Available in small cans, he foam can be injected into a large space through a small pening. It is permanent, and should only be used in hidden reas. While being applied, the foam is extremely sticky and xpands rapidly; practice first to get a feel for applying it. Do not overfill a gap; too much foam can open joints and push jambs apart.

Weather stripping provides a seal for movable joints, where two surfaces close against each other (a door and its stop) or slide past one another (a window sash and its channel). Choose weather stripping to suit its job. Simple styles, such as V strips and door sweeps, are the least expensive and tend to develop fewer problems over time. Factory-installed weather stripping, such as the pile strip along the edges of a sliding window sash, can be replaced when worn. Regular care and inspection of your home's doors and windows will keep them draft-free. Follow the maintenance procedures in this book and, in areas with cold winters, install well-fitting storm windows *(page 25)*, and doors *(page 64)*.

TROUBLESHOOTING GUIDE

SYMPTOM	POSSIBLE CAUSE	PROCEDURE
ir leaking around door or indow trim	Small gap between trim and wall	Caulk around trim *(p. 111)* □○
	Small gap between jamb and wall	Caulk behind trim *(p. 110)* ◨●
	Large gap between jamb and wall	Insulate with polyurethane foam *(p. 111)* ◨○
ir leaking around glass pane	Pane cracked or broken	Replace pane *(p. 76)* ◨●; or replace pane with insulating unit *(p. 83)* ■●▲
	Glazing compound deteriorated	Replace glazing compound *(p. 78)* ◨●
ir leaking between window ashes and jamb	Exposed pulley on double-hung window	Install pulley cover *(p. 114)* □○
	Weather stripping worn or non-existent	Replace or install weather stripping *(p. 114)* ◨○; install storm window *(p. 25)* ◨●
	Caulking cracked, worn or non-existent	Replace caulk at all fixed joints *(p. 110)* ◨○
	Window warped or house settled	Reposition interior stop *(p. 48)* ◨○; install weather stripping *(p. 114)* ◨○; install replacement channels *(p. 20)* ◨●▲; replace window *(p. 86)* ■●
ir leaking between door and amb	Weather stripping deteriorated or non-existent	Install weather stripping *(p. 114)* ◨○; install storm door *(p. 64)* ◨●
	Door warped or house settled	Reposition door stop *(p. 48)* ◨●; install weather stripping *(p. 114)* ◨○
ir or water leaking between ndow sash and stool or sill	Weather stripping deteriorated or non-existent	Install weather stripping *(p. 114)* ◨○; install storm window *(p. 25)* ◨●
	Wood worn or rotted	Remove rotted wood and patch with epoxy *(p. 123)* □○; replace sill *(p. 17)* ◨●
ir or water leaking between or and threshold	Threshold worn, weather stripping deteriorated or non-existent	Install door sweep *(p.115)* □○; install door shoe *(p. 117)* ◨●; install weatherproof threshold *(p. 116)* ◨●
	Sill worn or rotted	Replace sill *(p. 61)* ■●
indow or door rattling	Weather stripping deteriorated or non-existent	Install weather stripping *(p. 114)* ◨○
	Window or door warped	Reposition stops *(p. 48)* ◨○; install weather stripping *(p. 114)* ◨○
ondensation forming on side of storm window	Weather stripping on interior window deteriorated or non-existent	Install weather stripping *(p. 114)* ◨○; caulk interior fixed joints *(p. 110)* ◨○

DEGREE OF DIFFICULTY: □ **Easy** ◨ **Moderate** ■ **Complex**
ESTIMATED TIME: ○ **Less than 1 hour** ◨ **1 to 3 hours** ● **Over 3 hours**

▲ **Special tool required**

SEALANTS

TYPE	APPLICATION	DURABILITY	CHARACTERISTICS
Silicone caulk	Interior and exterior trim, sills, thresholds and glass panes.	Very durable. Paintable type may be less durable.	Colorless. Strong odor during application. Flexible; expands and contracts with joint. May require a primer.
Acrylic latex caulk (water-based)	Interior and exterior metal window frames and glass panes.	Moderately durable.	Available in colors, or paintable. For non-shifting joints. Metal surface may require primer.
Vinyl acrylic caulk (water-based)	Interior and exterior trim, sills, thresholds and metal frames.	Moderately durable.	Odorless. Available in colors. For small joints with limited shifting.
Acrylic caulk (solvent-based)	Exterior door and window trim, thresholds and sills.	Very durable.	Strong odor. Difficult to spread and touch up. For exterior use only.
Vinyl-acetate latex caulk (water-based)	Narrow joints between interior glass panes and wood or metal frames.	Not durable.	For non-shifting joints. Hardens and cracks. For interior use only.
Butyl rubber caulk	Exterior sill-to-masonry, or metal frame-to-masonry.	Moderately durable.	Paintable after curing for one week. For exterior use only.
Closed-cell foam rod	Cracks and small gaps behind trim.	Very durable.	Good insulator. Must be sealed over with caulk.
Polyurethane spray foam	Large gaps behind trim and weight pocket of double-hung windows.	Durable.	Good insulator. Expands on application. Must be covered and protected.

CAULKING GAPS BEHIND INTERIOR TRIM

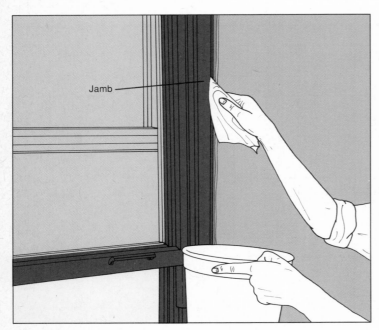

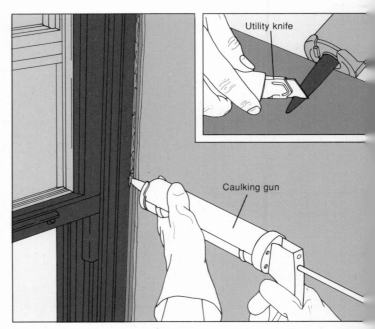

1 Preparing the surface. To stop air leakage around the window frame, look for gaps behind the trim. Score the paint between the trim and the wall, and carefully pry off the trim with a utility bar *(page 89)*. Using a wire brush or a utility knife, scrape old caulk and paint off the exposed surface, and out of any gaps between the window jamb and wall. Clean the area with a mild detergent-and-water solution *(above)*. Allow it to dry, then wipe the surface thoroughly with a clean cloth dampened with alcohol to remove all traces of moisture and adhesive. Seal gaps of 1/2 inch or less with a bead of caulk *(step 2)*. Fill larger gaps with insulating foam *(step 3)*.

2 Sealing a small crack. For gaps between 1/4 inch and 1/2 inch wide, first insert closed-cell foam rope or rods into the opening. Use an old screwdriver to push it in, until the foam is flush with the wall. Cut the tip of a tube of water-based acrylic or silicone caulk slightly smaller than the crack width *(inset)*. Hold the gun perpendicular to the crack, and squeeze the trigger, forcing a continuous bead of caulk along the crack. Move the gun steadily, completing one entire side of the window at a time. Turn the plunger handle down or snap the release lever to stop the flow. Reinstall the trim, driving slightly larger finishing nails through the old holes.

t only lets in air, but also water and dirt. The simple addition of a ...or sweep *(page 115)* will close off a narrow gap. An even better ...al can be obtained by installing a door shoe *(page 117)*, or replacing ...worn threshold with a weatherproof threshold *(page 116)*.
After choosing weather stripping, take time to prepare the surface ...d install it correctly. Carefully remove all traces of old caulk or

weather stripping with a utility knife or single-edge razor blade. Use rubbing alcohol or mineral spirits to remove old adhesive. Wash the surface with a mild detergent-and-water solution; residue from mineral spirits will damage many synthetic products. Finally, install the weather stripping carefully to ensure a snug, permanent fit, and inspect it periodically for damage.

TYPE	APPLICATION	INSTALLATION	DURABILITY
Spring-loaded jamb strip	A compressible seal for hinged doors and windows.	Screwed to jamb through attachment strip *(p. 115)*. Caulking behind attachment strip improves seal.	Long-lasting.
Magnetic jamb strip	A compressible seal for hinged steel doors and windows or, if a steel strip is attached, for wood windows and doors.	Screwed to jamb through attachment strip. Factory-installed on prehung units.	Long-lasting. Seal may deteriorate in extremely cold weather.
Partial threshold	A compressible seal for doors with no threshold, such as storm doors.	Screwed to door sill through metal plate.	Long-lasting. Replaceable rubber or plastic insert may wear out quickly.
Complete threshold	A compressible and sliding seal for replacement of a worn wood threshold.	Screwed to door sill through metal plate. Door may need to be trimmed *(p. 116)*.	Long-lasting. Replaceable rubber or plastic insert may wear out quickly.
Door sweep	A compressible and sliding seal for narrow gaps at bottom of exterior doors. May drag on carpeted floors.	Screwed to door bottom inside, through metal or plastic attachment strip. May be adjusted if gap widens *(p. 115)*.	Moderately long-lasting. Replaceable rubber, plastic or pile insert may wear out quickly.
Door shoe	A sliding seal for narrow or wide gaps at bottom of exterior doors. Comes in several styles.	Screwed to door bottom inside and outside, through metal or plastic attachment strips. Door may need to be trimmed *(p. 117)*.	Long-lasting. Replaceable rubber, plastic or pile insert may wear out quickly.

WEATHER-STRIPPING WINDOWS AND DOORS

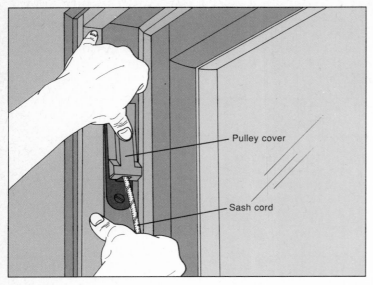

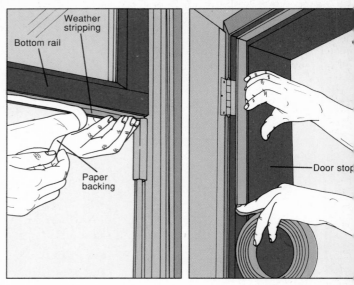

Installing a pulley cover. Clean the area around the pulley and wipe it with alcohol to ensure a clean, dry surface. Apply the self-adhesive gasket to the back of the pulley cover, leaving the backing paper on. Position the cover over the pulley and snap the sash cord into the opening at the bottom of the seal *(above)*. Trace around the cover with a pencil. Then peel off the backing paper and press the cover firmly in place. Make starter holes for the screws with an awl and a mallet, and screw them in until the gasket is slightly compressed. Pull the sash cord up and down a few times until it slides easily.

Installing foam-strip weather stripping. Apply closed-cell foam strips to compression surfaces such as the undersides of bottom sash rails *(above, left)* and the stops of hinged doors and windows *(above, right)*. Use a paint scraper to remove loose paint and old weather stripping or caulk from the area you are working on. Wash the surface with a detergent-and-water solution. Rinse and dry it, then wipe with a cloth dampened in alcohol to remove grease and adhesive. To install the foam strip, start at one end of the sash or stop and slowly peel off the paper backing as you press the strip into position. Cut the strip with scissors after applying it to each straight surface. Secure the strip with staples for a longer-lasting grip.

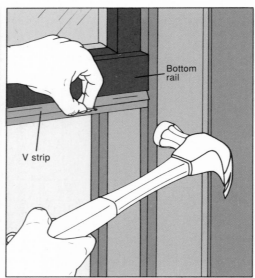

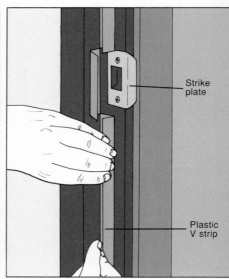

Installing metal or plastic V strips. Remove the interior stop on one side of a double-hung window, and then the lower sash *(page 15)*. If you plan to use the upper sash, remove it and weather-strip its channels as well. Otherwise, caulk the joint between the upper sash and parting strip *(page 111)*. Prepare the surface as for foam-strip weather stripping *(step above)*. Measure the sash channel from the stool to a point 2 inches higher than the bottom rail of the upper sash. Using tin snips, cut two pieces of metal V strip to this length. Measure the bottom rail of the upper sash and cut one more strip to this exact length. Position the strips in the lower sash channels, butting the V opening

against the parting strip. Nail the strips in place, using small flat-headed nails spaced at 1-inch intervals *(above, left)*. Position the shorter strip along the bottom rail of the upper sash, with the V opening downward *(above, center)*, and nail it in place. Finally, reinstall the lower sash, and apply closed-cell foam to the underside of the lower rail.

If you prefer, install self-adhesive plastic V strip, and staple the strips in place for better adhesion. Plastic V strip can also be used on compression surfaces, such as the stop of a door *(above, right)* or the bottom rail of a lower sash.

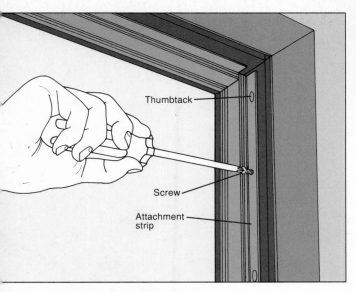

Thumbtack

Screw

Attachment
strip

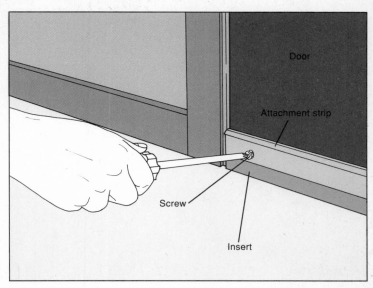

Door

Attachment strip

Screw

Insert

stalling spring-loaded weather stripping. Close the door and, from interior, measure the height of the jamb. Cut the strip to exact size a hacksaw and miter box. With thumbtacks, position the attach-nt strip on the door jamb, the contact surface against the door. u may need to cut out a section of the weather stripping for the ch plate. Open the door to test the spring mechanism; it should ress one third of the way into its channel when the door closes. position the weather stripping, if necessary. Then, removing one k at a time, fasten the attachment strip securely to the jamb with screws provided *(above)*. Cut and position a strip for the head b using the same procedure.

Installing a door sweep. To block a narrow gap between the door and the threshold, install a simple door sweep with a replaceable insert. Buy one the exact width of your door or cut it to size using a hacksaw and miter box. Close the door and, from the interior, place the attachment strip against the door bottom, ensuring that the flexible insert covers the gap entirely. Mark the positions of the screw holes. Drill pilot holes, then fasten the sweep to the door with the screws provided *(above)*.

EPLACING FACTORY-INSTALLED PILE STRIPS

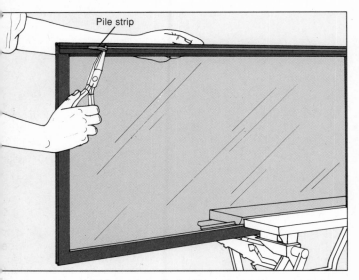

Pile strip

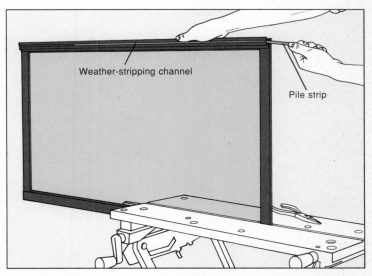

Weather-stripping channel

Pile strip

Removing a factory-installed pile strip. Most metal windows are available with pile weather stripping already installed. Replace it when the pile becomes matted or begins to look worn. Remove sash from its tracks. Check both ends of the pile strip for two tiny tal tabs that may be securing it. Bend them up gently with an old ewdriver. Using long-nose pliers, grasp the strip and pull it out of its rrow channel *(above)*. Take the strip to a window repair specialist for exact replacement.

2 Replacing the pile strip. Clean the weather-stripping channel with an old toothbrush. Cut the pile strip with scissors to the length of the channel. Feed a thick pile strip back into its chan-nel from one end *(above)*. Place a thin pile strip over the channel, then roll a splining tool along the pile to snap the strip back into its channel. Push the metal tabs back over the ends of the strip, and replace the sash in its track in the frame.

INSTALLING A WEATHERPROOF THRESHOLD

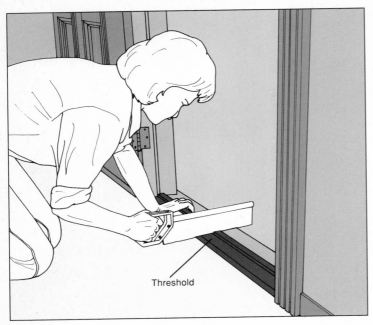

Threshold

1 Cutting through the old threshold. Remove a worn wood threshold and replace it with one that doubles as weather stripping. Cut away old caulk from around the threshold with a utility knife. If stops are nailed or screwed to the jambs, carefully remove them first *(page 48)*. If you can, tap the threshold out with a mallet, then go to step 3. If the jambs have built-in stops, use a backsaw to cut through the middle of the threshold *(above)*, taking care not to cut into the sill beneath it.

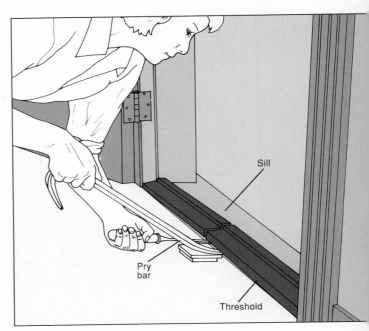

Sill

Pry bar

Threshold

2 Removing the old threshold. Push the end of an old screwdriver under the cut edge of the threshold, tapping it in with a mallet if necessary. Then fit the tip of a pry bar into the gap created, as shown, and remove the screwdriver. Place a block of wood under the pry bar to protect the sill, and ease up one cut end of the threshold. Pull the section out from under the door jamb by hand. Tap the other section out with a mallet. Use a hacksaw to cut off any nails protruding from the jambs.

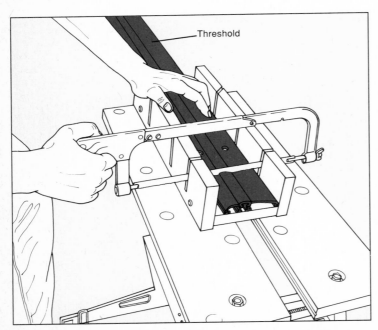

Threshold

3 Cutting the new threshold. Measure the old threshold and mark the new one to be cut to the same length and shape. Use a combination square to measure and mark any notches that need to be cut. Place the new threshold in a miter box and cut it with a hacksaw *(above)*. Position the threshold on the sill and close the door to ensure that the door contacts the rubber or plastic insert. Recut or reposition the threshold, if necessary. Mark the positions of the screwholes with a pencil, then remove the threshold.

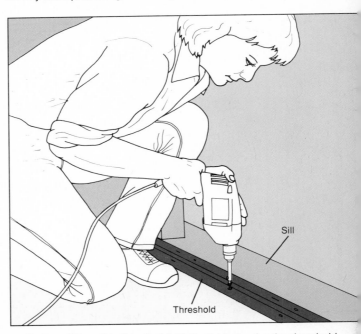

Sill

Threshold

4 Installing the threshold. Drill pilot holes for the threshold screws; wrap masking tape around the drill bit to gauge the depth of the hole. Apply caulk underneath the edges of the new threshold *(page 110)* and reposition it on the sill. Fasten the threshold with the screws provided, using a power drill fitted with a screwdriver bit *(above)*. If you removed the door stops, reinstall them *(page 48)*.

STALLING A DOOR SHOE

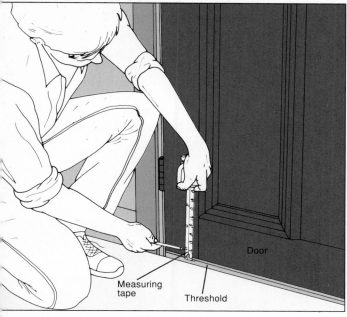

Measuring tape
Threshold
Door

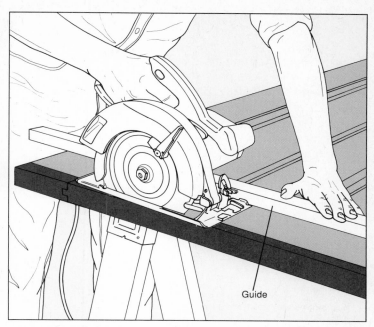

Guide

Measuring the shoe depth. If there is a gap between the door and the threshold, install a door shoe to stop air and water leakage. For the style shown here, hold the door shoe in place on the or, and measure from the door bottom to the shoe bottom. Remove shoe, close the door and mark this measurement on the door near h corner *(above)*, measuring up from the threshold.

2 Cutting the door. Remove the door from its hinges *(page 45)* and rest it across two sawhorses. Using a straightedge, draw a line connecting the two marks on the door. Clamp a straight piece of wood to the door, parallel with the line, as a guide for the base plate of a circular saw. Cut the door along the line. Smooth the rough edge with medium-grit sandpaper on a sanding block, and seal the bottom of the door with water-repellent preservative or varnish *(page 60)*.

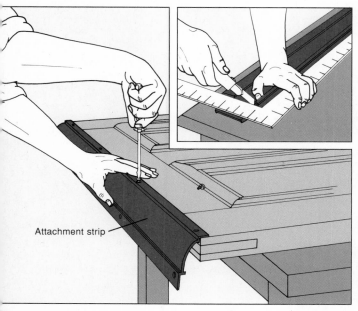

Attachment strip

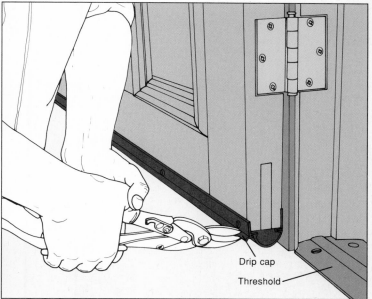

Drip cap
Threshold

Installing the shoe. Measure the exact width of the door and mark this measurement on the door shoe. Using a carpenter's square, cut through the rubber insert with a sharp utility knife *(inset)*, then cut through the attachment strips with a hacksaw. Position the e on the bottom of the door, with the drip cap on the exterior side of the door. Make starter es for the screws with an awl and screw the attachment strips to the door *(above, left)*. Re- g the door *(page 45)*. The shoe should fit snugly against the threshold and allow the door wing smoothly. Loosen the screws to adjust the attachment strip at the screw slots, if neces- y. Trim the drip cap at both ends with tin snips *(above, right)* if it impedes closing the door.

TOOLS & TECHNIQUES

This section introduces tools and techniques useful for repairing windows and doors, from drilling holes to patching rot. You can handle most repairs with the tools pictured below. Since many jobs fall into the realm of carpentry, you may need to do precision work with wood chisels or planes. If you haven't used them before, practice first to get a feel for them *(page 122)*. Power tools *(page 120)* make cutting and drilling much easier, and can be rented from a tool rental shop.

Accurate measuring is essential in carpentry. Use a carpenter's square to mark for square cuts and a combination square for marking 45-degree angles. A carpenter's level will help you to determine whether something is level (horizontal) or plumb (vertical). To operate a router, power drill or circular saw accurately, use a commercial guide *(page 120)* or clamp a straight piece of wood to the cutting surface *(page 121)*.

Avoid cheap tools and choose the right tool for the job. Clean metal tools with a cloth moistened with a few drops of light oil. (Avoid getting oil on the handles.) To remove rust, rub metal surfaces with fine steel wool or an emery cloth. Keep blades *(page 122)* and bits well sharpened; a dull blade can be dangerous. Protect tools in a sturdy toolbox, with a secure lock if you have children.

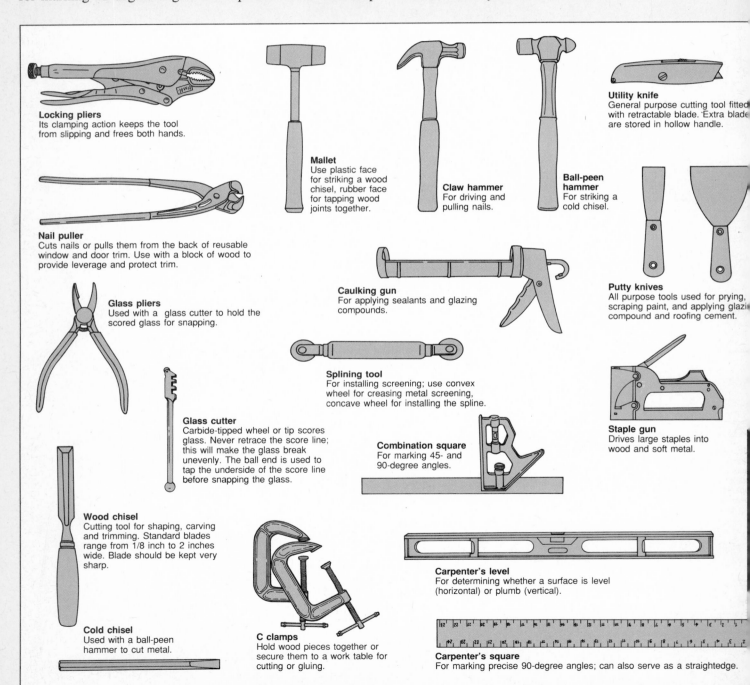

Locking pliers
Its clamping action keeps the tool from slipping and frees both hands.

Nail puller
Cuts nails or pulls them from the back of reusable window and door trim. Use with a block of wood to provide leverage and protect trim.

Glass pliers
Used with a glass cutter to hold the scored glass for snapping.

Glass cutter
Carbide-tipped wheel or tip scores glass. Never retrace the score line; this will make the glass break unevenly. The ball end is used to tap the underside of the score line before snapping the glass.

Wood chisel
Cutting tool for shaping, carving and trimming. Standard blades range from 1/8 inch to 2 inches wide. Blade should be kept very sharp.

Cold chisel
Used with a ball-peen hammer to cut metal.

Mallet
Use plastic face for striking a wood chisel, rubber face for tapping wood joints together.

Caulking gun
For applying sealants and glazing compounds.

Splining tool
For installing screening; use convex wheel for creasing metal screening, concave wheel for installing the spline.

Combination square
For marking 45- and 90-degree angles.

C clamps
Hold wood pieces together or secure them to a work table for cutting or gluing.

Claw hammer
For driving and pulling nails.

Ball-peen hammer
For striking a cold chisel.

Utility knife
General purpose cutting tool fitted with retractable blade. Extra blades are stored in hollow handle.

Putty knives
All purpose tools used for prying, scraping paint, and applying glazing compound and roofing cement.

Staple gun
Drives large staples into wood and soft metal.

Carpenter's level
For determining whether a surface is level (horizontal) or plumb (vertical).

Carpenter's square
For marking precise 90-degree angles; can also serve as a straightedge.

Cleaning and inspecting doors and windows regularly *(page 4)* keeps them operating smoothly. Repair minor damage immediately. Use epoxy to built up rotted wood *(page 123)*; it penetrates the wood fibers and stops rot from spreading. Adding sawdust to the mixture will help it blend with the wood; follow the manufacturer's instructions. Maintain a good coat of paint on doors and windows *(pages 124-125)* to prevent moisture from penetrating the wood.

A sturdy ladder is essential to reach high windows and skylights. When climbing, always keep your hips between the two vertical rails. Don't reach over; move the ladder. Don't stand on the top step of a stepladder, and keep your hips at or below the top step of a straight ladder. Before working on a roof, read the safety instructions on page 35.

To prevent accidents, keep the work area clean and uncluttered. Wear heavy work gloves to prevent cuts when working with sharp materials such as flashing, and rubber gloves when using chemicals. Wear safety goggles when working with power tools. When changing a bit or a blade, attaching a guide or making any adjustments, make sure the tool is turned off and unplugged. Always check for nails embedded in wood before using a power tool.

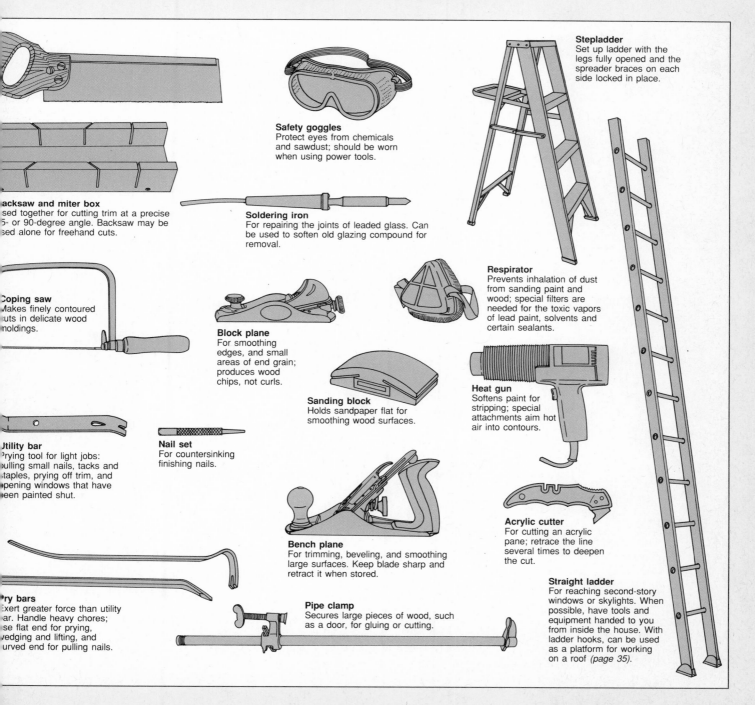

Backsaw and miter box
Used together for cutting trim at a precise 45- or 90-degree angle. Backsaw may be used alone for freehand cuts.

Safety goggles
Protect eyes from chemicals and sawdust; should be worn when using power tools.

Soldering iron
For repairing the joints of leaded glass. Can be used to soften old glazing compound for removal.

Stepladder
Set up ladder with the legs fully opened and the spreader braces on each side locked in place.

Coping saw
Makes finely contoured cuts in delicate wood moldings.

Block plane
For smoothing edges, and small areas of end grain; produces wood chips, not curls.

Respirator
Prevents inhalation of dust from sanding paint and wood; special filters are needed for the toxic vapors of lead paint, solvents and certain sealants.

Sanding block
Holds sandpaper flat for smoothing wood surfaces.

Utility bar
Prying tool for light jobs: pulling small nails, tacks and staples, prying off trim, and opening windows that have been painted shut.

Nail set
For countersinking finishing nails.

Heat gun
Softens paint for stripping; special attachments aim hot air into contours.

Bench plane
For trimming, beveling, and smoothing large surfaces. Keep blade sharp and retract it when stored.

Acrylic cutter
For cutting an acrylic pane; retrace the line several times to deepen the cut.

Pry bars
Exert greater force than utility bar. Handle heavy chores; use flat end for prying, wedging and lifting, and curved end for pulling nails.

Pipe clamp
Secures large pieces of wood, such as a door, for gluing or cutting.

Straight ladder
For reaching second-story windows or skylights. When possible, have tools and equipment handed to you from inside the house. With ladder hooks, can be used as a platform for working on a roof *(page 35)*.

POWER TOOLS

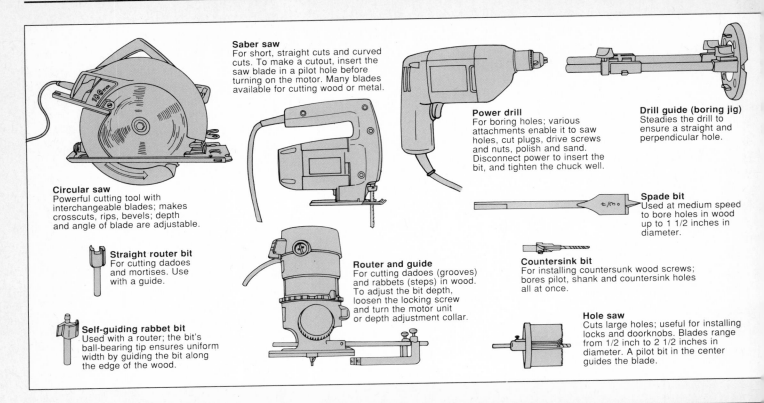

Saber saw
For short, straight cuts and curved cuts. To make a cutout, insert the saw blade in a pilot hole before turning on the motor. Many blades available for cutting wood or metal.

Power drill
For boring holes; various attachments enable it to saw holes, cut plugs, drive screws and nuts, polish and sand. Disconnect power to insert the bit, and tighten the chuck well.

Drill guide (boring jig)
Steadies the drill to ensure a straight and perpendicular hole.

Circular saw
Powerful cutting tool with interchangeable blades; makes crosscuts, rips, bevels; depth and angle of blade are adjustable.

Spade bit
Used at medium speed to bore holes in wood up to 1 1/2 inches in diameter.

Straight router bit
For cutting dadoes and mortises. Use with a guide.

Router and guide
For cutting dadoes (grooves) and rabbets (steps) in wood. To adjust the bit depth, loosen the locking screw and turn the motor unit or depth adjustment collar.

Countersink bit
For installing countersunk wood screws; bores pilot, shank and countersink holes all at once.

Self-guiding rabbet bit
Used with a router; the bit's ball-bearing tip ensures uniform width by guiding the bit along the edge of the wood.

Hole saw
Cuts large holes; useful for installing locks and doorknobs. Blades range from 1/2 inch to 2 1/2 inches in diameter. A pilot bit in the center guides the blade.

USING POWER DRILL ACCESSORIES

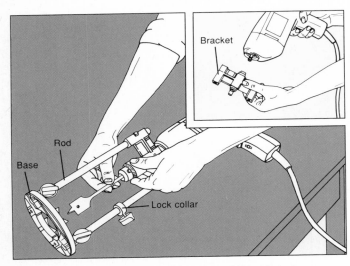

Bracket

Rod

Base

Lock collar

Assembling a power drill guide. Use a drill guide to bore a straight, perpendicular hole. To attach the guide, remove the chuck using its geared key. Screw the guide bracket on the end of the drill *(inset)*, then replace the chuck. Slide the rods, with the base attached, into the bracket and install the drill bit *(above)*. Position the base flat against the work surface, with the rods protruding if being used on a door edge. Adjust the drilling depth by sliding the base along the rods, and securing the lock collar at the desired stopping point.

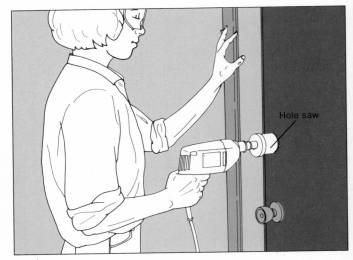

Hole saw

Using a hole saw. A hole saw can be used for installing a lock cylinder in a door, as shown here. Fit a power drill with a hole saw of the correct diameter, and wear safety goggles to protect your eyes from sawdust. Start the drill before applying it to the surface to be cut, and drill straight through the wood, keeping an even pressure on the drill. To avoid splintering, stop drilling as soon as you feel the pilot bit pierce the opposite side. Keep the blade spinning as you pull it out, then complete the hole from the other side.

MAKING STRAIGHT CUTS WITH A CIRCULAR SAW

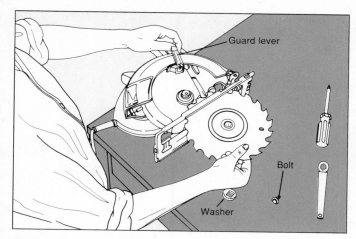

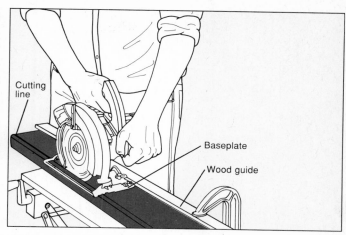

Changing a circular saw blade. Use a wrench to remove the bolt securing the blade to the saw shaft, or arbor; loosen it counterclockwise and pull the bolt and its washer free. Retract the blade guard by pulling its lever. Lift the blade off the arbor and slide in the new blade *(above)*. Resecure the washer and nut by hand. Then let the saw blade's teeth dig into a piece of scrap wood while you tighten the nut one eighth of a turn with the wrench. Do not overtighten.

Using a circular saw. Measure from the edge of the saw's baseplate to the blade, and clamp a straight piece of wood this distance from the cutting line as a guide. Remove any nails from the wood. Set the saw's cutting depth to the thickness of the wood. Wearing safety goggles, start the motor; let it reach full speed before cutting. Feed the saw steadily into the wood from one end, running the edge of the baseplate along the guide *(above)*. Wait until the blade stops revolving before putting the saw down.

ROUTING RABBETS AND DADOES

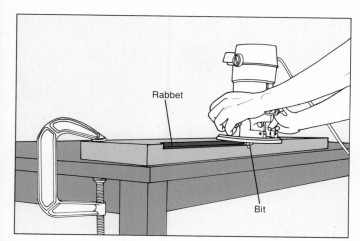

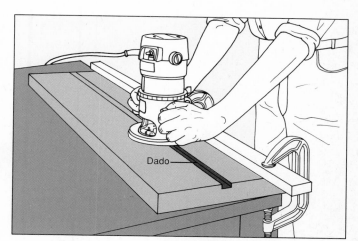

Cutting a rabbet. Clamp the wood firmly and remove any nails. Fit the router with a rabbet bit of the correct width; choose a bit with a built-in guide, called a pilot, to help you keep the rabbet straight. Set the baseplate on the wood with the bit hanging over the edge and adjust the bit to the correct depth. Wearing safety goggles, turn on the router, set the bit 1 inch from the left end along the side to be cut and feed the bit into the wood until halted by the pilot. Then move the router steadily from left to right *(above)*. Complete the rabbet by reversing the direction of the router to remove the uncut inch at the beginning.

Cutting a dado. Draw two lines indicating the width of the channel to be cut; fit the router with a dado bit of this width. Measure from the edge of the bit to the edge of the baseplate, and clamp a straight piece of wood this distance from one of the cutting lines as a guide. Adjust the bit to the correct depth. Wearing safety goggles, turn on the router and feed the bit into the wood at one end. Move the router from left to right, running the edge of the baseplate along the guide.

CHISELING A MORTISE

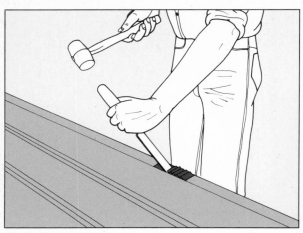

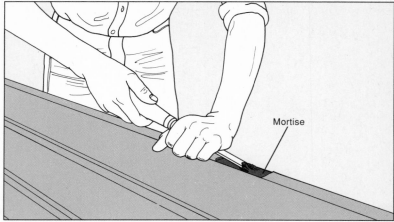

Mortise

Chiseling a mortise. Trace the outline of the mortise, then score the outline with a utility knife or a sharp chisel. Holding the chisel at a 90-degree angle to the wood and using hand force only, make a series of shallow parallel cuts within the outlined area. Then, holding the chisel bevel side down, position its tip at a 30-degree angle in each of these cuts, and tap the end of the chisel handle with a mallet *(above, left)*. Keeping the bevel side down to prevent the chisel from cutting too deeply, slice the wood away in thin layers. Repeat until you reach the desired depth, then turn the chisel bevel side up and carefully smooth out the recess *(above, right)*.

SMOOTHING WOOD WITH A PLANE

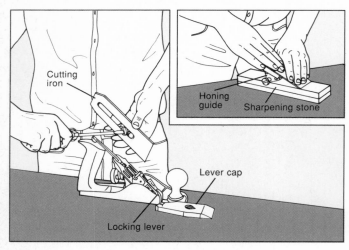

Cutting iron

Honing guide

Sharpening stone

Lever cap

Locking lever

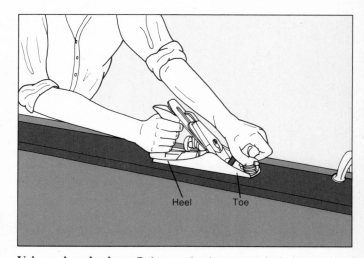

Heel

Toe

Sharpening the blade. Lift the locking lever to free the lever cap, loosening the lever cap screw if necessary. Lift out the irons. Wipe dust off the irons and the plane body. Separate the irons *(above)* by unscrewing them. Place the cutting iron in a honing guide at a 25-degree angle to maintain the bevel and rub it gently back and forth against an oiled sharpening stone *(inset)*. Turn the iron over and pull the blade flat against the sharpening stone to smooth the edge. Wipe the blade and reassemble the plane by reversing the steps you took to disassemble it.

Using a bench plane. Before cutting into a wood window or door, practice planing a scrap piece of wood. Check that the blade is sharp and not protruding more than 1/16 inch. Clamp the wood to a workbench. Always use a bench plane in the direction of the wood grain; use a block plane on end grain. Apply pressure to the toe of the plane at the beginning of each stroke, then gradually shift the pressure to the heel as you finish the cut. The wood should curl off in thin layers. If the plane jerks or cuts roughly, you are applying too much pressure or the blade is protruding too far.

ACKING A WORN SCREW HOLE

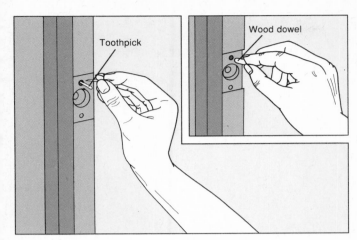
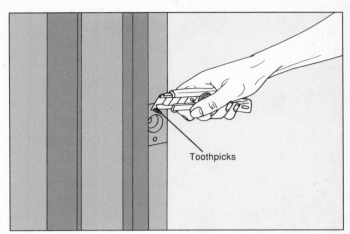

1 **Plugging a screw hole with toothpicks.** To refurbish a screw hole that is enlarged or stripped, pack it with wood. Remove the strike plate, hinge plate or other hardware. Apply carpenter's glue liberally to several toothpicks, and pack them tightly into the screw hole *(above)*. Alternatively, you can insert a wood dowel into the hole. Allow the glue to dry for at least 20 minutes.

2 **Reinserting the screw.** Use a utility knife to cut the toothpicks flush with the surface. If you used a wood dowel, trim it with a wood chisel, then drill a pilot hole into it for the screw. Replace the strike plate or hinge plate and use longer screws for more stability.

ATCHING ROTTED WOOD

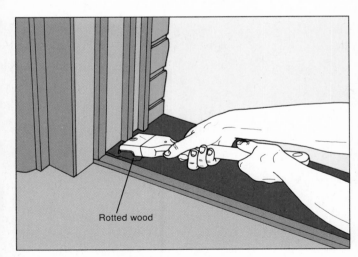

1 **Scraping away the rot.** Look for rotted wood on the top surface of a sill or threshold, at sash and frame joints and under areas of peeling or chipped paint. Scrape away paint flakes and check for loose, graying wood fibers. Push an awl into the wood to test the area for softness. Wood that crumbles instead of splintering is weakened by rot. Use a paint scraper *(above, left)* or a wire brush to scrape out the softened wood down to healthy wood.

2 **Applying the epoxy compound.** Mix epoxy resin and hardener according to the manufacturer's instructions. Wear safety goggles and heavy rubber gloves, and work in a well-ventilated area; choose a warm, dry day for best results. Use an old paintbrush to apply the epoxy compound to the damaged area, filling all cracks and holes completely. Then cover the epoxy with a sheet of plastic and smooth it with a block of wood. Allow the epoxy to cure overnight and remove the plastic. Smooth the surface with sandpaper or a metal file.

CLEANING WINDOWS AND DOORS

Washing a window. Use a squeegee and a solution of 3/4 cup ammonia and 2 1/2 gallons water to wash window panes. Scrub the glass with the squeegee sponge, then use the rubber blade to wipe off the solution *(above, left)*, angling the squeegee blade to force the liquid to drip into a lower corner. Dry the glass with crumpled newspaper, wiping in a circular motion *(above, right)*. Use a cloth with the same solution to clean the frame and sill. If you notice mildew, rinse the surface well and wash it with bleach *(next step)*. If there are signs of wood rot, treat it *(page 123)*.

Washing a door. Wash the door with a soft cloth and a mild detergent-and-water solution. If there are signs of mildew (dark green to black discolorations) wash the area with a solution of 1 cup household bleach and 1/2 gallon water, then rinse thoroughly. Examine the door carefully for cracking or peeling paint. If there is only slight damage to limited areas, sand them lightly and touch up with the same finish as the original, or repaint the door *(page 125)*. If there are signs of wood rot, treat it *(page 123)*.

PAINTING A WINDOW

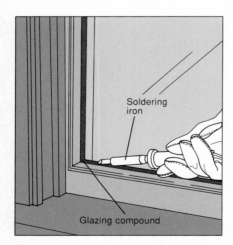

Removing glazing compound. Before painting a window, remove all cracked glazing compound. Heat a soldering iron and touch its tip to the glazing compound. Push the iron along the compound, lifting it from the pane *(above)*. Take care not to burn the wood. Scrape off the compound with a narrow, stiff putty knife and replace it *(page 79)*.

Painting a window. Remove window hardware. Scrape away peeling paint with a paint scraper or wire brush and wash all wood surfaces. Place masking tape on the glass 1/16 inch from the frame *(above, left)*, or from the glazing compound if you are painting the exterior side. Apply paint with a 1 1/2-inch sash brush. Pull down the upper sash and raise the lower one to paint the inside and top of the upper sash. The bottom edge of the upper sash rail should be painted with exterior paint. Then slide the sashes past one another, leaving them open a few inches at each end. Finish painting any previously inaccessible parts of the sashes, and the stool and the apron. Finally, paint the window jambs after all the other sections have dried.

AINTING A DOOR

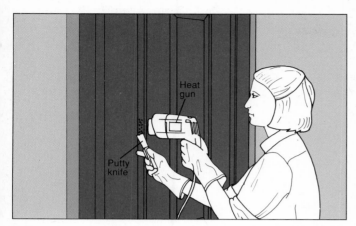

1 Preparing the surface. Remove door hardware. Use a heat gun to remove heavy paint buildup. Wear gloves and, if you suspect lead paint, a respirator. Working in a well-ventilated area, aim the gun at the door from several inches away. As the paint softens (a few seconds), move the gun ahead, scraping off the paint behind it with a stiff putty knife *(above)*. Remove as much paint as possible, taking care not to burn the wood. Clean off remaining paint with a chemical stripper and steel wool *(page 60)*. Wipe the door with a cloth dampened in denatured alcohol and allow it to dry overnight.

2 Painting a panel door. Protect door hinges with masking tape and lay newspaper on the floor. Sand the door lightly with medium-grit sandpaper on a sanding block. Load a 2 1/2-inch brush with paint to one half the bristle length and gently slap the bristles against the side of the can to knock off excess paint. Begin by painting the top edge of the door, then the panels *(above)*. Working from top to bottom, with even strokes, paint the rails and, finally, the stiles. Remove the masking tape right away, but wait until the paint is dry to reinstall the hardware. Clean the paintbrushes thoroughly *(step 4)*.

3 Painting a hollow door. Protect the door hinges with masking tape and lay newspaper on the floor. First paint the edges of the door with a brush. Then work paint into the nap of a paint roller until it is heavily loaded but not dripping. Starting at an upper corner, paint a rough W pattern. Then fill in between the strokes, spreading the paint evenly. Remove the masking tape right away, but wait until the paint is dry to reinstall the hardware.

4 Cleaning paintbrushes. When cleaning alkyd paint, first squeeze out as much paint as possible, wearing rubber gloves. Then fill a jar with paint thinner or turpentine and agitate the brush in the solvent. When the solvent becomes cloudy, use a fresh batch and work the solvent into the bristles by hand *(above)*. If necessary, leave the brush in the solvent overnight. Remove latex paint by working warm water through the bristles. Shake out excess water.

INDEX

Page references in *italics* indicate an illustration of the subject mentioned. Page references in **bold** indicate a Troubleshooting Guide for the subject mentioned.

ACKNOWLEDGMENTS

The editors wish to thank the following:
Alcan Building Products Division of Alcan Aluminium Ltd., Montreal, Que.;
American Architectural Manufacturers Association, Des Plaines, Ill.; Chris
Bradshaw, Montreal, Que.; Russell Caplette, Kennebunk, Maine; Colette
Caron, Montreal, Que.; Marty Cooper, Martin Industries, Montreal, Que.;
Dr. William Fiest, Madison, Wis.; Frank S. Fitzgerald, Fitzgerald Corpora-
tion and Association Management Company, Chicago, Ill.; Gerry Halton,
Robert Hunt Corporation, Montreal, Que.; Robert E. Hensley, Montreal,
Que.; Donald Huehnerfuss, Kolbe and Kolbe Millwork Co., Wausau, Wis.;
Larry Jones, Robert E. Meadows P.C. Architect, New York, N.Y.; Roger
Landreville, Montreal, Que.; Luc Lapierre, Gemico Windows Inc., Roxboro,
Que.; Ronald T. Lister, Ronald C. Lister Inc., Montreal, Que.; Steve Lodato,
Weiser Lock, Huntington Beach, Calif.; Tom Martin, SIGMA, Cherry Hill,
N.J.; Charles R. McCartney, United Skys, Inc., Round Lake, Ill.; Gregory
R. Moll, Torch Products Co., Grand Rapids, Mich.; J.D. Orrock, Imperial
Door Ltd., Montreal, Que.; Andy Petschner, Bennett Glass, Montreal, Que.;
Jack Starr, Crawford Garage Doors, Delray Beach, Fla.; Ron Ternoway,
Verrerie d'art classique, Montreal, Que.; Jacques Trépanier, RCR Interna-
tional, Inc., Longueuil, Que.; David Tovey, Ministry of Housing, Toronto,
Ont.; U.S. Consumer Product Safety Commission, Bethesda, Md.; Velux-
Canada, Inc., Kirkland, Que.; Cy Warner, Canam Corporation,
Mississaugua, Ont.

The following persons also assisted in the preparation of this book:
Marie-Claire Amiot, Philippe Arnoldi, Claude Bordeleau, Diane Denoncourt,
Fiona Gilsenan, Julie Léger, Serge Paré, Mark M. Steele, Dianne Thomas,
Natalie Watanabe and Billy Wisse.

Typeset on Texet Live Image Publishing System.